Sustainable Failures

SUSTAINABLE FAILURES

Environmental Policy and Democracy in a Petro-dependent World

SHERRY CABLE

TEMPLE UNIVERSITY PRESS
Philadelphia

Sherry Cable is Professor of Sociology and Faculty Fellow in the Tennessee Teaching and Learning Center at the University of Tennessee. She is coauthor (with Charles Cable) of *Environmental Problems/Grassroots Solutions: The Politics of Grassroots Environmental Conflict.*

TEMPLE UNIVERSITY PRESS
Philadelphia, Pennsylvania 19122
www.temple.edu/tempress

Library of Congress Cataloging-in-Publication Data

Cable, Sherry.
    Sustainable failures : environmental policy and democracy in a petro-dependent world / Sherry Cable.
        p.   cm.
    Includes bibliographical references and index.
    ISBN 978-1-4399-0899-0 (cloth : alk. paper)
    ISBN 978-1-4399-0900-3 (pbk. : alk. paper)
    ISBN 978-1-4399-0901-0 (e-book)
    1. Environmental policy.   2. Sustainable development—Government policy.
3. Environmental protection—Social aspects.   4. Industries—Environmental
aspects.   I. Title.
    GE170.C33 2012
    338.9'27—dc23   2012003240

♾ The paper used in this publication meets the requirements of the American National Standard for Information Sciences—Permanence of Paper for Printed Library Materials, ANSI Z39.48-1992

Printed in the United States of America

2 4 6 8 9 7 5 3 1

To Katy Cable, of course,
and her pop

And in memory of Kassady

Contents

PART IV   And So . . .

APPENDIX   Websites and Mission Statements:
NGO Partners for the Global Plan of Action for the Protection

Preface

If we do not change the direction we are going,
we will surely end up where we are headed.

—Ancient Chinese proverb

For months, oil gushes into the Gulf of Mexico from a runaway exploratory well, killing wildlife and livelihoods, all because the oil corporation lacks the technology to manage such a (predictable) disaster. Unusually damaging storms and extreme heat waves in 2010, 2011, and 2012 suggest that climate changes are upon us, while politicians continue to quibble over limits on carbon dioxide emissions. Babies in poor countries die from drinking water contaminated by sewage—a problem for which we have known the technical solution for centuries.

How in the world did we ever get ourselves into such a mess?

That question has driven me, as an environmental sociologist, for nearly three decades. I studied environmental problems in communities to see what the "little guy" did when confronting big government and big business. I learned much about the integrity, intelligence, and ferocity of ordinary people defending home and family. I learned that often there are not only two sides to every story but perhaps fifteen or twenty. But I did *not* learn why environmental problems are not fixed.

I had a eureka moment while interviewing a railroad worker and longtime activist who explained his persistence despite the costs: "Them Big Boys ought to have to obey the laws same as I do!" Eureka! Activists were not fomenting revolution or demanding that plants be closed down—they just wanted existing laws enforced. There are laws against environmental contamination; they are called "environmental policies."

I studied environmental problems at a federal nuclear weapons installation where contamination was epic but residents were virtually silent on the subject. I studied Persian Gulf War veterans denied medical care for their mysterious symptoms. I learned a great deal about social control—*subtle* social control—not just by officials but also by friends, neighbors, physicians. I learned that although exposure to environmental hazards makes people sick, nobody believes them, even when they are soldiers. I learned that—*guess who!*—poor and minority communities suffer disproportionately from environmental exposures and illnesses. I did *not* learn why the government routinely violates its own environmental laws.

I educated myself on subjects I had assiduously avoided as an undergraduate. I learned about ecological principles, carrying capacity, the evolution of humankind, the life cycle of stars, the gestation period of elephants, the wonder of worms, the physical and chemical processes that created the universe, and the rigid hierarchy of the beehive. I learned that we have sufficient knowledge to create environmental policies that will adequately protect us. I did *not* learn why environmental policies are more of a problem than a solution.

I believe that many people in powerful positions sincerely care about environmental problems: legislators around the world, presidents and prime ministers, activists and artists, and even some corporate types. I believe they do not want to destroy the environment. So why do environmental policies fail to work?

A trained scholar, I searched the library (and the Internet) to learn about environmental policy. I was disappointed. Environmental policy is most often analyzed by political scientists, economists, and natural resource managers. Certainly, I learned from my studies. But something was missing.

What about the big picture? Where is the big picture?

So I researched, pondered, conjectured, and finally wrote this book about the *sociology* of environmental policy. I learned that it is a sin that policymakers do not consult sociologists more often. Sociology's unique analytical lens yields an eminently useful view of environmental policy, illuminating the complex array of historical shifts, socially binding forces, cultural values, and economic imperatives that shape environmental policy processes at national and international levels. The more deeply I have immersed myself in this pursuit and the more I have learned, the more I am convinced that sociologists have substantial and consequential contributions to make to policymakers, environmentalists, and the public if only we can catch their ears. Toward that end, I declare this book a jargon-free zone. I have attempted to write in a style that is both accessible to non-sociologists and capable of conveying the power of the sociological imagination in interpreting social life.

Caution: Working on this book, I learned a great deal about how we got ourselves into this mess. But I learned considerably less about how, precisely, to get *out* of it. As I tell my students after I thoroughly depress them with analyses of the social forces that underlie environmental problems, I can't do *everything* . . .

I

Rationale for Sustainable Environmental Policy

1

The Shape of Sustainable Environmental Policy

Public policy regulates a variety of activities affecting our everyday lives, but we often take it for granted. Only when some event draws our attention to policy are we aware of its importance. The necessity of some types of policies is immediately apparent—for example, policies regulating traffic flow, product safety, and the substances permitted in foods. The need for other types—such as environmental policies—is far less obvious. Many people refer to environmental policy advocates as "tree huggers," "bunny lovers," and "radicals." Many believe that environmental policies negatively affect business.

So what is the necessity of environmental policies? Environmental policy is necessary for three critical reasons: to acknowledge ecological principles, to recognize the link between economic activities and environmental stability, and to enact democratic principles of fairness. In this chapter, I elaborate on these important societal requirements to identify significant criteria for defining sustainability and assessing the effectiveness of environmental policies.

The Acknowledgment of Ecological Principles

A number of analysts describe ecological principles. For example, the ecologist Garrett Hardin (1993) describes three ecological laws: we can never do merely one thing because everything is intermingled with everything else; we can never throw anything away because there is no *away*; and a nation's environmental impact is represented qualitatively by the relation $I = P + A + T$, where "P" is population size, "A" is per capita consumption rate (affluence), and "T" is a measure of damage done by technology.

The environmental scientist G. Tyler Miller (2008) describes the principles of ecosystem operations. For his first ecological principle, he applies the first law of thermodynamics—that energy can be neither created nor destroyed—to the one-way flow of energy through ecosystems. Solar energy entering an ecosystem undergoes sequential transformations. Photosynthesis processes convert solar to stored chemical energy; organisms transform chemical to kinetic energy to do their work; and the remainder exits the ecosystem as heat. Miller's second ecological principle is that functioning biological communities produce no wastes because wastes and dead bodies of one life form provide the nutrients required by other life forms. Another Miller axiom is that substances produced by humans should not interfere with any natural biological, physical, geological, or chemical cycles in ways that degrade the Earth's life-support systems for all species. The final principle is that we can never do just one thing in nature. Everything we do creates effects that are often unpredictable.

Perhaps the clearest description of ecological principles is offered in Barry Commoner's highly accessible delineation of four basic ecosystem laws (Commoner 1992).

Everything is connected to everything else.
The biosphere consists of all life forms and all the ecosystems that sustain them. It is an elaborate network of intrinsically linked component parts. In aquatic ecosystems, a fish is the following: consumer of oxygen produced by aquatic plants through solar-powered photosynthetic processes, producer of organic wastes that nourish microorganisms that support aquatic plants, the prey of birds, and a habitat for parasites. The fish is one element in a complex and coordinated network in which everything is connected to everything else in a balanced, stable equilibrium. Change in one element inevitably affects others, causing disequilibrium.

Everything has to go somewhere.
This ecological principle combines with the first to express the fundamental importance of cycles in ecosystems. Plants use solar energy to transform carbon dioxide from the air and nitrates from the soil in the production of biomass. Consumers—animals—eat plants and transform their stored chemical energy to kinetic energy for metabolism; other animals eat plant-eating animals. Animals excrete carbon dioxide and organic compounds. Microorganisms convert organic compounds into nutrients such as nitrates. Then the cycle begins again as plants use solar energy with the excreted carbon dioxide and nutrients to produce more biomass. In closed, cyclical systems, everything produced in one phase is used in a later phase. Ecosystems are the epitome of recycling systems: the identical *atoms* are recycled over and over.

Nature knows best.
Ecosystems' inner consistency and compatibility are the outcome of years of evolution. Ecosystems are conservative: the rate of evolution is slow, and the variety of surviving organisms limited. Temporary changes in an ecosystem generate a response that restores equilibrium: an overpopulation of rabbits is followed by an increase in the wolf population. "Nature knows best" represents the fact that, over several billion years, evolution has created a limited, self-consistent array of substances that are essential to life.

There is no such thing as a free lunch.
It appears to many people that few costs are associated with our exploitation of the environment. In actuality, the costs of disrupted ecological systems are

unavoidable but not immediately obvious. All interventions stress an ecological system, but responses to stress do not occur evenly and predictably
in a linear fashion. Initial adjustments may be minimal—hardly noticeable—
for some time. As stress increases, though, ecological responses may suddenly
become huge, even catastrophic. We deceive ourselves about no-cost environmental exploitation because of the lag time between stress and response.
But we cannot afford such deception. What looks like a free lunch is actually
a deferred debt—the bill will inevitably arrive.

Humans' violations of ecological principles inevitably degrade the environment, and the consequences for us are more severe than the aesthetic loss of a
salamander species or high gasoline prices—threats to human fertility, morbidity,
and mortality and destruction of the material basis for human survival. Yet many
people believe that humans are exempt from ecological principles. These beliefs
are based on a socially constructed duality between the biosphere and society.
The biosphere, created by physical, chemical, geological, and biological processes
over the planet's 4-billion-year history, is the land, air, and water that sustain all
living creatures. Society, created by humans in a mere 2 million years, consists of
cities, farms, wars, languages, music, landfills, televisions, poetry, factories, and
philosophies.

We separate the biosphere and society and perceive that we live only in society, viewing the biosphere as an object. Our attitudes toward the biosphere are
bifurcated. Sometimes we view it as beyond our influence: volcanic eruptions and
hurricanes are considered "acts of God." Other times, we view the biosphere as
subject to our manipulations. This erroneous perception leads us to believe that,
because the human species is not bound by ecological laws, we need not limit our
activities to comply with them. Yet our environmental problems derive directly
and fundamentally from violations of basic ecological principles. Consequently,
we require environmental policies that acknowledge ecological principles to ensure that our activities are consonant with them and that our life-support system
is protected.

The Link between Economic Activities
and the Environment

Despite our perception of dual worlds, there is only one—the biosphere. All
human activities are carried out in the biosphere through social institutions. The
economic institution is crucial in a consideration of environmental policy because it uses the very *substance* of the biosphere to provide humans' basic necessities of food, clothing, and shelter. Energy resources are humans' most fundamental requirement because we use them to extract materials from the biosphere
for our necessities. Food is the stored chemical energy that we acquire from our
consumption of plants and animals. The clothing and shelter that we require for
protection from physical elements are made from resources withdrawn from
the biosphere. We not only remove certain resources from the biosphere to

produce food, clothing, and shelter; we also add wastes to the biosphere via such production.

Both human and non-human organisms sustain themselves by extracting from and adding to the biosphere. But *every other species'* sustenance method—economic system—complies with ecological principles. Birds live in climates requiring nothing but their feathers for protection from physical elements. They use their own power to acquire the worms they eat and the sticks and grasses they use to build nests. Nature uses renewable solar energy to produce the nesting materials in the local environment. When the nest is no longer needed, it falls to the ground, where worms degrade it to build the soil that supports the plants that transform solar energy to the chemical energy that powers the birds.

In contrast, humans live in nearly all climates, seldom without clothing. We eat hamburgers and build skyscrapers. But our clothing, hamburgers, and skyscrapers are typically *not* produced entirely by nature in our local environments, and we rely on nonrenewable fossil fuels for many of our production processes. We wear clothing made from plants and animals grown and raised by farmers and sewn by factory workers outside our local environment. We produce hamburgers by razing rainforests for grazing and increasing the cattle population beyond nature's limit. We sustain cattle with synthetic growth hormones and grain grown from seeds manipulated in a laboratory to suit specific soil and weather conditions. Humans slaughter the cattle in one part of the world, process the meat, and transport it to other parts of the world to be cooked and presented to us in a Styrofoam box that we quickly discard as waste. We produce skyscrapers by removing resources from the earth, transporting them elsewhere to transform them into products, and transporting the products to a third site, where they are sold to contractors who transport them to a fourth site, where humans construct the skyscraper for the use of others. When the skyscraper is no longer wanted, humans knock it down and transport the disassembled materials to sites where the materials are sold for reuse or labeled "waste" that is either partially incinerated or buried in landfills.

Compared with the bird's worm-and-nest existence, humans' hamburger-and-skyscraper economy poses a much greater threat to our continued survival as a species. According to William Catton (1982), human survival depends on a carrying-capacity surplus, the excess of resource supply over human demand for resources. Carrying capacity is the population size that an environment can support. Catton declares that emphasis on increasing economic growth—increases in per capita consumption of resources—has turned us from *Homo sapiens* into *Homo colossus*. Technological innovation has temporarily expanded the available carrying capacity, but the finite planet inevitably imposes limits on our ability to fool ourselves with technological prowess. Humans are as dependent on the biosphere for survival as are birds. Economic activities are intrinsically linked to the biosphere. No alternative source exists. We *must* tread on the Earth to survive. Societies require environmental policies that reflect this crucial link, to guide our tread on the Earth in consonance with ecological principles.

The Enactment of Democratic Principles

A democracy is a political system in which supreme power is vested in the people and is exercised directly by them or their elected representatives. All citizens have an equal say in the decisions that affect their lives through their participation in the proposal, development, and passage of legislation into law. Participation is equated with citizens' power. Citizens require that political leaders respond to the general will and answer for their actions and inactions.

Democratic political systems adhere to democratic values. Three of the most characteristically democratic values are popular sovereignty, political inclusion, and equal opportunity (Olson 2006). Popular sovereignty holds that citizens themselves are the authors of the laws under which they live. The democratic value of political inclusion is the recognition that departures from popular sovereignty may occur, requiring extra measures to ensure that all citizens exercise sovereignty. The value of equal opportunity is rooted in principles of distributive justice and asserts that the state must maintain equal opportunities for political participation by counteracting social conditions, such as economic inequalities, that undermine participatory equality (Olson 2006).

Popular sovereignty in environmental matters means that citizens in a democracy have equal access to the natural resources that sustain life, are fully informed of potentially hazardous environmental exposures, and participate in laws and policies regulating resource use and hazardous exposures. Political inclusion in environmental matters demands that extra measures be taken to ensure that adequate and accessible information about resource use and potential hazardous exposures is available to all citizens so they can sustain themselves and choose the hazardous exposures that are acceptable to them. For equal opportunity participation, the state deliberately counteracts conditions inhibiting the participatory equality that allows citizens access to necessary resources and adequate information about hazardous exposures.

Because the biosphere is the basis for all human sustenance, we require environmental policies to enact democratic principles of fairness and justice in the production and distribution of life's necessities.

Sustainability:
The Promise of Environmental Policy

The outcomes of environmental policy extend well beyond the purposes of other types of policy. Policy failures in the areas of traffic flow, product safety, and food additives harm people by disrupting the *flow of life*. But failures in environmental policy disrupt the essential *material fabric of life*, eroding the biospheric life-support system of all organisms.

The promise of environmental policy is the assurance that we operate to maintain the material fabric of life. Some refer to such a state as sustainable. But "sustainability" remains a buzzword—prominently used, yet poorly defined.

- The United Nations World Commission on Environment and Development (1987: 43) offers an ethical definition: sustainability involves "development that meets the needs of the present without compromising the ability of future generations to meet their own needs."
- The definition of sustainability by environmental scientists is parceled out among disciplines. Sustainable agriculture grows crops and raises livestock using organic fertilizers, soil and water conservation, biological pest management, and minimal fossil fuels. Conservation is resource management that does not waste resources and interferes with non-human species only to meet important human needs. A sustainable society is based on recycling and reusing discarded matter, conserving matter and energy resources by reducing unnecessary wastes and use, not degrading renewable resources, and by building things that are easy to recycle, reuse, and repair (Miller 1991).
- Many environmental activists advocate sustainable growth: economic growth that focuses on making social, economic, and political progress to satisfy human needs, desires, aspirations, and potential without damaging the environment (McKinney and Schoch 1996: 622).

Confusion over an adequate definition of sustainability conveniently allows us to evade the crucial task of creating environmental policies that restrict our activities to the boundaries of ecological laws. The proliferation of definitions suggests that some of our confusion derives from difficulties in communication across disciplines. Because the biosphere crosses disciplinary boundaries, environmental problems can be sufficiently addressed only in a discourse that crosses all boundaries.

I use the reasons cited earlier as underlying societal requirements for environmental policy to assess the status of current environmental policy and recommend the shape of sustainable environmental policy. To what extent does environmental policy acknowledge ecological principles? Does environmental policy reflect the link between economic activities and ecological stability? Does environmental policy enact democratic principles of fairness and justice?

Organization of the Book

In Chapters 2 and 3, I extend my discussion of the rationale for environmental policy with a historical overview of humans' methods for sustaining themselves, from hunting-and-gathering times until the present. I define modes of subsistence in Chapter 2, based on technology—the tools and techniques used to access resources, the primary energy source used to implement the technology, the environmental impacts of the technology and energy source, and the policies devised to mitigate the impacts. I distinguish between hunting and gathering and agriculture as the modes of subsistence used until 1945. Chapter 3 analyzes humans' post-1945 method of sustenance: petro-dependency. I argue that the petro-dependent mode of subsistence inflicts greater and more deadly ecological damage than earlier modes and that the damage is less adequately addressed by policy.

In Part II, I provide a detailed analysis of the world's prototype petro-dependent society, the United States. In Chapter 4, I describe U.S. petro-dependent policies of resource management and pollution abatement, presenting the policies in the context of their relevant portions of the Earth's life-support system: lithosphere, hydrosphere, atmosphere, and biological resources.

In Chapters 5–7, I gauge evidence for the success of U.S. petro-dependent environmental policies by using the criteria cited earlier. How emphatically do the policies acknowledge ecological principles (Chapter 5)? How explicitly drawn is the link between economic activities and the environment (Chapter 6)? How substantially are democratic principles enacted (Chapter 7)? In Chapter 8, I use that evidence to analyze the institutional and cultural forces that push petro-dependent societies toward unsustainability.

In Part III, I examine petro-dependency's reflection in international environmental policy. Chapter 9 examines the international process of environmental policymaking and the substance of international treaties, offering details of the process in two case studies. Chapter 10 focuses on major environmental problems that persist despite global treaties: population growth, approaching peak oil production, and global climate change. In Chapter 11, I analyze institutional tendencies that impede environmental progress and identify the single largest barrier to sustainable international environmental policies: the transnational corporate state.

In Part IV (Chapter 12), I describe humanity's unwavering march away from sustainability since adopting the agricultural mode of subsistence, where the petro-dependent path could take us, and how we might change our path to move toward sustainability.

2

Modes of Human Subsistence, Environmental Impacts, and Environmental Policies

Humans' economic activities have not always violated basic ecological principles. For most of human history, we lived as harmoniously in the biosphere as do the birds, seemingly without constructing a false duality between the biosphere and society. Nor have human societies always been marked by economic inequalities. What happened?

Human efforts to obtain food, clothing, and shelter from the biosphere for survival are intrinsically linked to ecological stability because we strategically intervene in ecosystem processes to increase the resources available to us. We use energy to withdraw desired resources, and we unavoidably make additions to ecosystems with wastes from our transformation of resources. Depending on the intervention strategy, withdrawals from and additions to ecosystems can deplete and contaminate resources and simplify ecosystems, rendering them vulnerable to collapse. Since ecosystems are interdependent, severe degradation of the environment threatens the collapse of the entire biosphere. Humans devise rules to guide ecosystem withdrawals and additions. Rules guiding withdrawals of energy and other resources are resource management policies; rules guiding additions to the ecosystem are pollution abatement policies.

Economic institutions implement the intervention strategy chosen by a society. Intervention strategies always leave marks on the biosphere: you cannot catch a fish or grow a vegetable without withdrawals from and additions to the ecosystem. But some intervention strategies leave bigger marks than others. Gathering wood to build a fire to cook a fish caught from a local stream leaves far smaller marks than does extracting coal from the lithosphere to transport to a power plant for burning to generate electricity that powers the stove that cooks the fish trucked 500 miles to a store for purchase.

Historically, humans have chosen three intervention strategies, or three modes of subsistence: hunting and gathering, agriculture, and petro-dependency. Two elements distinguish intervention strategies: technology and energy source. Technology refers to tools and techniques used to extract food, clothing, and shelter from the environment. Energy source refers to the primary energy sources used to implement the technology. Each mode of subsistence has environmental impacts; the greater the impacts, the more restrictive are the policies required to address them sustainably (see Table 2.1).

Political systems changed with shifts in the mode of subsistence, a significant indicator of the link between political and economic systems: political systems are shaped in large part to protect economic systems. The tribal egalitarianism of the hunting-and-gathering mode of subsistence gave way sequentially to autocratic political systems in ancient and medieval agriculture, laissez-faire nation-states under mercantilist agriculture, and democratic political systems in industrialized agricultural societies.

In the next sections, I examine the shift from the hunting-and-gathering to the agricultural mode of subsistence, first as implemented in ancient societies, then with increasing focus on western European medieval, mercantilist, and industrialized agricultural societies.

The First Two Million Years: Hunting and Gathering

For about 99 percent of human history, the mode of subsistence was hunting and gathering—obtaining food, clothing, and shelter directly from the biosphere with hands or simple tools. Relying more on gathering than on the "difficult and hazardous activity" (Ponting 1991: 21) of hunting, humans gathered nuts, seeds, and plants produced by solar energy and occasionally hunted a few small mammals that fed on plants and other animals. Scholars believe that the diets of hunters and gatherers were nutritionally balanced, drawing on only a small proportion of the total available food and requiring only a small part of each day to collect it.

The technology required simple stone and bone tools and involved nomadic tribes of about fifty members roaming around a territory seeking edible plants and animals in the natural habitats in which they had evolved. Human muscle power was the primary energy source for implementing the technique. Available resources remained relatively constant, fluctuating around a stable average. Population size grew slowly, increasing only as tools were developed that made hunting and gathering more efficient, such as stone tools.

After the domestication of fire, wood was added to solar and human muscle power as an energy source. In his remarkable historical analysis of fire and civilization, Johan Goudsblom (1994) argues that the domestication of fire was humans' first great ecological transition, significantly influencing the relationship between humans and the biosphere. Fire was used for warmth, light, protection from predatory animals and rival clans, land clearing for campsites, and cooking food—which enhanced survival by dramatically improving food preservation. Goudsblom (1994) contends that use of fire elevated humans from an ecologically secondary to an ecologically dominant species.

The hunting-and-gathering mode of subsistence was preserved through a relatively simple political system. A chief, a council of elders, and a shaman typically made decisions for the collective. Aside from the chief, whose powers were

TABLE 2.1 Modes of Subsistence and Environmental Policies: Hunting and Gathering and Agriculture

Mode of subsistence	= Technology (techniques and tools to extract sustenance from the Earth)	+ Energy source (energy used to implement techniques)	→ Environmental impacts	→ Human response to impacts
Hunting and gathering: Evolution–8000 BC	*Technique:* Collection of foods from natural habitats through seasonal migration. *Tools:* Simple hand tools	Human muscle, wood	Negligible, local	Migration
Agriculture: 8000 BC–AD 1945	*Technique:* Replacement of natural selection processes with human selection processes. *Tools:* From stick and stone tools, to metal plow and metal tools, to machines, to electrical machines	From human muscle and wood, to animal muscle, water, and wind, to coal	From deforestation, overgrazing, soil erosion, stream siltation, desertification, salinization, species extinction, and water and air pollution, to flooding, resource depletion, and waste disposal and pollution problems	From migration, to urban policies and land use statutes, to conservation movements
Ancient agriculture: 8000 BC–AD 1100	*Techniques:* Domestication of some plants and animals via subsistence farming, irrigation. *Tools:* Stone and wood, wooden plow	Human muscle augmented with animal muscle; wood, water, and wind	Localized deforestation, overgrazing, soil erosion, stream siltation, desertification, salinization, species extinction, resource depletion, water and air pollution from stone, marble, and granite extraction	Migration, urban rules for traffic, sewage, green space
Medieval agriculture: AD 1100–1400	*Technique:* Intensification of domestication. *Tools:* Improved plow, some machines, iron tools	Human muscle augmented with better suited animal muscle; wood, water, wind, some coal	Wider deforestation, overgrazing, soil erosion, stream siltation, desertification, salinization, species extinction, resource depletion, flooding, water and air pollution from stone, marble, granite, iron, and coal extraction	Forest conservation, urban statutes, air and water pollution control laws; public works

Mercantilist agriculture: 1400–1750	*Techniques*: Intensification of domestication via specialized agriculture, trade and manufacturing, colonization. *Tools*: Improved machines and steel tools	Animal and slave muscle, human muscle, wood, increased coal, water, and wind	Increased deforestation, overgrazing, soil erosion, stream siltation, desertification, salinization, species extinction, resource depletion, flooding, water and air pollution from stone, marble, granite, iron, and coal extraction, spread of infectious diseases	Forest conservation, statutes regulating urban land use, litter, human wastes, air and water quality, waste disposal rules
Industrialized agriculture: 1750–1945	*Techniques*: Intensification of domestication via more highly specialized agriculture and hybridization, expanded trade and manufacturing via Fordism, increased integration of global market with expanded consumption. *Tools*: Electrical machines	Coal-fired electricity, wood, animal muscle, water, some petroleum, and wind	Massive deforestation, overgrazing, soil erosion, stream siltation, desertification, salinization, species extinction, resource depletion, flooding, water and air pollution from stone, marble, granite, iron, coal, and mineral extraction, and from coal combustion and internal combustion engines	Resource conservation, urban sanitation

usually hereditary, status differentiations were made on the basis of personal characteristics such as hunting prowess and leadership traits. Food was not owned but was readily available to all group members. Few goods were maintained because transporting them inhibited roaming and, besides, goods were easily made anywhere from materials at hand. With equal access to food and virtually no consumer goods, hunting-and-gathering societies were egalitarian.

The fossil record and anthropological studies of contemporary hunting-and-gathering societies indicate that this mode of subsistence was relatively sustainable, conforming to ecological principles with few seriously adverse effects on the functioning of the ecosystem. Keenly aware that they survived at the mercy of biospheric forces, hunters and gatherers possessed detailed knowledge of regional ecosystems that became part of tribal oral histories. Some evidence suggests that these societies engaged in resource conservation through totemic restrictions on hunting a particular species, the practice of rotational hunting, and prohibitions on hunting in sacred areas. Thus, for nearly 2 million years, human sustenance did not result in significant ecological impacts that required mitigating policies.

The Fundamental Alteration of the Biosphere: The Agricultural Mode of Subsistence, 8000 BC to AD 1945

About 40,000 years ago, hunters and gatherers were the dominant animals in every land-based ecosystem. Then a new mode of subsistence appeared. The agricultural, or Neolithic, revolution began simultaneously at several places in the world and gradually spread, replacing small hunting-and-gathering bands with settled agricultural communities. Agriculture generated the most fundamental alterations to the biosphere in human history.

In the transition to the agricultural mode of subsistence, food, clothing, and shelter were obtained from the biosphere with technologies for domesticating wild plants and animals. Domestication brought fundamental, transformative changes in the biosphere because it replaced the *natural* selection processes of ecosystems with the *human* selection processes of social systems. Supplanting nature's rules, agriculturalists shaped and controlled more and more of the Earth's surface by supplementing their muscle power with domesticated animals, wood, water, and wind and by creating complex social organizations to coordinate major projects such as timbering and irrigation. Wood was the main source of fuel because of it was easily collected, readily available, and frequently free, and it burned well (Ponting 1991).

For the first time in history, human subsistence produced a social surplus: more food was produced than was needed for the survival of society's members. The ramifications of a social surplus cannot be overstated. I highlight some of the more critical ones for this analysis:

- The most visible consequence of the surplus was population growth: an immutable biospheric law holds that, the more resources available in an ecosystem, the larger the population size at the top of the food chain. Population growth was significant even in ancient agricultural societies. The Inca Empire, for example, grew to a million or more citizens. Increasing population growth leads to greater consumption of resources and more waste.

- Social surplus was a consequence of humans' replacement of the natural selection processes of ecosystems with the human selection processes of domesticating plants and animals. Humans developed a biological hubris, an inflated view of our importance in the biological hierarchy as a conqueror of nature. Biological hubris was the ground floor for the construction of a false duality between the biosphere and society and for the belief that humans are exempt from biospheric laws.

- Social surplus was the basis of wealth, and land was the basis of the social surplus. For the first time, land was perceived as a strategic resource, as a *commodity*—to be bought or sold, nurtured or ruined, stolen or inherited. The result was increased conflict over land and territories.

- Since land was owned, social surplus was also owned, and owners determined the use of their portion of the surplus. They used it to increase personal wealth, directing part of it to the improvement of agricultural technologies and part to the manufacture of consumer goods. The unequal distribution and differential quality of land, food, clothing, shelter, and consumer goods generated an institutionalized social-stratification system in which individuals were evaluated and assigned life chances on the basis of their accumulated wealth rather than their personal characteristics or circumstances. Thus, agriculture emphasized ever increasing production and consumption rates and a considerable discrepancy between rich and poor.

- Owners' use of the surplus to increase wealth through increased production also substantially increased the environmental impacts of economic activities and set humans at odds with nature because of different utilizations of surplus by societies and ecosystems. Ecosystem surpluses result in increased growth in populations of organisms at the top of the food chain until the surplus is eliminated and ecological stability is restored. In contrast, humans use economic surplus to enlarge future surplus by channeling it back into production, expending it on the development of techniques to increase production efficiency (Schnaiberg 1980). The uses of surplus by the two systems contradict each other, resulting in ecological disruption and simplification.

- Technological improvements that increased agricultural efficiency permitted a relatively small proportion of the population to provide enough food for all. Consequently, specialized social roles developed: farmers, herders, traders, shopkeepers, constables, administrators, teachers, and priests appeared. The social roles reflected the hierarchical structure of the institutionalized stratification system.

I distinguish among ancient, medieval, mercantilist, and industrialized agricultural modes of subsistence to chart the increasing intensification of agriculture and to mark associated changes in environmental impacts and policies. I also describe changes in political systems as economic imperatives shifted with new variants of agriculturalism.

Ancient Agricultural Societies, 8000 BC to AD 476

Ancient agriculturalists' selection of plants for domestication replaced natural vegetation by supplementing solar energy with human energy and, later, domesticated animals. Selected animals were tamed using human muscle power. Agriculturalists used wood for warmth, light, protection, cooking, and land clearing. These subsistence farmers grew only enough food to feed their families. Initially, they employed slash-and-burn cultivation and used stick or stone tools to poke holes in the soil to plant roots and tubers. The wooden plow substantially intensified agriculture, allowing farmers to cultivate larger plots and more marginal lands. The soil was depleted after two or three years, and farmers migrated to new areas. Abandoned plots regained fertility after ten to thirty years.

Irrigation technologies further intensified agriculture, dramatically enlarging the surplus and increasing population growth. The enlarged surplus fostered increased accumulation of consumer goods and contributed to a stratification system based on the production of essential and non-essential consumer goods. Wealthy individuals developed the concept of private property to ensure that wealth remained in the family after their demise (Redman 1999). To protect land ownership and water rights as economic resources, armies were formed whose leaders claimed large areas of land and rose to powerful positions from which they forced slaves and peasants to produce food and to construct irrigation systems, palaces, temples, and tombs. Gideon Sjoberg (1960) emphasizes the wealth discrepancies that distinguished agricultural societies from hunting-and-gathering societies, estimating that less than 10 percent of the agricultural population accumulated the vast majority of wealth. About 90 percent of agriculturalists were peasants barely producing enough to meet family needs, cover ceremonial obligations such as weddings and deaths, and meet the mandates of large landowners and church and state officials.

Most political systems supporting ancient agriculturalism were autocratic. Democracy originated in the Greek city-state of Athens but excluded slaves and women and was short-lived. The Romans briefly embraced democracy before shifting to a monarchy in which a powerful military conquered other European civilizations to maintain the supply of resources and labor. As the empire declined, feudal systems emerged with power in the hands of warlords and their soldiers.

Significant environmental problems in ancient agriculture derived from increases in production, population size, wealth, and warfare. Because larger populations required more food and wood for fuel and housing, ancient agriculturalists decimated forest areas and plowed immense grasslands. Land clearing destroyed plant and animal habitats, some to the point of extinction. Poor land management techniques worsened deforestation, soil erosion, and the overgrazing of grasslands. Fertile lands transformed to deserts; rivers, lakes, and streams dried up; siltation rendered irrigation canals useless.

Because most environmental impacts in rural areas were localized, the most common response was migration rather than policies. But urban environmental degradation associated with high population density stimulated some of the world's first environmental policies. Ancient Greek and Roman laws banned cart and horse traffic at certain hours for residents' safety as they conducted business. Laws stipulated permissible times for dumping sewage into rivers and streams to ensure that the pollution did not coincide with families' laundering of clothes in the rivers. Codes mandated urban garden spaces for recreation.

Ancient agriculture's environmental policies, developed primarily to regulate urban land use and waste disposal, failed to alleviate environmental problems adequately because they emphasized local rather than regional issues. The Greeks' and Romans' worst environmental problem was deforestation. Forests were cleared for farmland, fuel, grazing, building construction, and shipbuilding. Deforestation brought soil erosion, water supply disruption, and lowland and coastal siltation. Soil erosion and irrigation caused salinization of the soil. Introduced domestic species such as goats and cats initiated competition with native species, causing habitat destruction and species extinction. In cities, crowding, tenement housing susceptible to fires, and waste disposal practices caused air and water pollution. Extractive industries produced pits, tunnels, and underground chambers that diverted and contaminated water, polluted air, exposed workers to hazardous materials, and eroded the landscape. Several analysts argue that ancient agriculturalists' environmental degradation was so severe and widespread that it substantially contributed to the civilizations' declines (Hughes 1994; Redman 1999).

Medieval Agricultural Societies, 476–1500

The fall of the Roman Empire in the West marked the beginning of the medieval era. Medieval agriculturalists further intensified domestication and enhanced efficiency with techniques such as seed planting, crop rotation, improved plows, and land management principles (Gimpel 1976). Energy sources were improved with better-suited domesticated animals—for instance, oxen before the plow were replaced with faster and more nimble horses.

Medieval agriculturalists domesticated seed plants in addition to roots and tubers, retaining seeds from a crop for the next year's planting. Three-field crop rotation reduced the percentage of fallow land, offered protection against failed crops, and fed draft animals (Gimpel 1976). Horses rigged with rigid padded harnesses and iron shoes could pull heavy-wheeled plows through denser soil, substantially increasing yields of high-protein grain (Gimpel 1976). Improved land management techniques that increased efficiency also created a new occupation of trained estate administrators (Gimpel 1976).

Police and the military enabled the aristocracy to coerce pauperized peasants to increase productivity and enlarge the social surplus (Wolf 1966). Commodification of land increased warfare among western European nations and led to the construction of walled cities for protection. War required considerable wealth to provide armor, lances, swords, and horses, but elites could afford armies only by allowing troops to conquer and plunder neighboring states. This expansionism fueled a medieval arms race.

Most political systems continued to be autocratic. Landownership was the principle source of wealth and power in rural, land-based feudal kingdoms. Under conditions of chronic warfare, the constant quest for physical security led people to swear allegiance to those who could organize and defend agriculture. Chronic warfare also consolidated power within the landed aristocracy, and the aristocrats found considerable benefits from vesting ultimate power in a monarch who protected them for a share of their plunder. Monarchs, feudal lords, and priests possessed exclusive and arbitrary power maintained through political repression and the exclusion of potential challengers. But as guild crafts and trade grew, city-states became centers of wealth, weakening the feudal system. The merchant class that emerged supported the monarch and flexed its economic muscles to gain greater economic freedoms.

Environmental problems escalated under medieval agriculture. Larger harvests, particularly grain, generated a tripling of the global population between 1000 and 1300 (Zupko and Laures 1996). Within the walled cities, water pollution, waste disposal problems, and littered and flooded roadways worsened. Millions of forested acres were destroyed for farming and grazing land and to meet increased demands for timber for fuel and for the construction of ships, buildings, water mills, bridges, and military installations. By the thirteenth century, wood was so scarce and expensive that the poor could not afford to buy coffins and were forced to rent them for burial ceremonies (Gimpel 1976). Wood for fuel was occasionally replaced by surface deposits of coal. As commercial enterprises grew, coal was increasingly extracted from deep pits for activities such as iron smelting.

Environmental policies developed in response to ecological disruptions lagged behind the magnitude of damage. Although some European forests were regulated as early as the thirteenth century, the greatest decimation of forestlands occurred in the medieval era (Gimpel 1976). Urban environmental problems were addressed only when trade was so impaired that the nobility, merchants, and artisans enacted statutes to facilitate commerce and nascent industrialization. Ronald Zupko and Robert Laures (1996) document policies in northern Italian cities that kept roadways clear for pedestrian and vehicular traffic, prohibited litter, restricted herd sizes to control wastes in the streets, and confined human waste disposal to covered sewers and drains. By the late thirteenth century, London had become the world's first city to suffer from man-made air pollution, caused by coal combustion (Gimpel 1976). London's air remained heavily polluted (Gimpel 1976) despite a royal proclamation in 1307 prohibiting the use of coal in kilns in certain areas.

Failed medieval environmental policies combined with natural climate changes to cause such deleterious effects on western European society that technological progress was substantially halted. Decreased temperatures and increased rainfall triggered an economic depression and famine contributing to the deaths of 10 percent of the population (Gimpel 1976). The bubonic plague spread quickly and reduced western Europe's population by 30 percent between 1378 and 1382 (Gimpel 1976).

Mercantilist Agricultural Societies, 1500–1750

The plague significantly slowed population growth in western Europe but did not destroy animal stocks or reverse agricultural improvements. Economic growth resumed within a century, and the nation-state emerged as the primary vessel of mercantilist agriculture. In this era, western European capital accumulation raised productivity to the highest levels in the world, providing more food per unit of human labor than ever before. Primary energy sources were human and animal muscle, wood, wind, water, and coal, which increasingly replaced wood as manufacturing became established, particularly in Great Britain.

Mercantilism emphasized private property and open market trading. States directed production, consumption, and trade relations, favoring a surplus of exports over imports that forced foreign states to pay in gold or silver. Mercantilists crucially depended on colonization to generate wealth, extracting resources and establishing new markets in conquered regions such as the New World. The increased flow of silver and gold from the Americas stimulated commercial land exploitation and the rise of a money economy.

The money economy and profit motive accelerated feudalism's decline and generated agricultural development. The profit motive changed agriculture from subsistence farming to commercial agricultural production. Mercantilist farmers improved the quality of crop yields through the careful selection of the seeds reserved for future planting, choosing seeds from the plants with the most desirable traits—better taste, greater resistance to pests, faster maturity, higher yield. Herdsmen achieved similar results from selection, breeding only the offspring of draft animals with prized traits. Increased agricultural productivity and enslavement of Africans displaced many farm laborers and forced them to migrate to the emerging urban factories as wage laborers, fueling the rapid urbanization of western Europe.

Mercantilism's political system consisted of a sovereign nation-state with power vested in monarchs, the landed aristocracy, and parliaments. States directed economies with the aim of accumulating capital and increasing the state's wealth.

Mercantilism's increased agricultural surplus not only fed a growing western European population but also generated a massive acceleration of international trade that considerably strengthened merchants' power. That power and the emergent money economy detracted from monarchs' financial security, making them increasingly dependent on parliaments for finances.

Continually challenging monarch rule, the expanding merchant class demanded rights to free trade in the pursuit of economic liberalism that upholds the autonomous character of economic order. England's economic growth seemed the proof of liberalism's advantages, and the political system began shifting to a laissez-faire liberalism. Trade restrictions were lifted, the government relinquished much economic power to the commercial classes, and new political associations were based on market operations. The developing aristocracy was rooted in agriculture and commerce.

Mercantilist agriculture intensified environmental problems. The greatly expanded social surplus fueled explosive population growth. The specialized agriculture necessary for export purposes quickly exhausted soil. Deforestation worsened with the extremely high demand for timber to build the naval fleets needed for colonization. Massive deforestation contributed to soil erosion and obstructed waterways. Large-scale irrigation projects increased soil salinization. Urban problems of waste disposal, air and water pollution, and the spread of infectious diseases were amplified as dislocated farm laborers moved to cities for factory work.

Mercantilist environmental policies mirrored medieval policies—particularly urban policies, but on a larger scale. Consequently, the policies lagged even further behind the damage and failed to address resource depletion and pollution problems.

Industrialized Agricultural Societies, 1750–1945

In late seventeenth century Britain, expanded global trading and scientific innovations combined to produce industrialized technology that further intensified agricultural and manufacturing production. Industrialization began in Britain in the mid-1700s, spread through western Europe, and extended to the United States by the late 1800s.

Because of my particular purpose, I differ from many social analysts who treat industrial societies as decidedly different from pre-industrial societies. I focus on the forms of humans' strategic interactions with the biosphere to gain food, clothing, and shelter; the environmental consequences of those forms; and the actions taken to address the consequences. Through that lens, industrialization does not represent a discontinuity from agriculture. The agricultural mode of subsistence initiated the solely human agenda of deliberately and permanently transforming all ecosystems—the entire biosphere—to satisfy singularly human desires. I observe that industrialized agricultural technology substantially accelerated the transformation of the biosphere and significantly widened the gap between agriculture's environmental damage and policies addressing that damage. But industrialization changed neither the fundamental nature of the technology nor its impacts.

Industrialization substantially enlarged the surplus by replacing small-scale, localized hand-production techniques with mechanized techniques, energized by coal and steam, in specialized rural agriculture and in centralized urban factories. Elites adopted these techniques to expand their personal wealth: replacing human labor with cheaper, more predictable machine labor decreased costs and increased profits.

Agriculture was mechanized with reapers, tractors, combine harvesters, and electric milking machines. More effective fertilizers developed from phosphates and nitrogen compounds replaced the farm byproducts of manure and compost. With electrical heating and lighting, livestock were raised more cheaply indoors in less space. Increased food production combined with steamships, refrigeration, and food-processing machines to foster the rapid growth of the international food trade. Industrialization supported with state subsidies transformed agriculture into an international industry in which food was produced as a commodity. Agribusiness became the world's largest industry.

Manufacturing productivity also improved with industrial techniques. Fordism used electrified assembly-line production processes that permitted mass-production and economies of scale that increased productivity and wages and decreased the price of consumer goods. Henry Ford originated the technique to increase workers' wages, recognizing that well-compensated workers constituted a lucrative market. As other manufacturers adopted the technique, higher wages and cheaper goods substantially enlarged the consumer society.

The shift in primary energy source from wood to coal underlay industrialization's success. Industrialization required monumental amounts of energy that wood could not supply. As wood became scarce, coal was mined on an ever larger scale. Global coal production in 1800 was approximately 15 million tons; by the end of that century, it was 700 million tons (Ponting 1991). Clive Ponting (1991: 281) explains per capita energy consumption's unprecedented increases: "The new rates of energy use simply could not have been sustained with wood—in 1900 the world's coal consumption was equivalent to destroying and transporting a forest three times the size of Britain every year. There were not enough forests in the world to sustain production on this scale for very long."

Oil and natural gas were other industrial energy sources. A byproduct of oil drilling, natural gas was minimally used until pipeline technology was developed after the 1930s. The world's first commercial oil was produced in 1859 in Pennsylvania. The initial motivation for extracting oil was to replace oil from nearly extinct sperm whales as a machine lubricant and illuminating fuel. The demand for oil increased with subsequent inventions of oil-burning furnaces and internal combustion engines and with the early development of the aviation industry.

Industrialized agricultural and manufacturing techniques created the modern production system. Analysts use a variety of terms for this. Harvey Molotch's (1976) urban growth machine model describes the power structure and economic growth agenda driving decisions over urban land use. Allan Schnaiberg's (1980) treadmill of production concept reveals capitalism's expansionist logic, emphasizing elites' direction of technology toward ever expanding production and its ecological impacts. John Logan and Harvey Molotch (1987) demonstrate expansionist logic in a modified urban growth machine model.

Many analysts refer to the modern industrialized production system as capitalism. But at least for my purposes, the terms "capitalism" and "socialism" best describe political ideologies used to justify modern systems. Capitalism is a belief system that supports economic growth through private ownership of the means of production in pursuit of private profits. Socialism is a belief system that supports economic growth through state ownership of the means of production in pursuit of government revenues.

In contrast, the concept of mode of subsistence focuses on the material links between economic and ecological systems. In that vein, I adopt Schnaiberg's term "treadmill of production" because it features those links in describing modern industrialized production systems.

The treadmill is characterized by continual expansion of production, the perennial pursuit of technologies that reduce labor's role while intensifying energy and capital use, and inevitable increases in environmental degradation. States subsidize production and encourage consumption to further expand production and provide higher employment. Expanded production generates profits for producers, creates employment for laborers, and provides revenues for the state. Because they all gain, corporate managers, laborers, and government officials bracket the conflicts that usually separate them and form a "growth coalition" (Schnaiberg 1980: 208), a solid consensus supporting expanded production. Ever increasing rates of production require resource extraction at rates that exceed ecosystems' capacity to reproduce or replenish those resources.

Industrialized agriculturalism's substantially enlarged surplus combined with Europe's eighteenth-century Enlightenment to shape new, democratic political systems that advanced and protected economic institutions. All citizens of a democracy were guaranteed equal say in decisions affecting their lives, including public policy decisions. Most political systems featured representative rather than direct democratic institutions. Representative democracies varied from constitutional monarchies consisting of a hereditary head of state and a parliament with lower and upper chambers to federal republics with officials elected for parliamentary or presidential positions and constitutional republics in which elected officials' power is constitutionally limited.

Most democratic states maintained a liberal, hands-off approach to economic matters until the Great Depression of the 1930s. Governments such as that of the United States responded to economic and social turmoil with a hands-on approach, instituting economic reforms and regulations that maintained the state's legitimacy while protecting private profits.

Industrialized agriculture's treadmill of production dramatically expanded environmental impacts. Increased global food production caused higher rates of population growth. Many impacts were age-old problems, significantly exacerbated: deforestation, soil erosion, siltation of streams, soil salinization, and species extinction. Highly specialized agriculture and the international food industry featured monocultures that heightened soil depletion and pest problems, requiring increased inputs of fertilizers and insecticides.

Industrialized manufacturing substantially intensified the usual urban problems of sanitation, waste disposal, and air and water pollution. Gwyndaf Williams (1996) describes Manchester, England, the world's first industrial city. Air and water pollution from diverse manufacturing quickly made Manchester the unhealthiest and most overcrowded locale in Great Britain. Mass-production of cheap consumer goods and the higher wages of Fordism enlarged and institutionalized a consumer culture. Consumers were urged to buy goods designed to become obsolete quickly.

The shift in primary energy source from wood to coal significantly intensified production's environmental impacts. Coal extraction caused severe land disturbance and soil erosion that could be only partially restored. Mine tailings polluted streams and groundwater with acids and toxic metal compounds. Coal-fired power plants were a major source of air pollution from sulfur dioxide, nitrogen oxides, mercury, and particulate matter—soot. Acids caused acid rain; nitrous oxides contributed to smog.

Policymakers in industrialized nations responded to resource depletion with more extensive conservation policies. The public was frequently made aware of the consequences of intense and careless resource extraction through disasters. For example, in 1889, the clear cutting of timber in the mountains near Johnstown, Pennsylvania, caused soil erosion that filled the Conemaugh River to the point that the South Fork Dam burst, releasing a wall of water a half-mile wide and seventy-five feet high that roared over the city and killed 2,209 residents.

Britain was the first nation to acknowledge resource depletion and host a conservation movement (Evans 1997). The U.S. conservation movement generated new government institutions to advance conservation, such as the U.S. Geological Survey and the U.S. Forest Service, and new public organizations, such as the National Audubon Society and the Sierra Club. In both nations, the conservation movement advocated policies to regulate resource use to sustain the basis of future economic expansion.

U.S. efforts at conservation were substantially upsized after the environmental disaster of the Dust Bowl. Prior to industrialization, the southern Great Plains were covered with hardy grasses that stabilized soil. Between 1887 and 1917, the grasses were plowed and replaced with wheat and grazing cattle, exposing the soil to wind erosion. In a period of severe droughts in the early 1930s, several inches of topsoil were blown away. President Franklin D. Roosevelt responded with multipurpose New Deal programs that advanced soil conservation and employed workers to strengthen the staggering economy. The Civilian Conservation Corps offered employment on conservation projects, such as planting trees across the Great Plains as windbreaks. The Soil Erosion Service assisted farmers with soil classification and analysis to promote conservation farming methods.

Policymakers also addressed urban problems. Britain's conservation movement coalesced with a reform movement to improve working conditions that blossomed into a broader progressive movement. In Manchester, housing and health problems were met with the Public Health Acts of 1875 and the construction of garden suburbs in the early 1900s (Williams 1996: 206). Britain's progressive movement spread to other industrialized nations, such as the United States, where problems with urban pollution brought calls for reform from middle- and upper-class women who formed civic organizations to monitor pollution and solve garbage and sanitation problems.

New Horizons

The necessity for environmental policies emerged and continually grew in urgency with the momentous shift in mode of subsistence from hunting and gathering to agriculturalism. Hunters and gatherers lived by ecological principles, acutely aware of the link between their subsistence and the environment. Their negligible environmental impacts necessitated no environmental policies for nearly 2 million years.

Agriculturalism's alteration of the biosphere immediately created environmental impacts that warranted a comparable regulatory response. The earliest environmental policies were associated with urbanization: the denser the population, the more obvious the environmental problems. These initial policies regulating urban traffic, waste disposal, and land use were often precipitated by problems impairing trade. Industrialized agricultural policies retained the urban focus, but extensive resource depletion and associated pollution fostered conservation policies.

As the magnitude of environmental problems multiplied, humans moved ever further from acknowledging ecological principles and the link between economic activities and the environment. Consequently, environmental policies consistently lagged well behind environmental problems. But by 1945, another shift in mode of subsistence was under way, a mode that would substantially enlarge the gap between environmental impacts and policies.

3

The Poisoning of the Biosphere

The Petro-dependent Mode of Subsistence

n 1945, the world stood poised on the threshold of a truly new age. At our backs was 10,000 years' use of a mode of subsistence that produced unprecedented wealth, continually enlarged the surplus, and supported an ever growing population. Before us on that threshold was the promise of even greater wealth and even higher standards of living for even larger numbers of people. The promise was offered by a new mode of subsistence: the petro-dependent mode.

The agricultural mode of subsistence fundamentally altered the biosphere by replacing natural selection processes with human selection processes. The petro-dependent mode of subsistence literally poisons the biosphere. Petro-dependent technologies manipulate nature's production processes to fabricate unnatural substances. The largely unregulated proliferation of these unnatural substances combines with the effects of massive increases in petroleum use not only to increase the scale and magnitude of agriculturalism's environmental problems but also to create problems never before encountered by the human species.

In this chapter, I present an overview of the petro-dependent mode of subsistence, describing its features and environmental impacts (see Table 3.1, which adds the period of petro-dependency to the periods covered in Table 2.1).

The Features of Petro-dependent Societies

Energy is the first priority for economic growth. Petroleum is the primary energy source for petro-dependent societies, although coal is used extensively for generating electricity. Petro-dependent techniques involve the use of a variety of hazardous substances, some produced in nature and others manufactured in laboratories. Petro-dependency is typically associated with democratic political systems dedicated to increasing economic growth as global integration of markets accelerates. Petro-dependency yields environmental impacts not encountered under agriculturalism.

TABLE 3.1 Modes of Subsistence and Environmental Policies: The Petro-dependent World

Mode of subsistence	=	Technology (techniques and tools to extract sustenance from the Earth)	+	Energy source (energy used to implement techniques)	→	Environmental impacts	→	Human response to impacts
		For modes and policies before the advent of petroleum dependency, 8000 BC–1945, see Table 2.1						
Petroleum dependency: 1945–2010		*Techniques:* Augmentation and intensification of domestication via manipulation of nature's production processes to fabricate hazardous unnatural substances: petrochemicals, transgenic organisms, and nanomatter. *Tools:* Oil-fueled and electronic machines, increased use of hazardous natural substances		Petroleum, coal, natural gas, nuclear, water, wind, and solar		(1) Exacerbation of agricultural-ism's impacts: deforestation, over-grazing, soil erosion, stream silta-tion, desertification, salinization, species extinction, resource deple-tion, and flooding; water and air pollution from stone, marble, granite, coal, mineral and hazard-ous natural substances extraction and from coal combustion and internal combustion engines; (2) More toxic waste stream from use of hazardous unnatural sub-stances: petrochemicals, transgenic organisms, and nanomatter; (3) Unprecedented global impacts: depletion of stratospheric ozone layer and global climate changes.		

Petroleum

Nonrenewable resources such as oil, coal, natural gas, and nuclear materials supply approximately 84 percent of the world's commercial energy; renewable sources—water, wind, and the sun—supply the remainder (Harper 2008). The portion of energy from coal peaked at 55 percent early in the twentieth century but had declined to 23 percent by 1999 (Harper 2008). In the same period, oil use increased from 2 percent to 39 percent, natural gas from 1 percent to 23 percent, and nuclear 1 percent to 6 percent. The use of renewable sources *de*creased from 42 percent to 16 percent

Still, coal is the world's most abundant fossil fuel (Miller 1991). About 60 percent of extracted coal is used to generate electrical power; the remainder is either converted to coke for steelmaking or burned in boilers to produce steam for manufacturing processes (Miller 1991). Coal is the cheapest energy source because the industry is subsidized in most countries, and costs are externalized (Harper 2008). Commercial energy consumption is expected to climb 50–80 percent in the early decades of the twenty-first century.

Petroleum is the world's largest industry, valued at $2 trillion–$5 trillion (Yeomans 2004). Oil is used as an energy source in gasoline and diesel fuel production and as a raw material for manufacturing petrochemicals, lubricants, and solvents. Oil is so crucial a resource in securing our food that we might refer to "petro-agriculture."

Petro-dependent Agriculture: Food Is Oil

Nearly all of agriculture's increased crop yield is due directly or indirectly to petroleum (Heinberg 2004; Weissman 2005). Energy expended for food production is estimated to be around ten times the energy produced by food (Manning 2004). Petro-agriculture uses machinery fueled by diesel and gasoline in plowing, sowing, and harvesting crops. Seeds, pesticides, fertilizers, and crops are transported great distances on oil-burning trucks and planes.

Petrochemical pesticides are a key factor in increased crop yields. Commercially bred high-yielding seeds boosted with genetic engineering accelerate crop growth in specialized monocultures. But petrochemical pesticides are required because monocultures invite increased pest populations, and hybrid seeds lack natural immunity to pests. Clive Ponting (1991: 247) emphasizes pesticide volume in his attribution of increased yields to "extra inputs that treat[ed] the soil less as a living organism and more as a medium to hold crops in position whilst various chemicals were poured on to them." The larger production scale significantly increases the capital costs of farming, intensifying the concentration of farm ownership and extinguishing family-owned farms.

Petro-agriculture's expanded food supplies combined with technological innovations to create the oil-dependent food industry. For example, new preservation techniques transformed food-processing industries. Affordable home food freezers led to the frozen food industry. Improved food-drying techniques enhance the preservation of milk, juice, eggs, potatoes, coffee, tea, meat, fish, fruits, and vegetables. Plastic packaging materials keep perishable foods fresh longer. Federally funded interstate highways and eighteen-wheel trucks expedite food transport, nearly eliminating seasonal fluctuations in foods' availability.

Food processing rather than food producing yields the highest profits in the industry, and 75 percent of all food sold is processed (Ponting 1991: 249). Additives such as artificial colorings, flavorings, preservatives, and emulsifiers ensure longer life, make poor food palatable, and raise profits (Ponting 1991: 250). Most brand-name foods are owned by only about six food conglomerates, dominated by Kraft, Beatrice, General Mills, and Con-Agra. Con-Agra, for example, owns more than eighty brands, including Hunt's, VanCamp's, La Choy, Wesson, Armour, Eckrich, Butterball, Hebrew National, and Banquet (Harper and LeBeau 2003: 114).

Petro-agriculture creates a cycle of petro-dependency (Weissman 2005). Mechanized farming fueled by oil favors large-scale agricultural production that impels further mechanization. Crops adapt to petrochemical pesticides, requiring newer petrochemicals. Oil-fueled transportation carries food farther and faster, increasing consumer demand. Richard Manning (2004: 42) states, "Ever since we ran out of arable land, food is oil. Every single calorie we eat is backed by at least a calorie of oil, more like ten."

Oil Production and Consumption

The potential for conflict over oil is high because it is the resource that greases the wheels of petro-wealth. Oil supplies are dwindling; the oil-rich Middle East is plagued with ethnic conflicts; and developing nations demand the same opportunities for economic growth that developed nations enjoyed. The more volatile the oil market, the more likely is conflict over adequate supplies.

To assess the oil market's volatility, I examined fluctuations in global oil production and consumption and shifts in top global oil producers and consumers. Table 3.2 presents annual global oil production and consumption measured in millions of barrels per day for five-year increments between 1960 and 2005. Analysis reveals two trends: production and consumption both rise substantially, and consumption consistently outpaces production.

Global oil production grew from 20.99 million barrels per day in 1960 to 73.65 million barrels per day in 2005—a 351 percent increase. But consumption increased even more—by 394 percent. The largest increases in production and consumption from one period to the next occurred between 1965 and 1970: production increased by 15.56 million barrels per day and consumption by 15.67 million barrels. The only decreases in production and consumption occurred between 1980 and 1985. From the point of highest increases in 1970, production increases ranged between 5.28 million and 6.77 million barrels per day (except for an increase of only 1.76 million barrels per day in 1990–1995). Similarly, increases in consumption ranged between 9.30 million and 6.46 million barrels per day (except for an increase of 3.43 million barrels per day in 1990–1995). Table 3.2 also shows that, for each five-year period, total consumption was greater than total production. Further, the gap between consumption and production increased in each successive period except 1985–1990. The greatest increase in the gap

TABLE 3.2 Global Oil Production and Consumption, 1960–2005

	World oil production (mbd)	World oil consumption (mbd)	Difference: production − consumption (mbd)
1960	20.99	21.34	−0.35
1965	30.33	31.14	−0.81
1970	45.89	46.81	−0.92
1975	52.83	56.20	−3.37
1980	59.60	63.11	−3.51
1985	53.98	60.09	−6.11
1990	60.57	66.55	−5.98
1995	62.33	69.98	−7.65
2000	68.37	76.62	−8.25
2005	73.65	84.04	−10.39

Source: From www.cta.ornl.gov/data/chapter1.shtml.

Note: mbd, millions of barrels per day.

occurred between 1970 and 1975, immediately followed by the smallest increase between 1975 and 1980. The nodes where changes occurred invite closer scrutiny for historical context.

- The unparalleled prosperity of militarily and economically dominant nations in the 1960s was reflected in unprecedented increases in global oil production and consumption between 1965 and 1970.
- The smaller production increase from 1970 to 1975 occurred when the Organization of Petroleum Exporting Countries (OPEC) imposed the oil embargo. Iran, Iraq, and Libya nationalized oil production, and Nigeria, Kuwait, Qatar, and Saudi Arabia substantially increased their shares in production. Increases in global oil consumption were not similarly slowed: this period showed the greatest increase in the consumption–production gap. A slowdown followed in the 1975–1980 period, with the smallest increase in the consumption–production gap.
- The only decrease in production or consumption occurred between 1980 and 1985, after the ouster of the shah of Iran in 1979 and the return of the exiled Islamist leader, Ayatollah Ruhollah Khomeini. Iranian militants seized hostages, many of them U.S. citizens, and canceled the country's contracts with U.S. oil companies. The Iran-Iraq War of 1980 substantially damaged both nations' petroleum infrastructure.
- The smallest increases in production and consumption in 1990–1995 were also related to tensions in the Middle East. To punish Iraq for invading Kuwait in 1990, the United Nations imposed economic sanctions, permitting only an oil-for-food program.
- The production–consumption gap widened from 2000 to 2005 because consumption increased sharply while production increases significantly slowed. In this period, Islamist militants launched terrorist attacks in the United States; coalition troops were shipped to Afghanistan to find Osama bin Laden; and U.S. troops invaded Iraq.

Table 3.3 identifies the top ten oil-producing and oil-consuming nations in 2000 and in 2006. Shifts in rankings also indicate global hotspots for oil conflicts. While Saudi Arabia remained the top oil producer, Russia moved up one ranking, and China, Canada, and the United Arab Emirates each rose by two ranks. Meanwhile, the United States and Norway dropped one and two rankings, respectively; Venezuela dropped four rankings; and Iraq dropped out of the rankings.

Simultaneously, the United States remained the world's top oil consumer. Russia and China each moved up one ranking; India, two; Canada, three; and Saudi Arabia, four. Japan, Germany, Brazil, and South Korea dropped one or two ranks, and Mexico dropped out.

These ranking changes suggest economic power shifts in a petro-dependent world. Saudi Arabia remained the top oil producer and broke into the ranks of the top ten consumers, indicating the nation's potential for economic power. The Saudis have long been U.S. allies, but the alliance is tempered by strong pro-Islamic sentiments. The United States remained the top oil consumer but slipped slightly in production. Close to the United States in rankings, Russia increased both production and consumption, indicating economic growth, while the United States was in near-recession. Iran continued high rates of oil production with relatively low consumption. With a somewhat unstable and strongly anti-American government, Iran could become a hotspot in a fight for control over its oil.

Venezuela dropped significantly in production without being a high-ranking consumer. The strongly anti-American government and significant oil reserves sit in the backyard of the world's top consumer. If Venezuelan economy declines from lack of oil revenues, political infighting could topple the government. Mexico remained a top producer but dropped in consumption, suggesting slowed economic growth and, perhaps, increased immigration to the United States. China's oil production dropped slightly, but consumption continued to increase, indicating the potential for China to become an economic powerhouse. Canada increased both production and consumption, reflecting the nation's growing economic power.

Japan, Germany, Brazil, South Korea, and India remained consumers only. All but India dropped in oil consumption. India is the only oil importer in which oil consumption increased, suggesting its rise as an economic power. Iraq's oil production suffered from the U.S. invasion; the nation dropped out of the top ten oil producers. Conflict is likely to endure for decades in a struggle for the control of oil production. The United Arab Emirates entered the production top ten without increased consumption, making it another hotspot for the control of oil.

Oil demand continues to outstrip supply as nations pursue the petro-dependency route to higher standards of living. China is a prime example: in 2003, China's economy grew 9.1 percent, and more than 2 million Chinese citizens bought their first cars. In 2004, China surpassed Japan as the world's second largest oil consumer. China is expected to replace the United States as the top oil consumer by 2020. The majority of that oil will likely be produced in the Middle East, where two-thirds of the world's known reserves lie. Middle East oil fields still operate below capacity production. Matthew Yeomans (2004: xix) warns, "The Middle East has not just the most abundant and deepest reserves of oil in

TABLE 3.3   Top Ten Oil Producers and Consumers, 2000 and 2006

2000	2006
Top Ten Oil Producers	
Saudi Arabia	Saudi Arabia
United States	Russia
Russia	United States
Iran	Iran
Venezuela	China
Mexico	Mexico
China	Canada
Norway	United Arab Emirates
Canada	Venezuela
Iraq	Norway
Top Ten Oil Consumers	
United States	United States
Japan	China
China	Japan
Germany	Russia
Russia	Germany
Brazil	India
South Korea	Canada
India	Brazil
Mexico	South Korea
Canada	Saudi Arabia

Source: From www.eia.doe.gov/emeu/cabs/topworldtables1_2_files/sheet001.htm.

the world but also the oil that is the cheapest to produce. . . . It's only a matter of time before the rest of the world's oil becomes uncompetitive compared to that of the Middle East. When that happens, Saudi Arabia, Iran, and Iraq will be able to set their price."

Noxious Substances

The widespread use of noxious substances in production processes is a second feature of petro-dependent societies. I define my use of concepts such as hazardous, toxic, natural, and unnatural substances because I find no consistent definitions or usages for them.

- I use "hazardous" as the broadest term for a variety of substances that have potentially harmful effects on living organisms.
- "Noxious" substances are hazardous substances produced naturally, in biological, physical, geological, and chemical processes in the biosphere. Noxious substances degrade in the environment. Uranium, mercury, and radon are examples.
- "Toxic" substances are hazardous substances produced unnaturally, in manufacturing processes. Toxic substances do not degrade in the environment; instead, they accumulate in the biosphere. Petrochemicals, transgenic organisms, and nanomatter are examples.

The agricultural mode of subsistence used noxious substances such as radioactive materials and heavy metals, but petro-dependency uses them on a far greater scale (Cable, Hastings, and Mix 2002; Commoner 1992; Schnaiberg 1980).

Radioactive materials include krypton, strontium, zirconium, silver, tin, antimony, iodine, cesium, thorium, uranium, and plutonium. They and their compounds are used in medicine, agriculture, and industry. In medicine, they are used in the diagnosis and treatment of diseases and the detection of tumors and blood clots. Radioactive materials are used in agriculture as an additive to fertilizers and to increase crop yields and reduce insect populations. Industry uses radioactive materials as a catalyst to study processes such as alkylation, polymerization, and catalytic synthesis; to test for wear inside a car engine; and to determine the surface area of solids and the thickness of films, paper, steel, and rubber. Uranium and plutonium are used in the construction of nuclear weapons and the generation of electric power.

Heavy metals such as arsenic, lead, mercury, cadmium, iron, and aluminum are used in manufacturing processes. Arsenic and its compounds are used in pesticides, herbicides, and insecticides and in various alloys. Lead is most commonly used in storage batteries, radiation shields, and computer screens. Mercury is used in dental restoration and lighting. Cadmium is used in batteries. Iron is the most widely used metal, most commonly used in steelmaking. Aluminum is used in cars, trucks, aircraft, boats, bicycles, packaging, windows, doors, siding, building wire, cooking utensils, street-lighting poles, consumer electronics, electrical transmission lines, magnets, electronics, compact discs, LED lighting, paint, and pyrotechnics.

Toxic Substances

The extensive manufacture and use of toxic substances is unique to the petro-dependent mode of subsistence. These substances are considered toxic because their unnatural production renders their effects on living systems unpredictable without considerable testing. Toxic substances are petrochemicals (man-made chemicals), transgenic organisms (man-made life forms), and nanomatter (man-made elements).

Petrochemicals

Petrochemicals are organic chemicals fabricated in laboratories using petroleum as the carbon base for manipulating amino acids into combinations that do not occur in the biosphere. Crude oil is refined to produce feedstocks for the petrochemical industry, which converts them into thousands of ubiquitous products.

Petrochemical pesticides are widely used in agriculture as the foundation of increased crop yields and the pillar of petro-agriculture. Manufacturing depends on petrochemicals to produce industrial chemicals, fibers, electronic equipment, and plastics. Industrial chemicals are used in paints, solvents, heating, street paving, Teflon, and an array of consumer products, such as aspirin, shampoo, shaving cream, deodorant, toothpaste, and glue. Fibers made from petrochemicals are used to manufacture sneakers, pantyhose, clothing, wallets, purses, and umbrellas. Electronic items such as telephones, computers, pacemakers, and blenders rely on petrochemicals.

Plastic is the most visible petrochemical product. Polyethylene terephthalate is used for containers such as bottles and jars. High-density polyethylene is used in heavier containers, such as milk jugs, plastic bags, and motor-oil and bleach bottles. Low-density polyethylene is in cellophane wrap, bread bags, and trash bags. Polyvinyl chloride is contained in vinyl siding, plastic pipes and hoses, shower curtains, and bottles for cooking oil and household chemicals. Polypropylene is used in packaging for foods such as margarine and yogurt. Polystyrene is incorporated in disposable coffee cups, plastic peanuts for packing, egg cartons, meat trays, plastic utensils, and videocassettes (McKinney and Schoch 1996: 545).

Transgenic Organisms

In genetic engineering, the genetic material of one organism is altered to emphasize prized traits, and the altered genes are inserted into the cell of a second organism, frequently across species boundaries, to create a new organism.

Genetic engineering was adopted as an agricultural technique in the late 1980s to create seeds to grow plants for consumption by humans and livestock that had substantial tolerance to insects, herbicides, and viruses. The most common transgenic food and feed crops are alfalfa, canola, chicory, cotton, corn, papaya, potato, rice, soybean, squash, sugar beet, and tomato. Genetically altered corn and soy are commonly used in food processing.

Genetic engineering is also used in livestock production. A primary example is the maintenance of dairy cows. To increase milk production, dairy cows for decades routinely were injected with natural growth hormones harvested from cow cadavers. Genetic engineering is used to create a synthetic bovine growth hormone (BGH).

Certain food crops are genetically modified for the production of industrial chemicals and pharmaceuticals. For example, rapeseed varieties are altered to produce oils used in lubricants, cosmetics, and soaps. A modified mustard family plant produces a biodegradable plastic similar to polypropylene. Synthetic insulin produced in 1978 stimulated significant research by the pharmaceutical industry to develop other medical applications. By 1988, four synthetic proteins had been approved for use: human growth hormone, hepatitis B vaccine, alpha-interferon for treating viral diseases including cancer, and tissue plasminogen activator for lysis of blood clots. More than 125 genetically engineered drugs had been approved for use by 1995.

By 2003, the United States produced 63 percent of the world's transgenic crops; Argentina, 21 percent; Canada, 6 percent; Brazil and China, 4 percent each; and South Africa, 1 percent. Transgenic crops cover more than 100 million hectares worldwide.

The newest development in genetic engineering techniques is the fabrication of DNA. The first altered chromosome copied a natural chromosome, but brand-new chromosomes are under construction, with the potential to create new life forms. Transgenic DNA could reprogram genetic codes to create metabolic machines with applications for fabrics, medicines, ethanol, and hydrogen.

Nanomatter

Nanotechnology, developed in the early 1980s, exploits the quantum properties of basic elements by processing, separating, consolidating, and deforming materials at the molecular and atomic levels. The altered element's structure has unique, commercially useful properties, such as exceptional strength combined with exceptional lightness. Nanomaterials are mostly used in health and fitness products such as skin care and suntan lotion, cosmetics, protective clothing, and stain-resistant clothing.

The number of nanotech patents has grown quickly. By 2003, more than 800 patents had been granted. Global investments in research and development topped $10 billion in 2004, led by the European Union, Japan, and the United States (Shand and Wetter 2006:78–79). More than 500 nanoproducts were commercially available by 2006 (Chatterjee 2007). The business community is optimistic about nanotechnology's potential: "Nanotechnology is considered a "platform technology," meaning that it has the potential to alter or completely transform the current state of the art in every major industrial sector, not just one. Nanotech offers the potential to develop stronger, lighter materials, low-cost solar cells and sensors, faster computers with more memory capacity, filters for cleaning contaminated water, cancer-killing molecules, and more" (Shand and Wetter 2006: 79). Lux Research, an independent research and advisory firm providing strategic advice on emerging technologies predicts that the value of commercial products will reach $2.6 trillion by 2014, affecting 15 percent of global manufacturing output. That proportion is ten times the output of genetic engineering and as large a total output as that of the information and telecommunications industries combined (NanoXchange 2004).

Democratic Systems and Global Economic Imperatives

Modern democratic states are charged with two often contradictory tasks: capital accumulation and legitimation (Cable and Shriver 1995; Cable and Benson 1993; O'Connor 1973). The accumulation task requires the state to facilitate conditions for capital accumulation, such as providing tax breaks, subsidies, and tariffs. The legitimation task requires that the state protect citizens from the negative impacts of capital accumulation. The tasks clash because they serve different class interests: capital accumulation benefits the corporate class and provides revenues for the state, while legitimation best serves the middle and working classes, protecting those with the least capacity to avoid accumulation's negative impacts.

Between 1945 and 1980, Western democracies led by the United States pursued capital accumulation by empowering corporations and maintained legitimacy with social safety nets and new regulations. Under prosperous conditions and propelled by social movements, legislators wove a substantial safety net of social security benefits, Medicare and Medicaid health-care coverage, and welfare programs aimed at eradicating poverty. The safety net mitigated the most gaping discrepancies between rich and poor, dampening potential grievances. Social movements successfully pressured policymakers for laws that guarantee equality across race and ethnicity, sex, and sexual orientation. New regulations placed some constraints on corporations. In the United States, for example, Congress established an environmental regulatory agency and passed so many resource management and pollution policies that the 1970s were known as "the environmental decade."

Since 1980, democratic political systems have adjusted to new economic imperatives associated with the acceleration of global economic markets. Rising oil prices, debt crises in developing nations, global economic recession, and the partnering of the like-minded world leaders President Ronald Reagan and Prime Minister Margaret Thatcher generated a neoliberal revolution. The linchpin was massive deregulation that freed corporations from regulatory restraint and more securely than ever cast the political system as the handmaiden of the economic system.

Petro-dependency's Unparalleled Environmental Impacts

Global economic integration promotes the petro-dependent mode of subsistence, increasing wealth and broadening the scope of petro-technology's use. The inevitable companion to petro-dependency's wealth is a trio of environmental impacts unparalleled in severity: the exacerbation of agriculturalism's impacts, the creation of novel impacts by toxic substances, and unprecedented global impacts.

Exacerbation of Agriculturalism's Impacts

Petro-dependency exacerbates agriculturalism's impacts through the intensification of agriculture, depletion and pollution from the expanded use of petroleum and coal, and the increased use of toxic substances.

Petro-dependency intensifies agricultural production with technologies that cultivate more land and increase the yield per land unit. The usual environmental impacts—deforestation, overgrazing, soil erosion, stream siltation, desertification, species extinction, water and air pollution, flooding, resource depletion, and waste disposal problems—are accelerated globally as individual subsistence farmers in poor countries are replaced by large, specialized agricultural corporations. Monoculture methods that suit the needs of global markets rapidly deplete soil, requiring larger and larger quantities of inorganic fertilizers and petrochemical pesticides. Agricultural runoff of fertilizers and pesticides combine with wastes from expanded livestock production to increase water pollution.

Petro-agriculture's substantially increased food surplus triggers explosive global population growth. Increased populations and displaced farmers accelerate urbanization processes. The usual urban environmental problems increase exponentially—inadequacies in sanitation, waste disposal problems, and water and air pollution. Manufacturing accelerates the depletion of resources and the extinction of species and enlarges the waste stream. Air pollution spreads: the World Health Organization (Cohen, Anderson, Ostro, Pandey, Krzyzanowski, Künzli, Gutschmidt, Pope, Romieu, Samet, and Smith 1996) estimates that more than 1 billion of the world's 1.8 billion urban residents breathe air polluted with sulfur dioxide, soot, and dust. Photochemical smog forms from a chemical reaction of sunlight and nitrogen oxides released by vehicle exhausts and industrial combustion. Smog causes eye irritation, respiratory problems, and damaged vegetation. Urban sprawl, extensive paving, and "McMansion" subdivisions destroy habitats. The rate of species extinction is such that analysts speculate we may be entering a mass extinction era, unseen since the dinosaurs' extinction 65 million years ago (McNeill 2000).

Petro-dependency exacerbates agriculturalism's impacts with greater energy demands that pollute and deplete energy resources more than ever before. Fossil fuel combustion is a substantial source of air pollution, releasing sulfur dioxide, nitrogen oxides, and particulate matter that contribute to acid deposition, corrode metals, and cause respiratory problems. More ominously, burning fossil fuel, especially coal, produces large amounts of carbon dioxide, the primary greenhouse gas contributing to global warming.

Marine oil pollution has several sources. Half is caused by people pouring oil and oil products into storm drains (World oil pollution n.d.). In descending order, the sources are routine ship bilge cleaning, atmospheric fallout, natural seepage from the ocean floor, oil tanker spills, and discharges and drilling accidents from offshore drilling operations.

Although oil spills make up a relatively small percentage of total marine oil pollution, they take an extraordinary toll on sea life. The pollution damages animals' fur and feathers, leaving them to freeze to death. Threatened and endangered animals such as sea turtles are injured, as are shorebirds, seabirds, crabs, shrimp, lobsters, and sport fish. Human livelihoods are threatened when beaches and fishing areas are closed.

Table 3.4 lists the twelve largest oil spills in history (Wright 2007). Nine spills were caused by collisions and groundings of oil tankers; the remaining three were caused by war, an oil well, and a pipeline. War is the source of the largest volume in a single spill, and oil tankers are the most frequent source of oil spills. Ranking sources by average spill volume yields the following: wars, 450 million gallons per spill; oil wells, 140 million gallons; pipelines, 84 million gallons; and oil tankers, 59.5 million gallons. Dropping wartime spills as an outlier, the oil well spill has the largest volume; its 140 million gallons volume is twice the average volume of 69 million gallons (759.5 million gallons divided by 11 spills equals 69 million gallons).

I grouped spills by oceanic region: the Persian Gulf and the Gulf of Oman in the Middle East, the Gulf of Mexico, the Arctic Sea, the Caribbean Sea, the South Atlantic, the North Atlantic, and the Mediterranean Sea. By percentage of the total spill volume (759.5 million gallons), the regions rank in the following order: South Atlantic, 19 percent; North Atlantic, 18 percent; Gulf of Mexico, 18 per-

TABLE 3.4 Top Twelve Global Oil Spills before April 2010

Name of oil spill and date	Location; region	Millions of gallons	Source
1. Arabian Gulf/Kuwait January 19, 1991	Persian Gulf, Kuwait; Middle East	380–520	War
2. Ixtoc 1 June 3, 1979–March 23, 1980	Bay of Campeche off Ciudad del Carmen; Gulf of Mexico	140	Oil well
3. *Atlantic Empress* July 19, 1979	Off the coast of Trinidad and Tobago; Caribbean Sea	90	Oil tanker
4. Kolva River September 8, 1994	Kolva River, Russia; Arctic Sea	84	Pipeline
5. Nowruz oil field February 10–September 18, 1983	Persian Gulf, Iran; Middle East	80	Oil tanker
6. *Castillo de Bellver* August 6, 1983	Saldanha Bay, South Africa; South Atlantic	79	Oil tanker
7. *Amoco Cadiz* March 16, 1978	Portsall, France; North Atlantic	69	Oil tanker
8. *ABT Summer* May 28, 1991	About 700 miles off the coast of Angola; South Atlantic	51–81	Oil tanker
9. MT *Haven* April 11, 1991	Genoa, Italy; Mediterranean Sea	45	Oil tanker
10. *Odyssey* November 10, 1988	Off the coast of Nova Scotia; North Atlantic	40.7	Oil tanker
11. *Sea Star* December 19, 1972	Gulf of Oman; Middle East	35.3	Oil tanker
12. *Torrey Canyon* March 18, 1967	Scilly Isles, U.K.; North Atlantic	25–36	Oil tanker

Source: From http://www.associatedcontent.com/article/454782/the_worst_major_oil_spills_in_history .html?cat=37.

cent; Middle East, 15 percent; Caribbean Sea 11.8 percent; Arctic Sea, 11.1 percent; and Mediterranean Sea, 5.9 percent.

The rankings shift when I account for number of spills per region: Gulf of Mexico, one spill at 140 million gallons); Caribbean Sea, one spill at 90 million gallons; Arctic Sea, one spell at 84 million gallons; South Atlantic, two spills at 145 million gallons (or 72.5 million gallons per spill); Middle East, two spills at 115.3 million gallons (or 57.7 million gallons per spill); North Atlantic, three spills at 140.2 million gallons (or 46.7 million gallons per spill); and Mediterranean Sea, one spill at 45 million gallons. The most spills occurred in the North Atlantic region, but the volume was relatively low for a major spill.

I calculated this information in January 2010 and concluded that the take-away lesson is to beware of oil wells in the Gulf of Mexico. On April 20, 2010, BP's Deepwater Horizon oil rig in the Gulf of Mexico exploded, killing eleven workers.

Two days later, the rig toppled and sank to the sea floor. Between the explosion and the subsequent sealing of the well in September, 206 million gallons of oil gushed into the Gulf, nineteen times greater than the *Exxon Valdez* oil spill.

Coal remains relatively plentiful. Identified reserves are expected to last 220 years at current usage rates (Miller 1991). Rapidly diminishing oil supplies signal a serious predicament for petro-dependent societies. The eventual *end* of oil is a critical problem, but looming much sooner is global peak oil production, the point in time at which half of existing oil reserves will be gone and the other half increasingly difficult to extract profitably or in the same amounts (Heinberg 2004). Increased oil demand will inevitably collide with decreased oil supply, and rates of economic growth will decline. Analysts estimate that oil production will peak between 2016 and 2030 (Weissman 2005) but suggest that the peak will be recognizable only in hindsight (Goodstein 2004; Heinberg 2003, 2004; Roberts 2004; Shah 2004).

The implications are ominous. Petro-agriculture's techniques will become obsolete. The price of gasoline and diesel fuel will increase dramatically, impairing crop tending and transportation of supplies and crops. Petrochemical pesticides will become expensive, yet without them monoculture crops from hybrid seeds will fail. Because of reliance on petroleum, "the agricultural miracle of the 20th century may become the agricultural apocalypse of the 21st" (McNeill 2000: 177).

Petro-dependency also exacerbates agriculturalism's impacts with the increased use of noxious substances in manufacturing processes. Exposure to radioactive elements and heavy metals derives from resource extraction, use in industrial processes, and acid rain. Radioactive elements such as radon, radium, uranium, and plutonium interfere with processes of cell division, which are associated with various cancers, genetic changes, and birth defects.

Acute radiation exposure causes burns and sickness. Radiation sickness can cause premature aging or death within two months of exposure (U.S. Environmental Protection Agency 2010). Chronic radiation exposure is associated with cancer. The longer the exposure, the more severe are the effects. Natural processes control the rates of cell growth and replacement. Chronic radiation exposure breaks the chemical bonds in atoms and molecules, disrupting natural processes and allowing uncontrolled cell growth. Exposures may cause DNA mutations that the body fails to repair. Teratogenic mutations are caused by exposure of the fetus and include small head or brain size, poorly formed eyes, abnormally slow growth, and mental retardation. Genetic mutations are passed on to offspring.

Organisms cannot metabolize and eliminate heavy metals such as arsenic, lead, mercury, cadmium, iron, and aluminum. Instead, noxious substances remain in the body, accumulating in soft tissue with subsequent exposure. Acute heavy metal poisoning is caused by inhalation of or skin contact with materials in the workplace and is characterized by cramping, nausea, and vomiting; pain; sweating; headaches; difficulty breathing; impaired cognitive, motor, and language skills; mania; and convulsions. Lower, chronic exposure occurs in residential settings, particularly in old homes with lead paint or old plumbing. Chronic heavy metal poisoning is associated with impaired cognitive, motor, and language skills;

learning difficulties; nervousness and emotional instability; insomnia, nausea, and lethargy; and damage to vital organs. Symptoms are difficult to associate with an exposure source because they develop slowly over months or years and mimic other diseases, such as Alzheimer's disease, Parkinson's disease, muscular dystrophy, and multiple sclerosis.

Novel Impacts of Toxic Substances

A significant feature of petro-dependency is an entirely new class of environmental impacts caused by the use of toxic substances in agriculture and manufacturing.

Petrochemicals

The pervasiveness of petrochemicals in our lives is impossible to overstate. Petrochemical products such as detergent, synthetic fiber, and plastic have replaced natural products such as soap, cotton, wool, wood, paper, and leather. Petrochemical pesticides have overtaken natural control methods such as crop rotation, ladybugs, and birds (Commoner 1992: 54). So unusual is the toxicity of petrochemicals that Erik Erikson (1991: 11) refers to the associated health risks as "a new species of trouble."

Petrochemicals are toxic to life because they do not evolve in the biosphere. After the Earth formed, hydrogen, ammonia, methane, water vapor, and carbon dioxide were exposed to an energy source—sunlight, lightning, or meteorites. The resultant chemical reaction produced 20 amino acids. Theoretically, the acids could have combined in many permutations to produce thousands of proteins. Instead, evolution ruled out most possibilities, constraining nature's production to a small fraction of potential combinations. These proteins remain the basis of all life. Nature's protein production is matched with enzyme production to catalyze protein degradation, so that each natural protein is degraded by its corresponding enzyme.

In stark contrast, petrochemicals are unnaturally produced by humans using petroleum as the carbon base to manipulate amino acids into combinations that do not occur in nature. No corresponding enzymes exist to biodegrade the artificial chemicals—they never go away. Instead, they accumulate in ecosystems and organisms, especially in the body's fatty tissues. Petrochemicals disrupt normal biochemistry, attack central nervous systems and nerve impulses, and can cause mutations and cancers.

Exposure to petrochemicals may have impacts beyond an exposed generation. Recent research suggests that some hormone-related changes caused by petrochemical exposure can be passed from one generation to the next (Montague 2006). Rodent studies have shown that exposure permanently reprograms genetic traits to cause a legacy of illness (Montague 2006).

Petrochemical pesticides have recently been implicated in Colony Collapse Disorder, a global syndrome observed since 2006 in which managed colonies of honey bees suddenly disappear in large numbers (Jacobson 2008; U.S. Department of Agriculture 2010). Honey bee colonies are crucial for agricultural pollination in the production of high-value crops such as nuts, berries, fruit, and vegetables. The Agricultural Research Service of the U.S. Department of Agriculture asserts a complex, "perfect storm" explanation for the syndrome, consisting of viruses or other pathogens, pesticides, poor nutrition, and exposure to limited or contaminated water (U.S. Department of Agriculture 2010). European officials indicate the role of a relatively new class of pesticides: neonicotinoids. When France, Germany, Italy, and Slovenia banned the pesticide, bee populations were restored (Cruger 2010).

Transgenic Organisms

Few tests have been conducted on environmental and health effects of genetically engineered crops. Concerns are expressed about the following: production of allergens and transfer of antibiotic resistance markers, effects of accidental human ingestion of food crops genetically engineered to produce drugs and industrial chemicals, unintended transfers of transgenes through cross-pollination, and unknown effects on other organisms.

A primary concern is that DNA could generate new seeds, either by the physical mixing of seeds and seed parts or by pollen carried by wind or insects to the female parts of plants. Hundreds of genes from pharmaceutical and industrial crops could potentially contaminate the traditional seed supply for food crops. Traditional seed supplies are crucial to farmers who export to organic farmers and to countries that reject genetic-engineering techniques.

Concerns are also expressed about the risk of BGHs to cows and humans. Although the European Union at first declared BGH safe, its members issued a moratorium on BGH sales in 1993 based on concerns about animals' health and welfare. BGH is not approved for use in European Union nations, Japan, Australia, New Zealand, and Canada, but it is still used in 17 percent of U.S. dairy cows.

Synthetic DNA raises concerns about contamination and contagion because of its capacity to make bacteria. Unlike viruses, bacteria can live and reproduce outside a living body. Some fear the development of biological weapons with synthetic DNA. Paul Rabinow contends that the fabrication of synthetic DNA "raises a range of big questions about what nature is and what it could be. Evolutionary processes are no longer seen as sacred or inviolable" (quoted in Weiss 2007).

Nanomatter

More than 720 products containing nanoscale particles are on the market, even though their environmental and health risks are less well known than those of genetic engineering. Some scientists believe that reducing even harmless elements to nanoscale can result in extremely dangerous substances (The Economist 2007). Nanoparticles' larger surface areas can make the matter chemically reactive— a normally inert substance may assume hazardous characteristics at the nanoscale.

Nanoparticles can be inhaled, ingested, or absorbed through the skin. They may evade the immune system and accumulate in the brain, blood, and nerves.

They can penetrate cell membranes, interact with biological processes, and affect regulatory mechanisms. Recent animal studies show cause for concern (Shand and Wetter 2006).

- A study of fish in 2004 associated nanomatter with rapid onset brain damage.
- In 2005, the U.S. National Aeronautics and Space Administration reported that commercially available carbon nanotubes injected into rats' lungs caused significant lung damage.
- A study by the National Institute of Occupational Safety and Health in 2005 reported substantial DNA damage in the hearts and aortic arteries of mice exposed to carbon nanotubes.

Unprecedented Global Impacts

Petro-dependency's environmental impacts include unprecedented global problems: depletion of the stratospheric ozone layer and global warming.

Sunlight and oxygen react to form the stratospheric ozone layer, which absorbs about 99 percent of the ultraviolet radiation entering the atmosphere. But this protective ozone layer is depleted by petrochemicals, primarily chlorofluorocarbons (CFCs), which require one hundred years to break down. As CFCs rise into the stratosphere, ultraviolet radiation initiates chemical reactions that destroy ozone. One chlorine atom can destroy up to 100,000 ozone molecules. The thinning ozone layer allows more ultraviolet radiation to reach the Earth, contributing to skin cancer, suppressed immune systems, and eye cataracts. Radiation damages soybeans, a major global crop, and phytoplankton, the base of oceanic food webs. Even with decreases in immediate emissions, atmospheric concentrations will continue to rise for at least another decade or two.

Climate change is the most devastating global environmental problem to confront the human species. It is caused by a severe escalation of the greenhouse effect, in which average global temperatures increase due to carbon dioxide, methane, and nitrous oxide levels in the atmosphere. Human economic activities have dramatically raised the proportions of those gases in the atmosphere: increases in carbon dioxide come from burning fossil fuels and destroying tropical forests; the release of methane comes from increased rice yields and domesticated animals; nitrous oxide comes from vehicle exhausts and nitrate fertilizers. The greenhouse effect causes unpredictable and potentially catastrophic global climate changes.

In 1988, the United Nations Environmental Programme (UNEP) and the World Meteorological Organization established the Intergovernmental Panel on Climate Change (IPCC) to assess data relevant to understanding the potential impacts of climate change and options for adaptation and mitigation. The IPCC issued assessment reports in 1990, 1995, 2001, and 2007. Some of the panel's conclusions are the following:

- Global atmospheric concentrations of carbon dioxide, methane, and nitrous oxides have markedly increased since 1750 as a result of human activities; concentrations now far exceed pre-industrial values.
- Climate system warming is unequivocal. The probability is more than 90 percent that human activities—particularly the burning of fossil fuels—account for most of the observed increase in global climate temperatures since the mid-twentieth century.
- Anthropogenic warming and sea level rise would continue for centuries even if greenhouse gas concentrations were stabilized.

Charles Harper (2008) illustrates the urgency of global warming with a sketch of the planet's climate history. An average warming of 1.5 degrees would match the climate 6,000 years ago, as agricultural civilization began. A climate warmed by 3–5 degrees has not occurred in human history—it would match the Pliocene era of 5 million years ago. An average warming of more than 5 degrees would represent the climate 40 million years ago, prior to the evolution of birds and mammals and the formation of glaciers.

Petro-dependency's Impacts on the Biospheric Foundation of Life

The environmental impacts of the petro-dependent mode of subsistence are substantial. To emphasize the striking departure of this mode from previous ones and to illustrate the unique nature of petro-dependency's human–environment interaction, I discuss petro-dependency's environmental impacts specifically as they affect the biospheric foundation of life (see Table 3.5).

The foundation of life consists of physical and biological resources. Physical resources are contained in three spheres. The lithosphere, the earth's upper surface, contains soil, which is built from decomposed minerals, rocks, and plant and animal remains, and mineral resources (metallic and non-metallic minerals, gemstones, semiprecious minerals, and energy minerals). The hydrosphere contains all of the Earth's moisture: ice, water vapor, salt water, and fresh water (surface water and groundwater). The atmosphere is a gaseous envelope extending above the Earth's surface, consisting primarily of nitrogen and oxygen, with smaller amounts of argon, neon, carbon dioxide, and ozone. Biological resources are plants and animals. Through our economic interactions with the foundation of life, we withdraw resources for the material support of production processes, causing resource depletion, and we add materials through production processes, causing pollution.

Withdrawing physical resources from the lithosphere, we clear land for food, fiber, forest products, and livestock grazing. We extract minerals for use in manufacturing and energy resources for fuel, electrical power, and manufactured products. Most mineral resources are nonrenewable for human purposes. Others, like copper, exist in fixed amounts. From the physical resources in the hydrosphere, we withdraw fresh water for consumption, irrigation, and manufacturing.

A potentially renewable resource, fresh water can be depleted in the short term. Except during respiration, we withdraw no physical resources from the atmosphere. The greater the rates of withdrawal from the lithosphere and hydrosphere, the more severe are problems of resource depletion.

We also withdraw biological resources from the lithosphere, hydrosphere, and atmosphere for the material support of production processes. Undomesticated plants and animals are extracted for land clearing, consumption and manufacturing, and extermination. They are potentially renewable resources that can be depleted or extinguished. The extraction of plants and animals triggers changes in population sizes that destabilize ecosystems. The greater the withdrawal rate of biological resources, the more severe is the problem of biodiversity loss.

Through our economic interactions with the foundation of life, we add materials from production processes to physical resources. Additions to the lithosphere and the hydrosphere are similar. Organisms such as bacteria, parasites, and viruses are added as a consequence of sewage treatment and livestock feedlots. Nutrients (phosphorus, iron, boron, and nitrates) enter from fertilizers and from manufacturing and meat-curing processes. Metals and acids come from manufacturing processes and plumbing infrastructures. Radioactive substances and heavy metals are deposited from mining activities and power plant operations. Inorganic chemicals penetrate physical resources from mine drainage and manufacturing processes. Petrochemicals from fertilizers, pesticides, and waste disposal infiltrate land and water. Transgenic organisms escape from confined areas, and nanomatter is released from manufacturing processes and waste disposal. Further additions to water include decomposed material from livestock and suspended and dissolved solids from agriculture, rangelands, and construction.

Petro-dependent additions to the atmosphere are substantial. Carbon monoxide, lead, nitrogen oxides, and particulate matter enter the air from internal combustion engines. Lead also comes from smelters and nitrogen oxides from power plants. Sulfur oxides are added from plant boilers, oil refineries, and petrochemical manufacturing. Particulate matter reaches the air from industrial combustion, windblown dust, and forest fires. Ground ozone forms in the atmosphere from the chemical reaction of nitrogen dioxide and hydrocarbons. Greenhouse gas emissions, particularly from fossil fuel combustion, contribute to global climate change. CFCs contribute to the hole in the stratospheric ozone level, increasing ultraviolet radiation reaching the Earth.

Failed Petro-dependent Environmental Policies?

Examination of the petro-dependent mode of subsistence's unparalleled resource depletion and pollution reveals that we are poisoning ourselves and destroying the basis of our future survival. The foundation of life—*all* life—is ailing. It appears that our policies are failing: failing to acknowledge ecological principles, failing to recognize the intrinsic link between economic activities and the environment, and failing to enact democratic principles.

TABLE 3.5 Petro-dependency's Impacts on Physical and Biological Resources

Biophysical foundation of life: Physical resources and biological resources	Withdrawal of resources for the material support of production processes = resource depletion	Addition of substances through production processes = pollution
Physical resources: Lithosphere Soil Minerals Energy minerals	Soil: land cleared for food, fiber, livestock, and forest products Minerals: metallic and non-metallic minerals extracted for manufacturing Energy minerals: petroleum and coal extracted for fuel, electrical power, and processed products	Organisms: from improper sewage treatment and livestock feedlots Nutrients: from manufacturing, meat-curing, and fertilizers Metals and acids: from manufacturing and plumbing infrastructures Radioactive substances and heavy metals: from mining and power plant emissions Inorganic chemicals: from mine drainage and manufacturing Petrochemicals: from fertilizers and production of synthetic organic substances Transgenic organisms: from food crops Nanoparticles: from production of manomatter
Physical resources: Hydrosphere Ice Water vapor Salt water Fresh water Surface water Groundwater	Fresh water: extracted for consumption, irrigation, and manufacturing	Organisms: from improper sewage treatment and livestock feedlots Nutrients: from manufacturing, meat-curing, and fertilizers Metals and acids: from manufacturing and plumbing infrastructures Radioactive substances and heavy metals: from mining and power plant emissions Inorganic chemicals: from mine drainage and manufacturing Petrochemicals: from fertilizers and production of synthetic organic substances Transgenic organisms: from food crops Nanoparticles: from production of nanomatter Low oxygen: plant and animal materials in runoff from livestock operations Suspended and dissolved solids: from agriculture, rangelands, and construction processes

Physical resources: Atmosphere Nitrogen Oxygen Argon Neon Carbon dioxide Ozone	Oxygen: extracted for respiration	Carbon monoxide: from motor vehicle emissions Lead: from motor vehicle emissions and lead smelters Nitrogen oxides: from motor vehicle emissions and electric utility boilers Sulfur oxides: from utility plant boilers, oil refineries, and chemical refineries Particulate matter: from motor vehicle emissions, industrial combustion, windblown dust, and forest fires Ground ozone: from the chemical reaction of nitrogen dioxide and hydrocarbons from motor vehicle emissions Heat = global climate change: from fossil fuel combustion Ultraviolet radiation = hole in stratospheric ozone layer: from chlorofluorocarbons
Biological resources: Undomesticated plants	Extracted for land clearing, consumption, manufacturing, and extermination	
Biological resources: Undomesticated animals	Extracted for consumption, extermination, and manufacturing	

At the end of World War II, the United States emerged as the first society to adopt the petro-dependent mode of subsistence. Four postwar conditions contributed prominently to that fact. First, the country's industrial and transportation infrastructures were intact because World War II was not fought in the continental United States. In contrast, would-be economic rivals in western Europe suffered devastation of their infrastructures.

Second, postwar prosperity was underwritten by the nation's military strength and the massive growth of the military-industrial complex. The nation emerged from World War II as a global economic and military power. The Cold War with the Soviet Union was an economic conflict as much an ideological one—the arms race, in actuality, was a production race. The Cold War "provided continuing markets for military production, as well as a military rationale for federal policies to keep these industries' productive capacities high" (Andrew 1999: 182).

Third, the government intervened substantially in economic activities, increasing cooperation with economic elites to plan a postwar strategy that maintained economic and military dominance by emphasizing a surplus of exports over imports, calculating that maintaining industry at wartime capacity would require exports at three times the prewar level (Block 1977). Under these conditions, the multinational corporation arose in "a most forceful convergence of state and corporation" (Marger 1987: 118).

Fourth, the United States possessed an abundance of oil that was reinforced by U.S. corporations' exclusive access to some of the Middle East's vast oil reserves. In Part II, I examine the United States as a case study of petro-dependent environmental policies.

II

The United States: Prototype Petro-dependent Society

4

Petro-dependent
Environmental Policies

As the first petro-dependent society, the United States exhibits all of the resource depletion and pollution problems described in the previous chapter. Environmental policies are the legislature's response to those problems within the context of constitutional authority. The constitutional bases for environmental legislation are the commerce, property, and federal supremacy clauses. The commerce clause (art. 1, sec. 8) grants Congress the power to regulate interstate and foreign commerce. The clause was originally intended to promote interstate commerce through federally funded projects, such as improving the navigable waterways and constructing buoys and lighthouses. It was subsequently expanded to justify federal regulation of interstate flows of natural resources and air and water pollution. The property clause (art. 4, sec. 3) grants Congress the power to regulate public lands for preservation, resource extraction, and sale. Article 6 establishes federal supremacy, ensuring the federal government's ability to set standards for air and water quality that states must meet.

Within the framework of the biospheric foundation of life, two types of policies are distinguished. Resource management policies regulate the withdrawal of physical and biological resources for the material support of production; they aim at conservation. Pollution abatement policies regulate the addition of substances to the biosphere from production processes; they apply end-of-pipe solutions, mitigating effects rather than avoiding them. Note that transgenic organisms and nanoparticles, the newest entries to petro-production, are largely unregulated. No statute was explicitly created for transgenic products. Regulatory statutes designed for other products are applied by an array of agencies. No statutes specifically address protection of the food supply from transgenic organisms. Nor do any statutes regulate the production, handling, or labeling of nanoparticles.

Most environmental statutes passed in the 1960s and 1970s use a federalist approach in which states take the lead in regulation with federal government oversight. In many cases, the federal government approves a state program and transfers regulatory authority if the state has a law at least as strict as federal law and a functioning regulatory agency. For example, the Surface Mining Control and Reclamation Act of 1977 regulates surface mining and reclamation. Most coal-mining states have approved regulatory programs that allow them to issue mining permits, inspect mines, and take enforcement actions.

I examine forty-seven U.S. environmental statutes (see Table 4.1) within brief historical contexts. My selection is not exhaustive but similar to those of specialists such as Richard N. L. Andrews, Michael E. Kraft, Jacqueline Switzer, and Norman Vig.

Statutes for Resource Management and Pollution Abatement in the Lithosphere

Soil Management and Pollution Policies

Concerns about widespread aerial spraying of pesticides on farmland and residential areas resulted in the Federal Insecticide, Fungicide, and Rodenticide Act of 1947. It required manufacturers to register new pesticide products but provided for neither the control of pesticide use nor the authority to prohibit pesticide marketing. In the late 1950s, the federal government launched two campaigns of aerial pesticide spraying. Thousands of acres in the Northeast were sprayed to halt the destruction of forests by the European gypsy moth caterpillar. Large areas of the Southeast were sprayed to eliminate two species of South American fire ants. Both efforts failed to eradicate the introduced "pests."

The Watershed Protection and Flood Prevention Act of 1954 authorized federal assistance for local governments "to prevent erosion, flooding, and sediment damage and to promote the conservation, utilization, and disposal of water" (Andrews 1999: 170). But economic imperatives contradicted conservation. In 1953, President Dwight D. Eisenhower authorized increased road construction in national forests to facilitate logging and meet postwar demands for single-family homes. The enlarged middle class and affordability of cars spurred tourism in national parks that generated two laws in 1964. The Wilderness Act authorized the permanent protection of 9 million acres as wilderness. The Land and Water Conservation Fund Act used sales of offshore oil and gas leases to aid state and local governments in acquiring recreational lands.

Reflecting growing concerns about aerial pesticide spraying, Rachel Carson's *Silent Spring* (1962) described the hazards of petrochemical pesticides and criticized both industry and regulators for failing to protect the public. The book substantially charged the modern environmental movement, which effectively lobbied for an unprecedented number of laws during the 1970s, beginning with the National Environmental Protection Act of 1970, which created the U.S. Environmental Protection Agency (EPA) as the premier environmental regulator.

A report by the President's Council on Environmental Quality in 1971 identified petrochemicals as a possible cause of cancers. Heightened public fears led to the Federal Environmental Pesticide Control Act (FEPCA) of 1972, which established a product registration process that authorized the EPA to suspend or cancel registration to protect public health. New pesticide products required the manufacturer's justification. Products sold prior to 1970 were granted registered status until reviewed by the EPA and could be banned if the review found unreasonable adverse effects on the environment. But the law did not establish standards based on public health. Instead, the EPA weighed "the environmental and health risks against the economic benefits of agricultural production, and even repaid the manufacturers and users for any stocks left unsold if a product was deregistered" (Andrews 1999: 243).

The Lands Policy and Management Act of 1976 terminated privatization of public lands and authorized the Bureau of Land Management to manage public lands for long-term benefits. A permit system was established in national forests and grasslands for logging, mining, and livestock grazing. Western legislators threatened the bureau's budget when permits favored protection over profit. Consequently, logging, mining, and grazing permits on public lands were routinely approved (Andrews 1999).

In 1978, Congress addressed pollution from noxious and toxic substances. Hazardous substances used in production processes are regulated under the Toxic Substances and Control Act (TSCA), which requires companies to notify the EPA of new chemicals prior to manufacturing and to maintain data on their effects. The TSCA requires the EPA to track 75,000 produced or imported industrial chemicals listed on the Chemical Substance Inventory. The EPA is authorized to screen chemicals and to require testing of those that pose hazards to the environment or to human health. Richard Andrews (1999: 244) brands the TSCA "one of the least effective EPA programs" because it assigns to the EPA responsibility for regulating tens of thousands of *substances* rather than a few hundred *firms,* imposing the burden of "generating and sifting huge quantities of scientific data and inferences, based on varying and uncertain evidence, for thousands of compounds and an almost unlimited range of possible effects." On average, 1,800 new chemicals are registered with the government each year, but few are tested (Montague 2006).

At the waste end of the production process, the Resource Conservation and Recovery Act (RCRA) regulates the treatment, storage, transportation, and disposal of solid and hazardous wastes generated after 1975. It sets standards, provides federal technical and financial assistance to states, and charges state and local governments with responsibility for compliance. Amendments in 1984 prohibited the land disposal of specified hazardous liquid wastes and mandated cradle-to-grave tracking and management of hazardous wastes.

The Soil and Water Resource Conservation Act of 1977 established nationwide inventories of soil and water resources to improve protection. The Alaska National Interest Lands Conservation Act of 1980 designated more than 100 million acres as national wilderness, forest, wildlife refuges, and parks.

In the late 1970s, residents of a blue-collar neighborhood in Niagara Falls complained about black ooze on basement walls and an unusual incidence of children's respiratory ailments. New York State health officials investigated and announced in August 1978 that a long-closed petrochemical waste landfill at the Love Canal posed a grave and imminent peril to residents' health. Congress

TABLE 4.1 Petro-dependent Policies Protecting the Biospheric Life Support System

	Regulation of economic activity	
Biophysical foundation of life: Physical environment and biological environment	Withdrawal of resources for the material support of production = resource management policies	Addition of substances through production processes = pollution abatement policies
Physical resources: Lithosphere Soil Minerals Energy minerals	*Management problems* Soil: land cleared for food, fiber, livestock, and forest products Minerals: metallic and non-metallic minerals extracted for manufacturing Energy minerals: petroleum and coal extracted for fuel, electrical power, and processed products	*Pollution problems* Organisms: from improper sewage treatment and livestock feedlots Nutrients: from manufacturing, meat-curing, and fertilizers Metals and acids: from manufacturing and plumbing infrastructures Radioactive substances and heavy metals: from mining and power plant emissions Inorganic chemicals: from mine drainage and manufacturing Petrochemicals: from fertilizers and production of synthetic organic substances Transgenic organisms: from food crops Nanoparticles: from production of manomatter
	Management policies: Soil 1954 Watershed Protection and Flood Prevention Act 1964 Land and Water Conservation Fund Act 1964 Wilderness Act 1976 Lands Policy and Management Act 1977 Soil and Water Resource Conservation Act 1980 Alaska National Interest Lands Conservation Act 1996 Agricultural Improvement and Reform Act	*Pollution policies:* Soil 1948 Federal Insecticide, Fungicide, and Rodenticide Act 1972 Federal Environmental Pesticide Control Act 1976 Toxic Substances Control Act 1976 Resource Conservation and Recovery Act 1980 Comprehensive Environmental Response, Compensation, and Liability Act 1984 Hazardous and Solid Waste Management Act 1986 Emergency Preparedness Community Right-to-know Act 1990 Pollution Prevention Act
	Management policies: Energy minerals 1946 Atomic Energy Act 1954 Civilian Nuclear Power Act 1975 Energy Policy and Conservation Act 1977 Department of Energy Organization Act 1978 Public Utilities Regulatory Policy Act 1978 National Energy Act 1992 Comprehensive Energy Policy Act 2005 Energy Policy Act 2007 Energy Independence and Security Act	*Pollution policies:* Energy minerals 1963 Limited Nuclear Test Ban Treaty 1970 Water Quality Improvement Act 1977 Surface Mining Control and Reclamation Act 1982 Nuclear Waste Policy Act

Physical resources:
Hydrosphere
Ice
Water vapor
Salt water
Fresh water
Surface waters
Groundwater

Management problems
Fresh water: extracted for consumption, irrigation, and manufacturing

Management policies: Fresh water
1968 Wild and Scenic Rivers Act

Management policies: Salt water
1972 Coastal Zone Management Act

Pollution problems
Organisms: from improper sewage treatment and livestock feedlots
Nutrients: from manufacturing, meat-curing, and fertilizers
Metals and acids: from manufacturing and plumbing infrastructures
Radioactive substances and heavy metals: from mining and power plant emissions
Inorganic chemicals: from mine drainage and manufacturing
Petrochemicals: from fertilizers and production of synthetic organic substances
Transgenic organisms: from food crops
Nanoparticles: from production of nanomatter
Low oxygen: plant and animal materials in runoff from livestock operations
Suspended and dissolved solids: from agriculture, rangelands, and construction processes

Pollution policies: Fresh water
1948 Federal Water Pollution Control Act
1965 Water Quality Control Act
1966 Clean Water Restoration Act
1974 Safe Drinking Water Act
1976 Toxic Substances Control Act
1976 Resource Conservation and Control Act
1986 Emergency Preparedness Community Right-to-know Act
1990 Pollution Prevention Act

Pollution policies: Salt water
1972 Marine Protection, Research, and Sanctuaries Act

(continued on next page)

TABLE 4.1 Continued

Biophysical foundation of life: Physical environment and biological environment	Regulation of economic activity	
	Withdrawal of resources for the material support of production = resource management policies	Addition of substances through production processes = pollution abatement policies
Physical resources: Atmosphere Nitrogen Oxygen Argon Neon Carbon dioxide Ozone	*Management problems:* Air None *Management policies:* Air None	*Pollution problems:* Air Carbon monoxide: from motor vehicle emissions Lead: from motor vehicle emissions and lead smelters Nitrogen oxides: from motor vehicle emissions and electric utility boilers Sulfur oxides: from utility plant boilers, oil refineries, and chemical refineries Particulate matter: from motor vehicle emissions, industrial combustion, windblown dust, and forest fires Ground ozone: from the chemical reaction of nitrogen dioxide and hydrocarbons from motor vehicle emissions Heat = global climate change: from fossil fuel combustion Ultraviolet radiation = hole in stratospheric ozone layer: from chlorofluorocarbons *Pollution policies:* Air 1955 Air Pollution Control Act 1963 Clean Air Act 1965 Motor Vehicle Air Pollution Control Act 1967 Air Quality Act 1976 Toxic Substances Control Act 1976 Resource Conservation and Control Act 1986 Emergency Preparedness Community Right-to-know Act 1990 Pollution Prevention Act

Biological resources: Undomesticated plants	*Management problems:* Plants Extracted for land-clearing, consumption, manufacturing, and extermination	*Pollution problems:* Plants None
	Management policies: Plants 1960 Multiple Use and Sustained Yield Act 1964 Wilderness Act 1973 Endangered Species Act 1974 Forest and Range Renewable Resources Planning Act 1976 National Forest Management Act 1995 Forest Health Act	
Biological resources: Undomesticated animals	*Management problems:* Animals Extracted for consumption, extermination, and manufacturing	*Pollution problems:* Animals None
	Management policies: Animals 1972 Marine Mammal Protection Act 1973 Endangered Species Act 1976 Fisheries Management and Conservation Act	

responded in 1980 with the Comprehensive Environmental Response, Compensation, and Liability Act (CERCLA), or the Superfund law. The law established a fund from taxes on petrochemical corporations for the federal cleanup of other abandoned or uncontrolled hazardous waste sites and directed the EPA to create a National Priority List of contaminated sites.

Continuing discoveries of contaminated communities stimulated a new wing of the environmental movement: the grassroots or anti-toxics movement. Residents of thousands of contaminated communities organized locally to pressure politicians for regulatory enforcement and neighborhood cleanup. The movement was composed primarily of working-class people—many of them women. Instead of lobbying legislators for *new* regulations, activists used protest tactics to pressure government agencies to enforce *existing* regulations.

The re-authorization of CERCLA in 1986 tightened cleanup requirements and added the Emergency Planning and Community Right-to-Know Act (EPCRA), a potentially powerful tool for activists. EPCRA requires corporations that emit certain hazardous substances to submit annual reports to the EPA listing facilities' on-site chemicals and the quantity of each chemical released to each environmental medium. Exempted industrial sectors are notable: utilities, mining, oil and gas production, agribusiness, municipal waste management facilities, and all federal facilities (Gottlieb 1995). Data submitted by corporations are not independently verified. The EPA uses these data to create a publicly available national toxic chemical inventory, the Toxic Release Inventory (TRI).

Disproportionate contamination of minority communities generated the environmental justice movement, originating in an incident in 1982 in which North Carolina state officials chose predominantly black Warren County as the site for a hazardous waste landfill. Residents protested the siting on the basis of racial discrimination. They were assisted in their struggle by the United Church of Christ's Commission for Racial Justice, the Southern Christian Leadership Conference, and the National Association for the Advancement of Colored People. Although the landfill was constructed, the environmental justice movement forced policymakers to recognize that environmental exposure is not evenly distributed in society. In 1992, the Office of Environmental Justice was established in the EPA with the mandate to encourage compliance with Title VI of the Civil Rights Act of 1964 in environmental use decisions.

The TSCA's deficiencies were first addressed by the Pollution Prevention Act of 1990, which attempts to control pollution at the source. But the act merely *encourages* source reduction, leaving it to voluntary action (Gottlieb 1995). A more substantial remedy to the TSCA is Senate Bill 847, the Safe Chemicals Act. First introduced in April 2010 and reintroduced a year later, the bill grants the EPA broad new powers to regulate new and existing chemicals. The EPA would create a public database with corporate-submitted information for every chemical produced. The law restrains industry's ability to claim exemptions on the basis that publicizing data would adversely affect business. The American Chemistry Council opposes the bill, claiming it could hamper innovation in new products and technologies and that it undermines business certainty by allowing states to adopt their own regulations. As of July 1, 2012, the bill remained in the Senate without a scheduled vote.

Energy Minerals Management Policies

Primary U.S. energy minerals include coal, petroleum, natural gas, and uranium. Besides products derived from petroleum, the minerals are used for fuel, heat, and the generation of electric power.

Public distaste for the U.S. atomic bombings of Japan led President Eisenhower in 1953 to initiate the Atoms for Peace program, promoting civilian uses for nuclear energy—particularly, the replacement of coal-burning power generation with nuclear power generation. The Civilian Nuclear Power Act of 1954 charged the Atomic Energy Commission (AEC) with developing plans for commercial nuclear power generation. It authorized federal licensing for commercial applications, allowed private electric utility companies to own nuclear materials, and directed the AEC to build experimental and demonstration reactors for civilian power generation. The government encouraged corporations to construct nuclear reactors through substantial subsidies and legislation that reduced capital risks, such as the Price-Anderson Act of 1957, which limited corporate liability for accidents at nuclear reactors.

Nuclear bomb research and production also continued. Between 1951 and 1958, the U.S. military carried out more than one hundred atmospheric nuclear tests in Nevada. The combination of the Cuban Missile Crisis in October 1962 and concerns by those living downwind of the bomb testing contributed to the Limited Nuclear Test Ban Treaty of 1963 between the United States and the Soviet Union, ending their atmospheric testing of nuclear weapons.

By the mid-1960s, large oil spills appeared from domestic oil rigs operating offshore on the Pacific and Gulf coasts and from huge tanker ships transporting oil around the globe. In 1969, an offshore oil rig poured millions of gallons of oil along the beaches of wealthy Santa Barbara, California. The spill drew far more international media attention than previous spills, and hundreds of photographs circulated of oil-soaked beaches and dying wildlife. Congress passed the Water Quality Improvement Act in 1970, authorizing the government's immediate intervention in oil spill cleanups and providing for judicial pursuit of reimbursement from polluters.

In 1973, OPEC reduced oil production levels and placed embargoes on oil sold to the United States, causing sudden shortages, drastically increased prices, and stark illumination of U.S. dependence on foreign oil supplies. The Energy Policy and Conservation Act of 1975 extended domestic oil price controls, mandated fuel economy standards for motor vehicles, and established the Strategic Petroleum Reserve to stockpile oil and minimize the effects of future oil embargoes.

Criticisms that the AEC could not adequately regulate commercial nuclear energy while promoting it led Congress in 1974 to replace the agency with two new ones. The Nuclear Regulatory Commission was established to regulate commercial applications of nuclear energy, and the Energy Research and Development Administration (ERDA) was assigned to oversee nuclear weapons activities and energy technology research. The more comprehensive Department of Energy Organization Act of 1977 replaced ERDA with the cabinet-level U.S. Department of Energy (DOE) and placed most federal energy agencies and programs under the DOE's control. The DOE's responsibilities included long-term, high-risk research and development of energy technology; federal power marketing; energy conservation; management of the federal nuclear weapons complex; energy regulatory programs; and a central energy data collection and analysis program used to create the National Energy Policy Plan, a biennial analysis of all aspects of the nation's energy.

The Surface Mining Control and Reclamation Act of 1977 is the primary federal law for regulating strip mining of coal. The act created the Office of Surface Mining within the U.S. Department of the Interior to disseminate regulations, fund state regulatory and reclamation efforts, and ensure consistency across state regulatory programs. It created regulatory programs for mining operations and for the reclamation of mined lands. The program for active mines sets performance standards, requires permits prior to mining operations, requires companies to post bonds to cover reclamation costs in case the company abandoned the mine, prohibits surface mining on lands such as national parks and wilderness areas, and allows citizens to challenge proposed surface mining operations. The reclamation program created a fund from coal taxes for the cleanup of mine lands abandoned before 1977. Amendments in 1990 allow the use of funds for reclamation of mines abandoned after 1977. Eighty percent of the fees are dispersed to states with approved reclamation programs. The remaining 20 percent is used by the Office of Surface Mining for high-priority cleanups in states without approved programs and for emergencies such as land subsidence.

The Public Utilities Regulatory Policy Act of 1978 was passed to keep power prices from escalating after the oil crisis. It increased competition in energy production by requiring utility companies to open national transmission grids to independent power generators. Similar intent underlay the National Energy Act of 1978, which partially deregulated natural gas pricing to make it more competitive with other energy sources. The 1992 amendments permitted utilities and other power producers to operate wholesale generating plants outside the utility's distribution region, breaking the "natural monopoly" (Andrews 1999: 301).

The Nuclear Waste Policy Act of 1982 was intended to resolve waste disposal problems with a permanent national repository, charging the DOE with evaluating three potential sites. Congressional legislation in 1987 directed the DOE to focus on the Yucca Mountain, Nevada, site, but local citizens and environmental groups strongly resisted (Kubasek and Silverman 2008). Debate raged for more than twenty years. The DOE recommended the site based on scientific and engineering studies that concluded it would protect public health and safety, preserve environmental quality, allow the environmental cleanup of Cold War weapons facilities, protect the nation from terrorist acts, and support sound energy policy.

Despite dissent by the governor of Nevada, Congress approved Yucca Mountain as the repository site in 2002. But the project was derailed when the DOE reported to Congress in 2009 that the site was no longer viewed as a viable option and that the government should develop new plans (Bryce 2009). Funding for development of the waste site was terminated under the Obama administration effective with the 2011 federal budget.

With the Soviet Union's invasion of Afghanistan in 1979, President Jimmy Carter declared the Carter Doctrine, warning that the United States would consider any Soviet attempt to gain control of the Persian Gulf region as an assault on U.S. interests. He created the Rapid Deployment Joint Task Force, later named the U.S. Central Command, to ensure the flow of Persian Gulf oil to the United States. Iran's Islamic Revolution of 1979 replaced the U.S.-friendly shah with the Islamic fundamentalist Ayatollah Ruhollah Khomeini. Iranians expelled all foreign oil companies. Although the Saudis increased oil production to meet the shortfall, oil prices continued to surge.

In 1989, the *Exxon Valdez* ran aground in Alaska's Prince William Sound, causing the largest oil tanker spill in history. About 11 million gallons of crude oil covered 900 square miles. Thousands of marine mammals were killed; hundreds of thousands of sea birds died; and fisheries supporting local residents closed. The Oil Pollution Act of 1990 streamlined and strengthened the EPA's ability to prevent and clean up catastrophic oil spills with a trust fund generated from oil taxes. The statute requires firms to submit plans for dealing with large discharges from oil storage facilities and vessels. The EPA established regulations for aboveground storage facilities, and the Coast Guard issued regulations for oil tankers.

In August 1990, Iraqi troops invaded oil-rich Kuwait. A United Nations Security Council resolution sanctioned member states' use of all necessary means to force Iraq from Kuwait. An international coalition assembled nearly a million troops using Saudi Arabia as the base. Coalition forces initiated an air assault against Iraq on January 17, 1991, followed on February 24 by a land offensive. Iraqi forces fell into disarray, and the Persian Gulf War ended on February 28. The Comprehensive Energy Policy Act of 1992, a direct consequence of the war, contained mandates to label alternative fuels and alternative-fuel vehicles, provide low-interest loans to small businesses for conversion to alternative fuels, promote increased use of renewable energy, and create programs for increasing energy efficiency. The statute also included tax breaks to independent oil and gas drillers.

In 2001, U.S. consumption of 7 billion of the world's 28.2 billion gallons of crude oil led President George W. Bush to appoint a task force to develop a new national energy strategy. The task force's report predicted an impending energy crisis with increased dependence on unfriendly foreign powers. The administration responded by increasing domestic oil production and prioritizing energy security in decisions on trade and foreign policy.

The Energy Policy Act of 2005 was the first significant energy law enacted in more than a decade. It made the most substantial changes in the Federal Energy

Regulatory Commission since the Federal Power Act of 1935 and the Natural
Gas Act of 1938, strengthening the commission's regulatory tools and reaffirm-
ing the commitment to competitive wholesale power markets—the third major
federal law in thirty years to do so. The Energy Independence and Security Act of
2007 aimed toward greater energy independence as a national security priority.
The statute promotes the production of clean renewable fuels; protection of consumers; efficiency of products, buildings, and vehicles; and research on options
for capturing and storing greenhouse gases.

By 2009, amid growing concerns about global warming, nuclear power generation became pivotal in debates over greenhouse gas emissions. Policymakers
looked more favorably than they had on nuclear power as part of the solution.
One-fifth of the nation's electricity and 70 percent of essentially carbon-free
power was provided by 104 reactors in 31 states (Hebert 2009). The NRC is considering applications for 30 new reactors that would be built only with government guarantees of private financing (Hebert 2009).

An oil spill that may be the largest such catastrophe in U.S. history began on
April 20, 2010, with an explosion and fire on an oil platform in the Gulf of Mexico
that killed eleven workers. The out-of-control exploratory well, owned by BP,
released between 20,000 and 40,000 barrels of oil per day until it was finally
capped in mid-July. The BP spill revealed the conflicting functions of the Minerals
Management Service: safety and environmental protection in offshore energy
activities, leasing federal waters for conventional and renewable energy resources,
and collecting and distributing revenues. Interior Secretary Ken Salazar abolished
the bureau in May, dividing the three missions across three entities: the Bureau
of Ocean Energy Management, the Bureau of Safety and Environmental Enforcement, and the Office of Natural Resource Revenue. A six-month moratorium was
imposed on deep-water drilling in the Gulf (Minerals Management Service 2010).

Thirteen mineral energy statutes regulate the production and use of petroleum, coal, natural gas, and nuclear technology. One might expect policy goals to
aim at the conservation of nonrenewable energy resources. But an examination
reveals three additional functions: pollution abatement, government control, and
promotion of resource use. Three mineral energy policies aim at petroleum; one
addresses conservation and two refer to pollution from oil spills. One statute
targets pollution associated with unburned coal. One natural gas policy, passed
after the oil crisis, deregulates pricing to promote production. Nuclear technology
is addressed by four statutes, two aimed at pollution abatement and two designed
specifically to promote the commercial use of nuclear power. Another four statutes concern fossil fuels without reference to specific minerals. Two of them
encourage fossil fuel conservation without establishing standards; instead, they
promote the use and development of alternative fuels with industry incentives.
The remaining two fossil fuel policies are aimed at increasing government control. In total, only three of the thirteen mineral energy policies aim at conservation, despite the dwindling of the oil and coal resources on which the petro-
dependent state crucially depends.

Statutes for Resource Management and Pollution Abatement in the Hydrosphere

Two policies address water conservation; nine address pollution. The Wild and Scenic Rivers Act of 1968 authorized the conservation of selected rivers for aesthetic reasons. Water pollution policies before 1972 aided states and municipalities in water quality management without setting standards. The Federal Water Pollution Control Act of 1948 extended grants to local governments to establish management programs and provided for federal lawsuits against interstate river polluters. The Water Quality Control Act of 1965 established the Federal Water Quality Administration to oversee an expanded grant program requiring states to set federally approved standards. The Clean Water Restoration Act of 1966 increased federal funding for the construction of wastewater treatment plants.

Two events in 1969 captured broad media attention and spotlighted the inadequacy of water pollution policies: the fire on the Cuyahoga River in Cleveland and the pronouncement of Lake Erie as dead. Industrial wastes on the surface of the Cuyahoga River ignited and burned for eight days, damaging two railroad bridges. Months later, Lake Erie was declared a fatal victim of eutrophication, a process of algal overgrowth caused by sewage wastes that consume oxygen, suffocating other aquatic life.

Both disasters were addressed by the Coastal Zone Management Act of 1972, which authorized state grants for developing management plans that balance economic development with environmental conservation. Amendments to the Water Pollution Control Act the same year strengthened the government's role in maintaining water quality: they set national water quality goals, established a permit system for waste discharges from point sources, required permits issued by the Corps of Engineers for draining or filling wetlands, and increased grants for modernizing wastewater treatment plants. The Marine Protection, Research, and Sanctuaries Act of 1972 authorized research and monitoring of the effects of pollution, overfishing, and other adverse activities on oceans.

Public concern about toxic substances led to the Safe Drinking Water Act of 1974, which directed the EPA to set maximum contaminant levels for drinking water, required local water authorities to monitor toxics, and assigned enforcement responsibility to the states. Amendments in 1996 permitted municipalities to apply cost-benefit analyses to regulations and required municipalities to provide consumers with annual water quality reports.

Statutes for Pollution Abatement in the Atmosphere

In 1948, residents of Donora, Pennsylvania, suffered a photochemical smog that killed twenty people. In 1953, a smog in New York City killed at least 200 people. Congress responded with the Air Pollution Control Act of 1955, the nation's first air pollution law. It emphasized state and local governments' primary responsibility for air pollution control but mandated federal research programs to investigate the health effects of air pollution and authorized technical assistance for state governments.

The Clean Air Act of 1963 authorized the surgeon-general's investigation of air pollution problems when requested by state or local governments. The law provided for development of air quality criteria for advisory purposes but did not *mandate* air pollution reduction. The Motor Vehicle Air Pollution Control Act of 1965 established federal emissions standards for all mobile sources of air pollution. Amendments in 1966 provided federal subsidies for state and local air pollution control programs.

Congress passed the Air Quality Act of 1967 after eighty New Yorkers died in a summer thermal inversion that trapped concentrated pollution near the ground. The law established a framework for defining air quality control regions based on meteorological and topographical factors. It authorized federal regulation of stationary sources of air pollution and directed the development of scientific criteria for specified air pollutants but failed to mandate pollution reduction.

Amendments to the Clean Air Act in 1970 made the act the principal source of statutory authority for controlling air pollution. The amendments ordered the phase-out of lead additives to gasoline; charged the EPA with establishing national ambient air quality standards and emissions limits and with regulating fuels and motor vehicle emissions; and provided financial and technical assistance to states to monitor, control, and prevent air pollution.

Substantial amendments to the Clean Air Act in 1990 renewed the emphasis on controlling emissions and inaugurated efforts to control acid rain and stratospheric ozone depletion. The law placed particular emphasis on benzene, beryllium, radionuclides, arsenic, mercury, asbestos, and vinyl chloride.

Statutes for Resource Management of Plants and Animals

When the timbering industry complained in the 1950s about surrendering national forest land to tourism (Andrews 1999), Congress passed the Multiple-Use Sustained-Yield Act of 1960. Although the act required forest management officials to consider diverse, even non-economic values, it established no priorities among multiple uses. Preservation activists complained that the law did not challenge the traditional priority of timbering and were rewarded with the Wilderness Act of 1964, establishing the National Wilderness Preservation System and authorizing permanent protection of about 9 million acres of national forest land as wilderness. Over the next twenty years, tourism boomed, but the policy emphasis remained timbering.

Increased environmental awareness included concerns about species extinction. The Marine Mammal Protection Act of 1972 established federal responsibility for the conservation of marine mammals and banned the importation of marine mammals and associated products. The Endangered Species Act of 1973 broadened the government's authority to protect species from extinction through an endangered species list and prohibited actions that are damaging to listed species or their habitats.

The Forest and Range Renewable Resources Planning Act of 1974 required five- and ten-year management plans for harvesting timber in national forests. Aimed at conservation, the act instead made it easier for decisions to be made about logging without public knowledge. Environmentalists resisted and, in 1975, won their Supreme Court suit against the Forest Service for violating the Forest Management Act of 1897 by authorizing clear-cutting in the Monongahela National Forest in West Virginia. The National Forest Management Act of 1976 issued restrictive guidelines for clear-cutting and provided for public input in management decisions. But loopholes allowed timber companies to continue unsustainable logging practices on public lands. The Forest Health Act of 1995 reinforced loopholes with its concept of "salvage logging," which justified the rapid expansion of logging on public lands.

Soviet encroachment on productive fisheries off U.S. coasts instigated the Fisheries Management and Conservation Act of 1976, which declared U.S. sovereignty over a 200 mile offshore zone. The statute established eight fishery management councils composed of fishermen. Andrews (1999: 294–295) describes how such a good conservation law went so badly. The act created an incentive program that provided financial subsidies to construct new commercial fishing vessels. Incentives triggered a rapid overexpansion of the fishing fleet that, by the 1990s, had nearly destroyed many major offshore fisheries.

Segueing from Account to Assessment

Four general trends in U.S. petro-dependent environmental policymaking are discernible. First, the foundation for environmental legislation constitutes a bias of economics over ecology and profit over protection. The commerce and property clauses were intended to regulate commerce. Citing them as the legislative basis indicates the government's priority of business over environmental concerns. Although Article 6 establishes federal supremacy, many pollution policies defer substantial responsibility to states and allow the states to weigh the economic costs of regulatory compliance.

The reasonable expectation of resource management policies is conservation. But a second trend in policymaking is that resource management policies, particularly those related to energy minerals, aim to *control* rather than *conserve* resources.

A third trend is that pollution policies emphasize mitigation over prevention. Instead of regulating substances *going into* production processes, policies regulate substances coming out of production, trying to catch pollutants after they enter the environment. Lead pollution in the air was dramatically reduced by laws prohibiting the addition of lead to gasoline, yet this success story has not influenced other policy content.

Decisions about production technologies are made by private corporations. This fourth general trend in environmental policymaking means that decisions with public consequences are made without public input. The federal government encourages new technologies instead of effectively regulating them—genetic engineering and nanotechnology are outstanding examples. The case of petrochemical pollution suggests that regulation of new technology comes only after a disaster, after citizens complain about the technology's environmental and health effects.

How effective are these statutes? In the next three chapters, I evaluate U.S. petro-dependent environmental policies with the framework established in Chapter 1. In Chapter 5, I ask this: To what extent does environmental policy acknowledge ecological principles? In Chapter 6, I attend to the following: Does environmental policy reflect the link between economic activities and ecological stability? And I devote Chapter 7 to this question: Does environmental policy enact democratic principles of fairness and justice?

5

Violations of Ecological Principles

Resource Depletion and Pollution

In the petro-dependent United States, the development of environmental policies lagged increasingly further behind petro-production's impacts. I demonstrate in this chapter that U.S. environmental policies only superficially acknowledge ecological principles. I first draw on a variety of sources to inventory resource depletion and pollution in the lithosphere, hydrosphere, and atmosphere. For a second and specific assessment, I analyze Toxic Release Inventory (TRI) data for pollution from hazardous substances.

The Status of the Biosphere

Resource Depletion and Pollution in the Lithosphere

A natural process, soil erosion becomes a problem when it outpaces soil replenishment. Petro-agriculture uses soil faster than microorganisms, which are killed by petrochemical pesticides, can convert minerals into usable forms for plants. The U.S. soil erosion rate is ten times the natural rate (Lang 2006). Erosion decreases productivity by diminishing the depth of soil and reducing its ability to store water and support plant growth. Erosion affects not only the quantity but also quality of food, because minerals and trace elements decrease as topsoil is stripped away. Consequently, food consumed today contains significantly less nutrition than food produced prior to petro-agriculture (Isaacs 2008). The economic impact of soil erosion on agriculture is approximately $37 billion per year (Lang 2006).

Eroded soil becomes a pollutant. Approximately 60 percent of eroded soil enters rivers, lakes, and streams, causing flooding and waterways polluted with fertilizers and pesticides. Airborne soil causes dust pollution that carries approximately twenty infectious disease organisms, such as anthrax and tuberculosis (Lang 2006). A study measuring dust deposited in western states reports that dust levels have increased 500 percent in the past 150 years because of large-scale agriculture and livestock industries and urbanization (Dunham 2008). The chemical composition of dust changed, with higher levels of phosphorus and nitrogen.

The livestock industry is a primary source of land and air pollution. Animal digestion and wastes release approximately 65 percent of the world's nitrous oxide and 37 percent of methane, a significant greenhouse gas. According to data from the Census of Agriculture, the production of hogs, cattle, poultry, and sheep generates nearly 910 million tons of animal waste per year. A 2008 report by the Pew Commission found that most animal waste at factory farms is either spread on the ground without treatment or placed in poorly treated waste lagoons (Block 2008). The report identifies concentrated animal feeding operations (CAFOs) as substantially contributing to contaminated drinking water and reduced oxygen in aquatic ecosystems.

Minerals are depleted because the government gives them away. Nearly one-third of the continental United States is resource-rich public land. A study by the Environmental Working Group in 2004 found that the government sold millions of these acres to mining companies for extraordinarily low prices (Environmental News Service 2004). For example, the Phelps Dodge mining company bought 155 acres in Colorado for $875. In California alone, mining corporations control 645,000 acres of public land. Foreign-owned corporations from ten countries control approximately 1.2 million acres of public land. The study concluded that more than 28,000 companies gained control of metals and minerals on 9.3 million acres of public land across twelve western states. Corporations will pay neither for the value of minerals extracted from public property nor for the environmental costs: the Environmental Protection Agency (EPA) estimates that 40 percent of western headwaters are contaminated by mine wastes and that $35 billion is needed to remediate a half-million abandoned mines in thirty-two states.

Energy mineral depletion is difficult to assess not only because of measurement problems but also because of the government's classification system. Resource reserves are categorized as "proved" or "undeveloped." "Proved resource reserves" refers to already developed sites with a 90–95 percent probability of containing the estimated amount. "Undeveloped resource reserves" refers to lands that likely contain resources with a 50 percent probability that the estimated amount will be found. "Undeveloped possible reserves" indicates a 5–10 percent probability of containing the amount specified.

In 2005, amendments to the Energy Policy and Conservation Act (EPCA) mandated an inventory of oil and natural gas resources in federal land with the identification of impediments in developing the resources. The EPCA Phase III Inventory, released in 2008, listed 279 million acres of federal land with potential for oil or natural gas resources. The inventory estimated proved oil reserves at 5.3 billion barrels and undeveloped oil reserves at 30.5 billion barrels. Approximately 24.2 billion barrels of undeveloped oil reserves are "possible" reserves, and 6.3 billion barrels are "probable" reserves. The inventory estimated proved natural gas reserves at 68.8 trillion cubic feet and undeveloped gas reserves at 231 trillion cubic feet. Undeveloped gas reserves consist of 214.1 trillion cubic feet of possible reserves and 16.9 trillion cubic feet of probable reserves. The report places public land in three categories, indicating impediments:

- Only 17 percent of the lands are accessible for oil and natural gas extraction under standard lease terms. These highly accessible lands contain 8 percent of all oil reserves and 10 percent of all gas reserves.
- Twenty-three percent of the lands are accessible for extraction with additional restrictions. These lands contain 30 percent of all oil reserves and 49 percent of all gas reserves.
- Sixty percent of the lands are inaccessible for oil and natural gas extraction and contain 62 percent of all oil reserves and 41 percent of all gas reserves.

Pollution in the Hydrosphere

Drinking water is contaminated by microorganisms, lead, chloroform, leaking underground waste storage tanks, landfills, and agricultural runoff. A study by the Natural Resources Defense Council in 1995 found that 53 million citizens drank water that violated standards under the Safe Drinking Water Act. A study by the Associated Press (2008a) found that water supplies in twenty-four major cities serving 41 million people are contaminated with trace amounts of pharmaceuticals, including antibiotics, anticonvulsants, mood stabilizers, and sex hormones (Down, Mendoza, and Pritchard 2008). The pharmaceuticals were found in twenty-eight of thirty-five watersheds. Water providers are not required to test for pharmaceuticals, and the government has no recommendations for safety limits.

The EPA uses data supplied by states to conduct periodic evaluations of the water quality in rivers, streams, lakes, ponds, reservoirs, bays, and estuaries. Under the evaluation system, "good" water quality signifies that water quality standards are met; "threatened" means that standards are met but quality is predicted to violate standards by the next report; and "impaired" means that water quality standards are not met. The National Water Quality Inventory of 2002 reports the following assessments:

- Rivers and streams: 51 percent were assessed as good, 4 percent as threatened, and 45 percent as impaired. Primary contaminants were siltation, pathogens, and habitat alterations. Top sources of contaminants were agriculture and hydrologic modifications.
- Lakes, ponds, and reservoirs: 48 percent were assessed as good, 5 percent as threatened, and 47 percent as impaired. Primary contaminants were nutrients, metals (especially mercury), and low dissolved oxygen. Top sources were agriculture and deposition from the atmosphere.

Sediments and agricultural runoff from the agricultural Midwest enter surface water, drain into the Mississippi River, and empty into the Gulf of Mexico to create a dead zone, a vast expanse of water that is oxygen-depleted each year from spring to early fall. Excessive plant nutrients increase phytoplankton populations, whose decay removes dissolved oxygen and kills fish and other marine animals. The dead zone has grown significantly since the 1980s. It covered approximately

6,000 square miles in 2007, but record-breaking floods in 2008 expanded it to more than 10,000 square miles (Gulf Dead Zone 2008).

Bays and estuaries are polluted by nutrients and metals, especially mercury. The National Water Quality Inventory of 2002 assessed 66 percent of bays and estuaries as "good," 2 percent as "threatened," and 32 percent as "impaired." The inventory warned that more than a third of U.S. bays and estuaries are in non-compliance or soon will be. Forecasts for the next decade by the NOAA indicate that conditions will likely worsen in 65 percent of estuaries and improve in only 20 percent (NOAA 2008b).

The NOAA study examined fifteen ecosystems within U.S. states and territories, finding nearly half in poor or fair condition because of rising ocean temperatures, corrosive water from the ocean's absorption of carbon dioxide released by burning fossil fuels, and land-based pollution such as sewage, beach erosion, coastal development, and overfishing (Associated Press 2008g). For the first time, acidified water was found to have infiltrated the continental shelf, less than twenty miles off the western coast of North America (NOAA 2008a). Marine life is likely to be seriously affected, particularly corals, mussels, and mollusks. Researchers had not anticipated this extent of ocean acidification until near the end of the twenty-first century.

Pollution in the Atmosphere

The EPA maintains a database on daily air quality in areas with populations that exceed 350,000. More than a thousand monitoring stations record daily measurements of the concentration of five common air pollutants: carbon monoxide, nitrogen dioxide, ground-level ozone, sulfur dioxide, and particulate matter.

- *Carbon monoxide* derives from the incomplete combustion of fossil fuels, affecting mental alertness and vision and aggravating cardiovascular and respiratory diseases.
- *Nitrogen dioxide* is produced when oxygen combines with nitrous oxides emitted from internal combustion engines, power plants, and pulp mills. It is generally associated with decreased lung function, aggravated asthma and allergies, and sudden infant death syndrome. It significantly contributes to so many other pollutants—notably, ozone and particulate matter—that identifying the health effects solely attributable to nitrogen dioxide is difficult.
- *Ground-level ozone* forms when pollutants emitted from motor vehicles, power plants, chemical plants, industrial boilers, and refineries chemically react in sunlight. One out of three healthy people is susceptible to the effects of ozone: respiratory irritation and infections, decreased lung function, and aggravation of asthma.
- *Sulfur dioxide* is produced in the combustion of sulfur-laden fuels such as coal and oil. It is associated with bronchoconstriction, shortness of breath, respiratory illnesses, and aggravation of asthma and cardiovascular diseases.

- *Particulate matter,* a combination of solids and liquid droplets, is either emitted directly or forms in the atmosphere. Fine particulate matter, less than 2.5 micrometers in diameter, cannot be seen without a microscope. The primary source is combustion from motor vehicles, power plants, residential wood burning, forest fires, and industrial processes. Coarse particulate matter, 2.5–10 micrometers in diameter, derives mainly from crushing and grinding operations and dust. Both forms are associated with heart and lung diseases, respiratory infections, and aggravation of asthma.

The EPA uses daily measurements of these pollutants to calculate values on the Air Quality Index (AQI), which are reported to the public in daily newspapers. The index is a 0–500 scale in which 100 indicates that air standards are met. The AQI value for a given day is the highest AQI value of the five pollutants. The values are categorized to aid public interpretation.

- AQI values between 0 and 50 are categorized as "good": air pollution poses little or no risk to anyone.
- AQI values between 51 and 100 are categorized as "moderate": air quality is acceptable, but some pollutants carry moderate health concerns for a small number of unusually sensitive people, such as those with respiratory problems. The accompanying cautionary statement advises that unusually sensitive people should consider reducing prolonged or heavy exertion outdoors.
- AQI values between 101 and 150 are categorized as "unhealthy for sensitive groups." For example, exposure to ozone will affect those with lung diseases, and exposure to particulate matter will affect those with lung or heart diseases. The cautionary statement advises that active children and adults and people with lung diseases such as asthma should reduce prolonged or heavy exertion outdoors.
- AQI values between 151 and 200 are categorized as "unhealthy": the general public will experience health effects, and sensitive groups will experience more serious effects. The cautionary statement advises that active children and adults and people with lung diseases such as asthma should avoid prolonged or heavy exertion outdoors, while everyone else, especially children, should reduce prolonged or heavy exertion outdoors.
- AQI values between 201 and 300 are categorized as "very unhealthy." A health alert is issued because everyone will experience serious health effects. The cautionary statement advises that active children and adults and people with lung diseases such as asthma should avoid all outdoor exertion while everyone else, especially children, should avoid prolonged or heavy exertion outdoors.
- AQI values between 301 and 500 are categorized as "hazardous." Health warnings of emergency conditions are issued. The cautionary statement advises that everyone should avoid all physical activity outdoors.

The Air Quality Index Report for 2007 (U.S. Environmental Protection Agency 2007) summarizes data for 304 Metropolitan Statistical Areas (MSAs).

Some limitations are noteworthy. Of 304 MSAs, eight-six (28%) failed to report AQI values for the entire 365 days. Forty-eight MSAs (16%) reported fewer than 329 days (90%). Since states are responsible for reporting data, I searched for patterns in the forty-eight MSAs that potentially indicated differences in states' emphases on air quality. Nearly half of the deficient MSA reports were from seven states. Alaska has one MSA, and Wyoming has two; neither state reported full data on any MSAs. Maine and Michigan failed to report fully on 75 percent of their MSAs. (Maine failed on three of four MSAs, and Michigan failed on six of eight MSAs.) Alabama and North Carolina each failed to report fully on four of ten MSAs. Wisconsin failed to report fully on five of eleven MSAs.

Because of missing data, I examined information for only the 256 MSAs reporting AQI values at least 90 percent of the required time. Several findings in particular stand out:

- Only 30 MSAs (12%) were in compliance with standards on all reported days.
- Of the 88.3 percent of the MSAs that broke the law at least one day of the year, the level of noncompliance varied from 1 noncompliant day to 205:
  - Of the 256 MSAs, 145 (64.2%) broke the law for more than one week.
  - Of the 256 MSAs, 98 (43.3%) broke the law for more than two weeks.
  - Of the 256 MSAs, 17 (7.5%) broke the law for more than six weeks.
  - Of the 256 MSAs, 6 (2.7%) broke the law for more than 100 days.
- By substantial margins, the two most frequent pollutants were ozone and fine particulate matter.

Substantial air pollution plagues urban areas, despite policies that set standards, require full reporting, and provide the basic infrastructure for accurate records. Noncompliance among nearly 90 percent of MSAs guarantees that even healthy people—active children and adults—are exposed to levels of air pollutant that are likely to have negative effects.

The EPA classifies recognized carcinogens as "hazardous" air pollutants and lists the top eight as diesel emissions, benzene, carbon tetrachloride, chromium compounds, polycyclic organic matter, 1,3-butadiene, formaldehyde, and coke oven emissions (Scorecard 2008a).

Diesel emissions contain fine particulate matter, nitrous oxides, and more than forty other chemicals identified on federal regulatory lists. Diesel emissions are associated with lung cancer, respiratory problems, asthma, pneumonia, heart disease, and asthma. Children and the elderly, smokers, and those who exercise outside are most at risk.

Benzene, a flammable liquid derived from crude oil and gasoline, is used to manufacture plastics, resins, synthetic fibers, rubber, lubricants, dyes, and pesticides. Benzene appears on eight federal regulatory lists and is a recognized carcinogen and developmental and reproductive toxicant. It is a suspected toxicant in cardiovascular, endocrine, gastrointestinal, immune, neurological, respiratory, skin, and sensory systems. Benzene production exceeds 1 million pounds annually.

Carbon tetrachloride, a petrochemical, was banned for use in refrigerants, pesticides, propellants, solvents, and degreasers and is still used in industry. It is a recognized carcinogen and a suspected toxicant in cardiovascular, blood, development, endocrine, gastrointestinal, liver, kidney, neurological, reproductive, respiratory, skin, and sensory systems. Carbon tetrachloride depletes the stratospheric ozone layer. It appears on eight federal regulatory lists. Production exceeds 1 million pounds annually.

Chromium compounds are manufactured in industrial processes and are used in steel making, chrome plating, dyes and pigments, leather tanning, and wood preserving. They are recognized carcinogens and suspected respiratory system toxicants. Chromium compounds appear on at least one federal regulatory list.

Polycyclic organic matter consists of more than 100 compounds produced in the incomplete combustion of fossil fuels, in wood combustion, in petroleum refining, and in the manufacture of industrial machinery, paper, and petroleum products. A recognized carcinogen and a suspected respiratory toxicant, polycyclic organic matter appears on two federal regulatory lists.

The chemical 1,3-butadiene is made from petroleum and used to manufacture synthetic rubber for truck and car tires. It is a recognized carcinogen and a developmental and reproductive system toxicant. It is also a suspected cardiovascular, blood, gastrointestinal, neurological, respiratory, skin, and sensory system toxicant. It appears on five regulatory lists. Production exceeds 1 million pounds annually.

Formaldehyde is a petrochemical used in the production of fertilizer, paper, plywood, particleboard, and veneers. It is used for embalming and as a preservative in food, antiseptics, cosmetics, and medicine. Formaldehyde is a recognized carcinogen and a suspected gastrointestinal, liver, immune, neurological, reproductive, respiratory, skin, and sensory toxicant. It appears on eight federal regulatory lists. Production exceeds 1 million pounds annually.

Coke oven emissions are a fraction of the total particulate matter produced in the carbonization of bituminous coal to make coke, the main fuel used in blast furnaces. Coke oven emissions consist of coal and coke particles, vapor, and tar containing polycyclic aromatic hydrocarbons, benzene, naphthylamine, cadmium, arsenic, beryllium, and chromium. They are recognized carcinogens and suspected gastrointestinal, liver, kidney, respiratory, skin, and sensory toxins.

Depletion of Biological Resources

The Endangered Species Act of 1973 was intended to conserve biological resources by protecting ecosystems on which threatened and endangered plant and animal populations depend. Amendments in 1978 obliged regulators to consider the economic impacts of designating a habitat as critical and narrowed the definition of species to limit the term "population" to vertebrates. Many development projects have received exemptions. For example, the government approved the Tennessee Valley Authority's construction of Tellico Dam on the Little Tennessee River to build a high-income retirement and summer-home community, even though altering the river habitat is likely to extinguish the endangered snail darter fish.

Since 1974, 14 species have been confirmed or believed by experts to be extinct. They include five fish species from the Chesapeake Bay, Great Lakes, and Texas habitats; two mammal species from Washington State; three bird species from habitats in the mid-South, Southeast, and Washington; two plant species from Gulf states and Arizona; and two mollusk species from Nevada, Tennessee, and Virginia habitats.

The Fish and Wildlife Service lists 609 animal species and 744 plant species as threatened or endangered, a total of 1,353 species. The animal species include 82 mammals, 90 birds, 37 reptiles, 23 amphibians, 139 fish, 70 clams, 75 snails, 57 insects, 12 arachnids, 22 crustaceans, and 2 corals. The plant species include 713 flowering plants, 3 conifers and cycads, 26 ferns, and 2 lichens. Many analysts are particularly alarmed by the decline and extinction of amphibian populations because it is a sign that the biosphere is significantly and rapidly changing (World's frog species 2006).

Pollution from Hazardous Substances: Toxic Release Inventory Data

The EPCRA established the TRI program, which requires corporate emitters to report to the EPA releases of listed chemicals to the land, water, and air. I obtained TRI data through 2006 (U.S. Environmental Protection Agency 2008c) documenting that 22,880 facilities, including 306 federal facilities, reported 4.25 billion pounds of nearly 650 toxic chemicals.

Nearly 88 percent of the waste was disposed of on-site: 44 percent to land, 33 percent to air, 6 percent to water, and 5 percent to underground injection. Approximately 12 percent of the waste was disposed of off-site: 8.5 percent was released to land, 3.3 percent to air and water, .4 percent to underground injection, and .1 percent to municipal treatment plants.

Metal mining facilities reported 29 percent of the total production-related waste; electric utilities reported 24 percent; petrochemical manufacturers reported 23 percent; primary metals processors reported 11 percent; paper production and hazardous waste and solvent recovery processors each reported 5 percent; and all other facilities reported 10 percent.

Known and suspected carcinogens accounted for 19 percent of production-related waste, mostly lead, lead compounds, arsenic, and arsenic compounds released to land. Styrene air emissions accounted for 45 percent of air emissions of carcinogens. Land releases of mercury and mercury compounds increased by 17 percent between 2005 and 2006, and releases of dioxin and dioxin-like compounds increased by 52 percent. Total production-related waste managed at federal facilities, such as nuclear weapons plants, increased by 6 percent.

Rupture of the Material Fabric of Life

Data on resource depletion and pollution demonstrate that U.S. petro-dependent policies do not acknowledge ecological principles. As a consequence, we have ruptured the material fabric of life. U.S. policies not only fail to abide by ecological principles; some actually encourage violation.

The first ecological principle, "everything is connected to everything else," asserts that the biosphere is a complex and coordinated network in which everything is connected in a balanced, stable equilibrium. Change in one ecosystem inevitably causes disequilibrium in others. We violate the first principle with our nearly complete alteration of the biosphere. The consequences are rapid soil erosion that threatens food supplies, CAFOs that feed us but are cruel to animals and cause substantial land and water pollution, contaminated drinking water for a sizable proportion of the population, the growing dead zone in the Gulf, and air pollution so bad at times that people are advised to stay indoors.

The second ecological principle, "everything has to go somewhere," refers to the process of matter cycling in ecosystems. In cyclical systems, everything produced in one phase is used in a later phase so that the same atoms are continuously recycled. We violate this principle with an economic system that operates in contradiction to ecosystems. Instead of a closed cycle, we use a linear system, the materials economy. The stages in this linear production system are resource extraction, production, packaging and distribution, consumption, and disposal. Throwaway products and planned obsolescence are the basic elements of the materials economy. Throwaway products maintain a perpetual round of supply and demand; planned obsolescence ensures that consumers will continue to purchase products. Waste produced at each stage is not cycled; it accumulates in the biosphere and degrades ecosystems.

"Nature knows best" is the third principle, stating that ecosystems' inner consistency and compatibility is the outcome of 4 billion years in which evolution has created a limited, self-consistent array of substances essential to life. We violate this principle by manipulating nature's processes to manufacture materials that are inconsistent and incompatible with ecosystems: petrochemicals, transgenic organisms, and nanomatter.

"There is no such thing as a free lunch," the fourth ecological principle, says that humans are not exempt from ecological principles, even though it appears that we are—in the short-term. We violate this principle with our biological hubris. Our interventions in the biosphere always stress ecological systems, and ecosystems always respond. But response to stress does not occur evenly and predictably in a linear fashion; initial adjustments may be barely noticeable. Later, as stress increases, responses suddenly become huge. In that lag time between stress and response, we kid ourselves that we are unaffected by nature's laws, and our biological hubris is fortified. But our perceived free lunch is actually a deferred debt. The bill is now in the mail.

Petroleum sits at the center of policymakers' failure to acknowledge ecological principles. Agriculture, so dependent on petrochemicals as to be called "petro-agriculture," is the source of substantial land and air pollution. Petrochemicals pollute air, land, and water with unnatural substances. Routine and catastrophic oil spills endanger marine life, and wars over oil reserves take human lives. Much urban air pollution comes from oil-derived fuel.

Logically, acknowledgment of ecological principles should reveal the material link between economic activities and the biosphere. Environmental policies' superficial acknowledgment blatantly and dangerously denies the link. The next chapter examines the consequences of living in such denial.

6

Living in the State of Denial

Conflict and the Contamination of Workplaces, Communities, and Citizens

ollowing implementation, the policy process usually includes an evaluation stage, a measurement enabling comparison of policy intent with policy outcome. Evaluation allows adjustments for errors. If the measured outcome indicates persistence of the initial problem, policymakers amend and improve policies.

When ecological principles are not recognized in environmental policies, the outcomes are resource depletion and pollution. If the state denies the link between economic activities and the environment, policies are not amended and the problems continue and worsen. And we all live in a state of denial.

Official Denial: Resource Scarcity and Social Conflict

As I demonstrated in the previous chapter, resource management policies violate ecological principles, with the outcome of resource depletion or resource scarcity. Resource scarcity is associated with conflict in both nature and societies. In nature, conflict in the form of competition underlies population dynamics, and equilibrium is maintained. In contrast, human competition over scarce resources causes social conflict that indicates policy failure. Does the state respond with policy adjustments to conserve resources and increase access to them?

Basic Resources

To a point, an expanding society can intensify or adapt its exploitation of resources to satisfy the needs of an ever-increasing population. Two fundamental resources, however—water and land—will inevitably limit that expansion and become a source of conflict.

Snapshot: Watering Los Angeles. Water is frequently the scarce resource causing social conflict. Los Angeles is a premier example. When Spaniards founded it,

Los Angeles was an arid coastal basin, its sole water source the Los Angeles River. The small river rapidly alternated between a dry bed most of the year and a torrential stream in the winter when tropical rains flooded and washed out neighborhoods. In his history of the American West, Marc Reisner (1993: 53) writes, "Had humans never settled in Los Angeles, evolution, left to its own devices, might have created in a million more years the ideal creature for the habitat: a camel with gills."

While San Francisco grew into one of the largest U.S. cities and one of the world's busiest ports, Los Angeles languished until the late nineteenth century. Southern California oranges attracted crowds at the New Orleans World's Fair in 1884, and oil was discovered in Beverly Hills. Budding entrepreneurs moved to Los Angeles to farm: the semitropical, ocean-cooled, sunny climate was suitable for growing widely diverse crops. Water was the only impediment to agricultural fortunes.

Unable to support irrigation and the enlarged population, the water flow of the Los Angeles River had dropped from 100 cubic feet per second in the 1880s to 45 cubic feet per second by 1902 (Reisner 1993). City leaders identified the Owens River, 250 miles away, as the only feasible water source. The sole water source for farms in the Owens Valley, the river drained the eastern slope of the mountains for more than 150 miles before taking a downward course that would permit construction of a system of aqueducts and reservoirs using gravity to transport water. Historians document that the Owens River was brought to Los Angeles through "chicanery, subterfuge, spies, bribery, a campaign of divide-and-conquer, and a strategy of lies. . . . [Officials] milked the valley bone-dry, impoverishing it, while the water made a number of prominent Los Angeleans very, very rich" (Reisner 1993: 62).

A city official acquired rights in 1905 to more than 50 miles of river land by intimating that the land was intended for a proposed U.S. Reclamation Service project. Others posed as ranchers to purchase land. Landowners then proposed that the city buy their water rights and options to water Los Angeles.

The Owens Valley Land Registrar protested the purchases to the Commissioner of the General Land Office and to President Theodore Roosevelt. An appointed special investigator blamed the city for "not at once present[ing] their claims to the Secretary of the Interior so that the situation might have been determined on its merits in the beginning" (Los Angeles Department of Water and Power 2008). But the investigator concluded that no crime had been committed.

In 1906, a state legislator from Owens Valley organized opposition to a bill granting Los Angeles rights of way across federal land to construct an aqueduct. He argued that irrigation in Southern California should not occur at the expense of irrigation in the Owens Valley and appealed to Roosevelt, who expressed regret to residents of the valley but concluded, "Yet it is a hundred or a thousand fold more important to the state and more valuable to the people as a whole if [the water is] used by the city than if used by the people of the Owens Valley" (Los Angeles Department of Water and Power 2008). The aqueduct opened in 1913.

Providing water to Los Angeles dried up Owens Lake, an area three times the size of Manhattan island. The dryness generated toxic dust storms that for decades made the lake's salty, mineral-laced basin the country's largest source of particulate matter pollution. Complaints led to an agreement in 1998 by city officials and local regulators to comply with federal requirements to control the dust (Archibold 2007). When the city moved slowly, a county judge in 2005 imposed fines of $5,000 a day. The city has spent $400 million on dust control for approximately 30 square miles and has agreed to treat another 12.7 square miles.

Snapshot: Land Use and the Megamall. Prioritizing the expansion of production and land's status as a commodity drive urbanization, converting natural ecosystems into built environments. Continually bought and sold to generate profits, land yields greater profits the more "developed" it is. Federal, state, and local governments promote economic development to generate tax revenues. Policymakers adopt land-use statutes that foster development and establish tax structures. Thus, cities' shape and development is determined by profit seeking through the intensification of land use.

The post-1945 development imperative changed the standard growth pattern in metropolitan areas to urban sprawl. Sprawl is promoted by planners, developers, bankers, mortgage companies, real estate agents, and the construction industry. It is aided and abetted by local governments. Sprawl rapidly consumes farmland, forests, and pastureland, causing considerable environmental problems and exacerbating social inequities (Brannon 2007). The megamall is a recent form of development that causes conflict.

The population of Ashbury, New York, a small farming town in the upper Hudson River Valley, increased after the war because IBM constructed several plants and a teachers college was incorporated into the state system. Completion of the New York State Thruway further increased population because it facilitated the commute to New York City. In the late 1960s and 1970s, the university's expansion drew artists and craftspeople to town. By 1992, commercial farms dominated family farms, and overall farming had declined by two-thirds since 1950. Abandoned farmland met expanding residential needs with the construction of suburban subdivisions and apartment complexes.

David Porter and Chester Mirsky (2002: 27) describe a shift in land-use policies in Ashbury from a "minimalist" to a "pragmatic capitalist" orientation, led by local powerbrokers determined to bring economic growth to the town. Without much community input, local elites encouraged development through land-use decisions that consistently diminished Ashbury's rural small-town character. In 1993, the Magellan Construction Group proposed a development project to the town's planning board: a 178,000 square-foot megamall consisting of a 100,000 square-foot Wal-Mart, a 65,000 square-foot grocery store, miscellaneous retail stores in two other buildings, and an 18 acre paved parking lot. The selected site contained a natural wetlands area that recharged a high-quality aquifer.

Conflict erupted when citizens from two grassroots organizations opposed the development project. Citizens Linked for Environmental Action and

Responsibility (CLEAR) was initially formed in 1985 by experienced community activists to oppose construction of a 700 unit residential and conference center. Ashbury Citizens Together (ACT) formed in 1994 specifically to oppose the megamall. The organizations mobilized a substantial portion of citizens who engaged in letter writing, petitioning, and picketing and educated themselves about zoning laws and U.S. Environmental Protection Agency requirements. Activists pressured the town's planning board to reject the proposed megamall.

Porter and Mirsky (2002: 297) emphasize that, without the persistent efforts of activists, the megamall would have been built. A local newspaper editorial also credited the groups:

> [If] it were not for the Herculean efforts of Ashbury Community Together and CLEAR, our local grassroots watchdog groups, this monster-mall would probably already be built. In the early stages of this project, the *Tribune* was also guilty of not doing its job. Of listening to but a few select voices on the planning board.

The Magellan Construction Group gathered its blueprints and moved the project to a nearby community whose citizens accepted the proposal.

Scarce Energy Minerals

Few energy policies aim at conservation; most concern pollution. Most energy-related conflicts center on pollution or safety in mineral extraction.

Petroleum: Powering the Powerful

I distinguish modes of subsistence largely by the primary energy source used. Petroleum defines the petro-dependent society and, through its multiple applications, underlies expanded agricultural and manufacturing production. Yet only three policies address petroleum: one weak policy for conservation and two for pollution from oil.

The Oil Pollution Control Act of 1990, passed after the *Exxon Valdez* spill, did little to help economically and emotionally devastated residents of Alaska. A federal jury initially awarded damages of $5.5 billion to about 33,000 commercial fishermen, Alaska natives, and property owners in 1994. Exxon Mobil appealed, and in 2008 the court reduced the award, first to $2.5 billion and then to $507.5 million, amounting to about $15,000 per victim. Exxon Mobil's posted earnings in 2007 were $40.6 billion. It would have taken less than four days for the company to earn back the $2.5 billion award (Vicini 2008).

Government investigations of the BP oil spill in 2010 documented that a series of internal investigations over the past decade had warned managers that the company repeatedly disregarded safety and environmental policies, risking a serious accident (Lustgarten and Knutson 2010). Four previous accidents at BP facilities confirmed the warnings: an explosion at a Texas oil refinery that killed fifteen workers and injured 170 in 2005; a pipeline spill in Prudhoe Bay, Alaska, that released 267,000 gallons in 2006; the blowout of a 28 foot section of the Alaska gas pipeline in 2008 (Lustgarten and Knutson 2010); and three similar pipeline accidents in 2009, including a near-explosion. Because of that record prior to the Gulf spill, BP already faced a possible ban on its federal contracting and new drilling leases (Lustgarten and Knutson 2010).

Around the first anniversary of the spill, an investigation by a presidential commission concluded that a cascade of technical and managerial failures— including a faulty cement job—had caused the disaster (Burdeau and Weber 2011). Tar balls still occasionally roll up on the beaches; fishermen face uncertain futures. A married couple whose livelihood was crabbing received $53,000 in compensation from BP. They reported that the sum covered only three months' debt (Burdeau and Weber 2011).

Coal (Company) Power

Although oil defines the petro-dependent society, coal remains king in power generation. Coal extraction and burning have long been sources of conflict— between labor and management and between communities and the coal industry.

Snapshot: Explosion at Upper Big Branch Mine. In April 2010, twenty-nine miners were killed in an explosion at Massey Energy's Upper Big Branch coal mine in West Virginia. It was the nation's worst mining disaster since 1970. Nineteen miners died from carbon monoxide intoxication and ten from injuries sustained in the explosion (Vanden Heuvel 2011). Massey Energy claimed that the explosion was a natural phenomenon, a large methane bubble that unpredictably popped up from the ground (Tavernise 2011). But Governor Joseph Manchin's Governor's Independent Investigation Panel (GIIP) asserted that the blast could have been prevented if Massey had observed minimal safety standards.

Based on months of interviews and document analysis, the panel explained that a spark from cutting coal ignited an explosive accumulation of methane, causing a fireball. The fireball ignited coal dust that carried the explosion throughout more than two miles of the mine (Governor's Independent Investigation Panel 2011). Methane and coal dust accumulated because of an inadequate ventilation system, for which the company had received sixty-four violations in 2009 (Tavernise 2011). The fire spread because Massey failed to maintain safety equipment such as water sprays. The panel attributed miners' deaths to a "shocking corporate culture of illegality, [including] 'enemies lists,' 'codes of silence,' and a 'too big to be regulated' attitude." In this culture, "wrongdoing became acceptable" and "deviation became the norm." Autopsies revealed the extent of Massey's negligence: seventeen of twenty-nine victims tested positive for black lung disease (Vanden Heuvel 2011). The national rate of miners' black lung disease is 3.2 percent; West Virginia's rate is 7.6 percent.

An investigation by the Mine Safety and Health Administration found that managers at Massey pressured workers to omit safety problems from official records. The result was two sets of books: an accurate set for Massey and a sanitized set for regulators (Huber and Smith 2011). Massey had been cited for 600 violations in the eighteen months before the explosion (Huber and Smith 2011).

Massey merged with a competitor, Alpha Natural Resources, in June 2011 to create the nation's second largest coal company.

Nuclear Power Trips

The nuclear power industry is enjoying a resurrection. The industry had stalled with the partial reactor meltdown at the Three Mile Island plant in Pennsylvania in 1979. Investigations revealed substantial problems with reactor design, operator knowledge, and corruption. Concerns about the safety of nuclear power were underscored with the 1986 reactor explosion at the Soviet Union's Chernobyl plant. U.S. utility companies cancelled orders for new reactors and abandoned many plants under construction.

Heightened public pressure to replace coal-fired power generation because of pollution has inspired policymakers and industry advocates to revive nuclear power. Critics have responded. An investigation of safety issues at nuclear power plants by the Associated Press (AP) concluded that the U.S. Nuclear Regulatory Commission (NRC) has relaxed safety standards to keep aging reactors operating (Donn 2011). Using NRC records, the AP investigation found that radioactive tritium had leaked from corroded underground piping at forty-eight of sixty-five aging plants. Nearly two-thirds of the leaks had been reported in the previous five years. Although tritium is not known to have reached public water supplies, it contaminated private wells at three sites.

Subsurface water corrodes pipes, many of which carry cooling water to reactors. Much piping is buried in concrete and thus inaccessible. Water damages other underground components, including cables that take signals to control operators. The AP investigation revealed that improved earthquake science led to the NRC's identification of twenty-seven reactors in eastern and southern states that are at greater risk from earthquakes than previously realized. Reactors are indirectly at risk from earthquake damage to water tanks and mechanical and electrical equipment that can disable reactor cooling. Similar risks are posed by floods, tornadoes, and hurricanes.

Snapshot: Tennessee Valley Authority. The Tennessee Valley Authority (TVA), the only federally owned utility company, provides coal-powered electricity for 9 million southerners. Persistently pressed by the EPA to close half of its coal-fired plants, the agency is a prominent cheerleader for nuclear power generation. In 2007, the TVA initiated a plan to finish construction of the Unit 2 reactor at the Watts Bar nuclear power plant. Construction that had begun in the early 1980s was halted in 1988 (Flessner 2009). Under the revived plan, Unit 2 construction was expected to be completed and the reactor started in 2012. But continuing problems and cost overruns delayed the startup, now projected for December 2015 (Marcum 2012).

Critics cite the TVA's record as a reason for opposition. The trouble-plagued Browns Ferry plant is the TVA's problem child. It was the largest nuclear plant in the world when it went online in 1974. In 1975, a fire significantly damaged Unit 1's cabling when a worker using a candle to search for air leaks ignited a cable seal. The reactor was shut down for repairs, restarted in 1976, shut down for operational and management issues in 1985, and restarted in 2007. But problems continue:

- Between May 2009 and January 2010, air was discovered in piping eleven times in Unit 1's coolant system.
- Although TVA publicly reported no problems after a series of tornadoes in April 2011, formal documents filed with the NRC show a different picture. Operators manually operating water flow to Unit 1 failed to notice immediately that water was boiling off faster than it was replaced; operational failures occurred in a valve and a diesel-driven fire pump; warning sirens were inoperable; and a small brass fitting broke, causing a fluid leak that instigated voltage fluctuations, which shut down an emergency generator that maintained a cool water flow to Unit 1.
- In May 2011, the NRC issued a rank ordering of unsafe reactors and rated Unit 1 first. Yet conditions are not deemed serious enough to warrant a permanent shutdown. Unit 1 is licensed to operate through 2033.

In June 2011, TVA officials announced two plans: (1) to complete a partially built reactor at its thirty-five-year-old Bellefonte Nuclear Plant; and (2) to contract for the design, licensing, and building of six to twelve small, prefabricated underground nuclear reactors that, if licensed, would be the first commercially viable small nuclear plants.

Natural Gas: What the Frack?

Geologists have long known about rich natural gas reserves in shale, particularly the Marcellus shale formation covering large parts of New York, Pennsylvania, Ohio, West Virginia, Maryland, and Virginia. Spurred by rising oil prices, drilling companies have developed a technique to extract natural gas that is driving a new "gold" rush.

High-volume horizontal hydraulic fracturing—fracking—involves injecting huge amounts of water mixed with sand and chemicals at high pressure to break up rock formations and hold shale layers open to release natural gas. Total reserves are estimated to be enough to supply gas for heating, power generation, and vehicle fuel for a hundred years. Fracking is welcomed by energy companies as a profit maker, by some environmentalists as a strategy to reduce carbon emissions, and by lawmakers as a source of jobs in a sputtering economy. The number of natural gas wells doubled between 1990 and 2009 to 493,000; 90 percent use fracking (Urbina 2011).

The U.S. Constitution's federal supremacy clause ensures that federal laws supersede state laws. In 2005, Congress amended the Safe Drinking Water Act specifically to *exclude* the regulation of fracking. Critics refer to it as the "Halliburton Loophole" (Zeller 2011) because of intense lobbying by Halliburton, the world's second largest provider of technical products and services for oil and gas exploration and production. Since no federal legislation regulates fracking, states are free to set their own standards.

Fracking has substantial environmental impacts. One well can produce over a million gallons of wastewater containing naturally occurring corrosive salts, carcinogens, and radioactive elements. In addition, hazardous materials such as diesel fuel are added in the technique (Urbina 2011). Between 2005 and 2009, oil and gas companies injected tens of millions of gallons of diesel fuel into fracking wells in more than a dozen states (Zeller 2011). The industry claims that using diesel fuel is legal because the EPA has not developed rules and procedures for this. The *New York Times* obtained EPA documents revealing that wastewater is frequently routed to sewage treatment plants unequipped to remove hazardous substances and then is discharged to rivers, lakes, and streams.

Official Denial: Contamination of Workplaces and Communities

The previous chapter documented that pollution abatement policies violate ecological principles. The outcome is the contamination of workplaces, communities, and citizens. Does the state instigate policy adjustments?

Snapshot: The Love Canal Disaster. The public's first intimation of the particularly harmful effects of petrochemicals—and the first policy response to contaminated communities—was forced by events in a neighborhood of Niagara Falls. In the 1930s, Hooker Chemical Company purchased the abandoned Love Canal, which the company and the city of Niagara Falls used as a landfill for municipal and chemical waste. In 1952, 21,000 tons of waste later, Hooker closed the landfill, capped it with indigenous soil, and sold the 16 acre site to the city for $1 with a deed stipulating that Hooker was not responsible for injury, death, or loss of property caused by the landfill's industrial wastes.

The city promptly built an elementary school atop the chemical waste landfill. The school attracted developers, and postwar prosperity allowed first-time homeowners to create a working-class community. The young families had no knowledge of the landfill but soon observed strange phenomena in the neighborhood: intermittent caustic odors, occasional exploding rocks, and skin irritations after children played barefoot near the school (Cable and Cable 1995). They reported their concerns to city officials. The city ignored their concerns.

By the mid-1960s, homeowners were complaining about a noxious substance oozing from basement walls. City inspectors found holes in the schoolyard from collapsed underground waste drums, some of which had broken through the ground and protruded into the children's playing fields. The city covered the holes and the protruding drums with dirt.

In the 1970s, residents observed that strong odors were worse after heavy rains. Rainwater puddles did not evaporate for days. Gardens withered and died. Sinkholes appeared overnight. A joint U.S.-Canadian commission found traces of insecticide in Lake Ontario fish and tracked the source to Hooker's dumpsite in 1976. Local media coverage of the report revealed to unaware residents that a chemical waste dump lay at the heart of their neighborhood. A journalist had a sample of the basement ooze tested and traced the chemicals revealed by the analysis to Hooker and the Love Canal. A city-funded study found that most homeowners at the landfill's southern end reported persistent chemical residues and strong odors in their basements; storm sewers contained polychlorinated biphenyls; and, in multiple sites, corroded waste drums lay within three feet of the ground's surface (Cable and Cable 1995). The study recommended a cleanup, estimated at $425,000. The city rejected the recommendation, for lack of funds.

The New York State Health Department conducted tests on the contents of the landfill and found more than 200 chemicals, many of them known or suspected carcinogens, and notified the county's Health Department to act to reduce health threats. The county covered exposed waste drums with dirt, fenced off an area of the landfill, and provided free fans for residents to ventilate their basements.

Continuing complaints motivated state officials to convene a public meeting to assure residents that appropriate protective measures were under way. When residents were not reassured, the meeting transformed into a mobilizing event. Of several citizens' groups formed, the most enduring was the Love Canal Home-owners Association (LCHA). Lois Gibbs, a working-class housewife, walked door-to-door collecting health information and recruiting others in efforts to close the elementary school, remediate the landfill, and obtain compensation for property losses.

At a press conference in August 1978, the state's health commissioner pronounced the landfill "a public nuisance and an extremely serious threat and danger to the health, safety, and welfare of residents" (quoted in Levine 1982: 28). Declaring an emergency, he ordered the city of Niagara Falls to halt chemical leaching from the landfill, conduct studies of residents' chronic illnesses, and close the elementary school. He urged pregnant women and preschool children to evacuate. The governor announced that the state government would purchase land bordering the landfill if residents could demonstrate that their health problems were directly related to landfill leachate. President Jimmy Carter approved disaster aid for residents—a first for a non-natural disaster.

Residents were dissatisfied with the limitations of the state's buyout offer and feared that remediation would release additional chemicals. Most preferred permanent relocation of the residents who lived closest to the landfill. LCHA members hired an attorney, conducted health surveys, spoke publicly, marched on City Hall, picketed the landfill site, and burned the health commissioner and the governor in effigy. The U.S. Justice Department filed suit in December 1979 against Occidental Petroleum Corporation, Hooker's new owner, seeking reimbursement for remediation and relocation costs. The EPA ordered a pilot sample of thirty-six residents for chromosomal damage tests, and the results, released in May 1980, showed that eleven residents were affected.

President Carter authorized a federal buyout of homes. Sewers were severed in 1982; an expanded 40 acre landfill cap was installed; and a long-term monitoring system was implemented in 1984. By 1987, nearly a thousand families had relocated; homes adjoining the canal had been demolished; and the community, known to the world as "Love Canal," was virtually a ghost town. The government's lawsuit was settled in 1989 with a consent order obliging Occidental to manage waste disposal and destruction (U.S. Environmental Protection Agency 1989). The company did so but rejected liability claims and refused to pay relocation costs.

A state official, Eckardt Beck (1979), wrote about the incident in the January issue of the *EPA Journal*: "I have been very pleased with the high degree of cooperation in this case among local, State, and Federal governments, and with the swiftness by which the Congress and the President have acted to make funds available. But this is not really where the story ends. Quite the contrary. We suspect that there are hundreds of such chemical dumpsites across the Nation." Beck was wrong about "hundreds" of dumpsites—the number was far larger. Policy fallout from Love Canal was the passage of the Comprehensive Environmental Response, Compensation and Liability Act (CERCLA), or Superfund, in 1980, which was intended to prepare for future Love Canals. CERCLA requires the EPA to conduct habitability and land use studies to assess risks associated with inhabiting a remediated hazardous site. The resulting study by the state's Department of Health in 1988 stopped short of declaring the area safe but concluded that portions of the neighborhood were as habitable as the rest of Niagara Falls. Young working-class families again bought homes in Love Canal. When regional bankers balked at providing mortgage loans, the Federal Housing Administration agreed in 1992 to provide mortgage insurance for new homeowners.

Superfund and the National Priority List

Love Canal's policy legacy, the Superfund, guides a process from identification of a hazardous site as a priority for cleanup to implementation of a cleanup remedy and deletion from the National Priority List (U.S. Environmental Protection Agency 2008b). The Superfund law epitomizes petro-dependent policies for three reasons. First, entire communities are contaminated. Second, corporations typically escape responsibility for contamination—*all* costs are externalized. Third, even weak policies are frequently unenforced.

Individuals or organizations may petition the EPA Regional Administration for listing, describing the site's location and the effects on the petitioner of actual or potential release of harmful substances. If the EPA approves, the agency conducts a Preliminary Assessment/Site Inspection to determine whether the site poses a threat to human health and the environment and whether the threat requires further investigation. If further investigation is recommended, site inspectors collect data to rank the site with a numerically based Hazard Ranking System that assesses three categories of risk factors: likelihood of a release of hazardous substances; toxicity, quantity, and other characteristics of waste; and the people or sensitive environments affected by releases. Four pathways are scored: groundwater migration, surface water migration, soil exposure, and air migration. The site is proposed for NPL listing if the score makes the threshold.

TABLE 6.1   Distribution of All National Priority List Sites by Stage of Progress

Initial study to collect data for design of remedy not yet begun	17
Study to collect data for design of remedy under way	125
Pre-remedy construction for emergency response or data collection	170
Data collected, design of remedy under way	85
Final remedy selected	58
Post-remedy construction; implementation of remedy under way	106
Completed construction	708
Restored to National Priority List and new data collected for design of remedy	1
Total sites	1,270

Listing initiates the remediation process. First, data are collected to design the remedy's technical specifications. If necessary, pre-remedy emergency construction reduces the threat. More data are collected as the remedy design is under way. Then the remedial action is selected and implemented. Remediation is complete when physical construction is done, even if final requirements have not been achieved, if the EPA limits actions to non-construction measures, or if the site qualifies for deletion from the list. Because exposures remain possible, post-construction monitoring assesses the remedy's effectiveness through five-year reviews. If the monitoring shows an effective outcome, the site is deleted. At least one of the following criteria must be met for deletion: the EPA and the state determine that responsible parties have completed all required actions; the EPA and the state determine that all actions financed by the Superfund have been implemented and no further response is appropriate; or releases pose no significant health or environmental threat.

I obtained NPL data in August 2008. Since Superfund, 1,630 total sites have been listed on the NPL; 360 sites (22.8%) have been deleted. Sixty potentially hazardous sites were proposed but rejected for listing. Currently, the total number of sites on the NPL is 1,270. I combed the EPA's site-specific Cleanup Progress Summaries and determined the distribution of listed sites by stages of progress (see Table 6.1).

No data have yet been collected at seventeen listed sites. Initial study is under way at 125 sites. Emergency response construction is required at 170 sites. Remedy design is under way at eighty-five sites, and remedies have been selected for fifty-eight sites. Remedy implementation is taking place at 106 sites. Construction has been completed at 708 sites. One site was remediated, deleted, and later returned to the list.

To clarify the status of sites, I bracket those where remediation construction is complete and post-remedy monitoring is in place. Bracketing leaves *562 active sites* (44.3% of all listed sites) where continuing exposures may harm residents (see Table 6.2). Of the 562 active sites, 70.8 percent have no remedy even identified. Emergency response construction is under way at 18.9 percent of sites. At only 10.3 percent of active sites have remedies been identified, but construction has not started.

TABLE 6.2   Distribution of Active National Priority List Sites by Stage of Progress

No remedy yet identified	70.8%
Under remedial construction	18.9%
Remedies identified but construction not under way	10.3%

The time required for completed remediation is curious. I examined 290 sites placed on the NPL in 1983: remediation is still not complete at nearly 30 percent of them, nearly thirty years later. Even these numbers tell only part of the story. I describe illustrative cases in three Superfund snapshots.

Snapshot: Nyanza Chemical Waste Dump, Ashland, Massachusetts. The Nyanza Chemical Waste Dump is a 35 acre site adjacent to an active industrial complex near Boston, used from 1917 to 1978 to produce textile dyes. Approximately 10,000 people lived within three miles of the site. Production generated large volumes of wastewater containing high levels of acids and numerous organic and inorganic chemicals. Some wastes were discharged after partial treatment into a small stream emptying into the Sudbury River. More than 45,000 tons of chemical sludge from wastewater treatment processes, spent solvents, and other chemical wastes were buried on-site. Mercury contaminated wetlands and river fish. Spent solvent vapors were detected inside several buildings.

The site was listed on the NPL in 1983. Emergency response construction in 1987 and 1988 excavated an underground storage vault containing 12,025 tons of waste. Three-hundred tons of contaminated soil were incinerated, and 356 tons were buried at an off-site facility. The Superfund site contains four Operable Units (OUs).

- OU 1 concerned source control and soil contamination. The source control remedy was excavation of all outlying sludge deposits, contaminated soil, and sediments, consolidating the material with on-site sludge deposits and placing a 13 acre cap on the area. The site was fenced; final construction of the cap was completed in 1991; and all cleanup actions were completed in late 1992.
- OU 2 is a contamination plume in off-site groundwater. An interim remedy was selected in 1991, but further contamination was discovered, requiring additional data collection. Modifications were made in 2006, and the remedy is under way.
- OU 3 addressed heavy metal contamination of wetlands and drainageways between the site and the Sudbury River. Initial construction in 1993 excavated and landfilled the contaminated sediments from the wetlands. A remedy was selected in 1999. More than 45,000 cubic yards of sediment contaminated by mercury were excavated from four areas and disposed in an on-site landfill. The EPA completed all remedial and restoration activities in 2001.

- OU 4 is 26 contaminated miles of the Sudbury River. Initial investigations showed sediments and fish contaminated with mercury and other heavy metals. Further data collection was completed in 1997. In 2003 and 2004, the EPA conducted biota sampling and identified four major habitats: reservoirs, fast-flowing river reaches, slow-flowing river reaches, and the Great Meadows National Wildlife Refuge. The EPA is reviewing data prior to conducting further investigations before selecting a remedy.

The Massachusetts Department of Public Health announced in 2006 that a multiyear study showed a consistent association between past site exposure and rare cancers. The findings held for individuals who self-reported cancer diagnoses, for individuals with confirmed cancer diagnoses, and for individuals with rare cancers. The findings suggest a gene–environment interaction between exposure to the Nyanza site involving water contact and participants with a family history of cancer (Department of Public Health 2006).

Snapshot: Ringwood Mines and Landfill, Ringwood Borough, New Jersey. Ringwood Realty, a subsidiary of Ford Motor Company, used as waste repositories 500 acres of abandoned magnetite mines. Between 1967 and 1974, Ford dumped waste, including car parts and paint sludge, in mine pits and on ground surfaces. In 1970, Ringwood Realty donated 290 acres of waste to the borough for a municipal landfill that operated until 1976. Groundwater from the site discharged to surface streams and the Wanaque Reservoir, a source of drinking water for 2 million people. Twenty wells drew water from the aquifer for households and industries. Approximately 13,000 people lived in Ringwood Borough.

The site was listed in 1983. The EPA ordered Ford International Services to remediate soil contamination and eliminate health and environmental risks. In 1987 and 1988, Ford removed 7,000 cubic yards of paint sludge and associated soil and disposed of them off-site. The EPA selected a remedy in 1988. In 1990, sixty waste drums were discovered and subsequently removed and disposed of off-site. Remedial construction was completed in 1993, and the site was deleted from the NPL in 1994.

The next year, another 5 cubic yards of solidified paint sludge were discovered; 50 more cubic yards were discovered in 1997. When still more significant amounts of paint sludge were found in 2004, the EPA ordered Ford to conduct a comprehensive investigation. The site was restored to the NPL in 2006. Sludge removal is still under way.

Snapshot: PCBs in the Hudson River. Two General Electric capacitor manufacturing plants discharged 209,000–1.3 million pounds of polychlorinated biphenyls (PCBs) into the Hudson River, contaminating a 200 mile stretch from Hudson Falls to the Battery in New York City. Albany, the largest city in the basin, has more than 100,000 people, and Fort Edward has 6,480 people. Agriculture, service, and manufacturing are non-residential land uses. The Hudson River, designated an American Heritage River, is a significant source of hydroelectric power, public water supplies, transportation, and recreation. In 1977 and 1978, approximately 180,000 cubic yards of contaminated sediments were dredged from the east channel at Fort Edward to improve navigation. Those and another 14,000 cubic yards of contaminated sediment were placed in a clay-lined containment cell.

The site listed for remediation in 1984 was the Upper Hudson River, a 40 mile stretch from Hudson Falls to Troy. It includes five remnant deposits—river sediment exposed when the water level was lowered in 1973 to remove Fort Edward Dam.

Two long-term remedial phases were instigated under a consent decree between the EPA and General Electric. The remedy for shoreline remnant deposits was in-place containment, a covering consisting of a geo-synthetic clay liner and two feet of soil, and grading and re-vegetating to minimize erosion. River banks were stabilized with rock to prevent scouring. Cap construction and gate installation to limit access was completed in 1991. The EPA decided in 1984 to take no more action on river sediments. But after a comprehensive reassessment of its earlier decision, the agency opted in 2002 to address the contamination further by dredging 2.65 million cubic yards of PCB-contaminated sediment from the river—nearly 65 percent of the PCBs present in the river. Remedy construction is under way.

In 2002, General Electric agreed to conduct extensive sediment sampling to identify dredging areas. In 2003, the company agreed to design the remedy and begin implementation of the first dredging phase in 2008. At the last update, General Electric had paid the EPA approximately $37 million, with an agreement to pay $78 million more.

Contaminated Citizens and Environmental Illness

On August 8, 2008, Lois Gibbs and 100 others gathered at LaSalle-Griffon Post 917 of the Veterans of Foreign Wars (Bonfatti and Hayden 2008). They met to commemorate the thirtieth anniversary of the New York State Health Commissioner's declaration of a state of emergency at Love Canal. Former residents shared stories of illness and death. A woman interviewed for the *Buffalo News* motioned to a vacant lot and said, tears trickling down her face, "My niece lived right there and she died of cancer at 32." Another, much younger woman recalled the death of her baby sister. A current resident, a young man with three young sons who arrived after the resettlement of the neighborhood, expressed shock at discovering what lay a few vacant blocks from the house he had begun renting the previous December.

Superfund sites represent the massive externalization of the social and environmental costs of petro-dependent societies. They are the cesspools of the risk society. And they are communities where families work, live, play—and become contaminated. Following are two snapshots of contaminated communities.

Snapshot: Dioxin Beach. Times Beach was a 480 acre lower-middle class, suburban community on the Meramec River, 17 miles west of St. Louis, Missouri. Lacking funds for road paving, city officials contracted with a waste oil hauler to spray dusty lanes in summer with waste oil from 1972 to 1976. The waste hauler also sprayed stables at a horse farm. When horses died, the owners contacted the Centers for Disease Control and Prevention (CDC), whose investigation in 1979 revealed that the wastes were produced at the Northeastern Pharmaceutical and Chemical Company. In 1982, a local reporter's investigation led to findings that the wastes contained dioxin levels 2,000 times higher than the herbicide Agent Orange. The EPA confirmed the information but did not conduct soil tests for nine months (Leistner 1985).

The Meramec River flooded in December 1982, and the community evacuated just as the EPA completed soil tests revealing dioxin. Evacuees were encouraged not to return home, and non-evacuees were advised to leave. Residents were eventually housed under the Flood Insurance Program. Many who tried to clean up from the flood suffered painful rashes. Citizens and officials wrote letters and signed petitions requesting a federal buyout and relocation of the town. Marilyn Leistner (1985) reports that depression increased as many residents' health and financial concerns mounted. Conflicts erupted between residents who favored a buyout and those who wanted to remain.

A one-square-mile site within a twenty-five-year floodplain was listed in September 1983. EPA officials announced a $32 million voluntary buyout of the town—the first in history. Residents found initial offers for the property low, but the government threatened condemnation within thirty days if the offers were rejected (Leistner 1985). By 1986, Times Beach was deserted and had been disincorporated by executive order and quarantined. Thousands filed lawsuits against the waste hauler, the chemical company, and the company's subcontractors. The hauler claimed ignorance and was never charged criminally.

In 1996 and 1997, 265,000 tons of contaminated soil and debris were removed from Times Beach and 28 other sites in eastern Missouri. The EPA built an incinerator in Times Beach, incinerated contaminated soil, and promptly dismantled the incinerator. The site was deleted from the NPL in 2001 and relinquished to the State of Missouri. Officials converted it into the Route 66 State Park, which includes picnic sites, boat ramps, and seven miles of hiking trails with wildlife viewings of turkey, geese, deer, and forty bird species. No public records indicate the final tally of dioxin victims.

Snapshot: Childhood Leukemia in Woburn. Woburn, Massachusetts, one of the oldest communities in New England, lies northwest of Boston near the head of the Mystic River Valley. Many residents criticized the quality of the city's public wells in the 1960s for foul odor, discoloration, and nasty taste.

In 1972, Ann Anderson's son was diagnosed with acute lymphocytic leukemia. She met and talked at the hospital with parents of other childhood leukemia patients and suspected the city water (Brown 1991, 2000). In 1975, she requested that state health officials conduct tests of city wells. Her request was granted only after many other residents complained. City officials commissioned a water study by private consultants that found high levels of carbon-chloroform extract. Assuming that chlorine's interaction with minerals caused pollution, city officials petitioned the Massachusetts Department of Public Health to change the city's chlorination method. State health officials granted the petition but advised the city not to rely on Wells G and H because of high salt and mineral concentrations.

When the state analyzed samples from Wells G and H and found high concentrations of organic compounds known to be carcinogenic, particularly trichloroethylene (TCE) and tetrachloroethylene (PCE), they closed both wells. Soon after, an engineer's complaint of Wetlands Act violations near an industrial complex in Woburn led to EPA testing that identified dangerous levels of lead, arsenic, and chromium. The EPA did not notify the public; residents found out only when local reporters published the study's findings.

Anderson's pastor placed a newspaper notice asking people who knew about childhood leukemia cases to contact him. He identified twelve cases, six of them closely grouped. He notified City Council, whose members requested an investigation by the CDC. Its report in 1981 found 12 cases of childhood leukemia where 5.3 would be expected, but it could not definitively link the diseases to the water supply. Anderson's son and five other children had died.

The state's hydrogeological investigations determined in 1982 that the source of the TCE and PCE contamination was W. R. Grace's Cryovac Division and Beatrice Foods' tannery. Leukemia victims' families filed a $400 million suit against Grace and Beatrice for poor waste disposal practices leading to groundwater contamination and fatal disease. In 1983, Wells G and H were listed as NPL sites. A study by researchers at the Harvard School of Public Health in 1984 found that Woburn's childhood leukemia cases were significantly associated with exposure to water from Wells G and H. Exposure was also linked to perinatal deaths, eye and ear anomalies, chromosomal and oral cleft anomalies, kidney and urinary tract diseases, and lung and respiratory diseases.

In 1986, a federal court absolved Beatrice but found Grace negligent in dumping chemicals on its property. Studies in 1995 established that between 1966 and 1986, the childhood leukemia rate in Woburn was four times higher than the national average, at twenty-eight cases where six were expected. The CDC referred to Woburn as the most persistent leukemia cluster in the nation.

The Woburn Superfund site consists of four OUs. Remedial construction is not completed at any of them. The EPA is still considering whether contaminated groundwater migration is sufficiently under control. No public records indicate the final tally of leukemia victims.

Denial and Democracy

The snapshots reveal that policymakers *do* recognize the link between economic activities and the environment—evidence lies in their routine tolerance of violations of environmental policy in the name of economic growth. They are *acutely* aware that petroleum greases the global economy as fuel, fertilizer, and fabric. But instead of treating petroleum as the endangered energy source it surely is, policymakers follow the path of least resistance: their recognition of the economy–environment link is not reflected in the environmental policies they formulate. Petro-dependency strangles policymaking processes, forcing policymakers not only to deny the economy–environment link but also to maintain the ruse of denial by severing economic from environmental policy as though they really were separate realms.

And ironically, if policymakers did *not* maintain the ruse, they likely would not be re-elected to office. Withholding information from the public is elites' essential strategy. Devra Davis (2007) provides startling insight into authorities' efforts to turn attention in cancer research away from the heavy metals and synthetic organic chemicals on which petro-dependent production depends. She documents four strategies used by policymakers, corporate authorities, scientists, judicial officers, and physicians to hide the health effects of petro-production substances, aided by a "revolving door of cancer researchers in and out of cancer-causing industries" (D. Davis 2007: xvii). First, authorities assert that no records connect workers' health issues to hazardous exposures—no data, no problem. Second, they create evidence refuting a problem and sponsor carefully designed studies in low-risk populations to produce confusing results. Third, they fund further studies to indicate remaining doubts, even though dangers appear to be clearly defined. Fourth, they use litigation, political lobbying, and confidentiality clauses to delay the publishing of research results as long as possible.

Without adequate information such as research findings on hazardous exposure, citizens are denied the right to choose their exposures. Excluded from democratic participation in decisions that affect our lives, we stroll confidently down the path of least resistance.

7

Broken Promises

Environmental Injustices

Popular sovereignty, political inclusion, and equal opportunity are overlapping, characteristically democratic values (Olson 2006). Applied to environmental policy, popular sovereignty ensures that citizens have equal access to necessary resources, grants full information about potentially hazardous exposures, and maintains citizen participation in forming regulations. Political inclusion provides for extra measures, if needed, to ensure access for *all* social groups to adequate information about resource use and potentially hazardous exposures. Equal opportunity tasks the state with not only providing favorable conditions for participatory equality but also counteracting *un*favorable conditions. Environmental injustices result when the state breaks democracy's promise of fairness and justice in environmental matters. Environmental injustices threaten the state's legitimacy.

In this chapter, I examine evidence of environmental injustice through statistical analyses and through narratives of people's experiences living in contaminated communities.

Statistical Analyses of Environmental Injustice

Many studies demonstrate environmental injustices with statistical analyses of disproportionate exposure to a variety of environmental threats. The most studied threat is hazardous waste facilities; others include workplace hazards, air pollution, and Superfund sites. Some examples follow:

- An investigation in 1983 by the U.S. General Accounting Office of demographic characteristics of four southern communities hosting commercial waste sites found that in three communities, blacks were the majority of the population, and in all communities, at least 26 percent of the population lived below the poverty level and most of this poor population was black.
- M. Lavelle and M. Coyle (1992) referred to a *National Law Journal* study on racial bias in environmental enforcement, finding that in all environ-

mental lawsuits concluded in the previous seven years, penalties against violators were lower in minority areas than in largely white areas.

• R. Zimmerman's (1993) nationwide study of 800 Superfund sites in 600 communities concluded that race and ethnicity were more strongly related to Superfund sites than was severe poverty.

In 1990, EPA Administrator William Reilly charged an agency workgroup with reviewing evidence for disproportionate environmental burdens and recommending remedial policies. The workgroup's report in 1992 was the first federal acknowledgment of environmental injustices. Reilly created the Office of Environmental Justice in the EPA. In 1994, President Bill Clinton signed Executive Order 12,898, "Federal Actions to Address Environmental Justice in Minority Populations and Low-Income Populations," requiring federal agencies to include potential environmental justice outcomes in all actions.

A report by the U.S. Office of General Counsel for the Commission on Civil Rights (2003:8) criticized implementation of the executive order by the EPA and the Department of the Interior, the Department of Housing and Urban Development, and the Department of Transportation. It charged that violations seldom resulted in revoked permits or withheld money; regulation guidance failed to consider the totality of a community's risk of exposure and failed to use cumulative risk assessments that consider all environmental and social factors; agencies failed to incorporate environmental justice into their core missions; and the agency's leadership frequently lacked commitment to environmental justice.

Debates over environmental injustices flare periodically. Claims of weakness in empirical evidence for environmental injustice are easy to make because of the inherent difficulties of designing an adequate methodology for separating effects of class and race. But whether or not evidence of discrimination can be found that fits the specifically bounded discourses of science or law, the unequal distribution of hazardous exposures is a logical deduction from well-established evidence of enduring stratification systems based especially on class, race/ethnicity, and gender.

State Rankings in TRI Releases

The Toxic Release Inventory (TRI) is a database containing information on releases of nearly 650 hazardous chemicals. In 2006, the EPA reported total emissions of 4.25 billion pounds of chemicals.

Table 7.1 displays the top- and bottom-ranked fifteen states by pounds of TRI chemical releases in 2006. The only discernible patterns are tendencies for southeastern and midwestern states to carry the heaviest TRI poundage and for northeastern states to carry the lightest.

I adjusted TRI releases for the state's area to obtain the pounds of TRI per square mile (Table 7.2). Adjustments mostly affected rankings of large and small states. Most states either retained their rankings (Alaska and Georgia) or moved up or down by no more than four rankings. Ohio, Pennsylvania, North Carolina,

TABLE 7.1 Top and Bottom Fifteen States Ranked by Total Pounds of TRI Releases, 2006

Top fifteen states by releases		Bottom fifteen states by releases	
State	TRI releases (pounds)	State	TRI releases (pounds)
Alaska	667,622,176	Minnesota	26,103,867
Ohio	291,343,874	Colorado	24,700,682
Texas	238,458,603	New Jersey	21,763,587
Indiana	236,869,696	Oregon	23,856,697
Nevada	217,099,056	New Mexico	23,713,415
Pennsylvania	154,077,302	Delaware	15,826,260
Utah	148,194,599	Wyoming	15,439,288
North Carolina	134,094,779	Maine	10,552,141
Louisiana	131,580,448	South Dakota	7,202,736
Tennessee	131,417,536	Massachusetts	6,969,912
Georgia	129,762,605	Connecticut	4,927,560
Alabama	121,070,327	New Hampshire	4,173,403
Florida	119,400,281	Hawaii	3,019,263
Illinois	112,558,536	Vermont	604,304
Missouri	109,861,126	Rhode Island	493,668

Source: U.S. Environmental Protection Agency, 2006 report, available online at http://www.epa.gov/tri/tridata/tri06/pdr/SectionB.pdf (accessed September 3, 2008).

TABLE 7.2 Top Fifteen States Ranked by Pounds of TRI Releases per Square Mile

Geographical unit	TRI releases per square mile of state's area (pounds)	State's area (square miles)
Alaska	10,172.71	656,425
Indiana	6,503.84	36,420
Ohio	6,499.15	44,828
Delaware	6,358.48	2,489
Pennsylvania	3,345.29	46,058
Tennessee	3,118.15	42,146
Louisiana	2,538.06	51,843
New Jersey	2,495.25	8,722
North Carolina	2,491.50	53,821
Alabama	2,317.45	52,423
Georgia	2,210.89	59,441
Nevada	1,963.51	110,567
Illinois	1,943.41	57,918
Florida	1,815.75	65,758
Utah	1,745.44	84,904

Sources: U.S. Environmental Protection Agency, 2006 report, available online at http://www.epa.gov/tri/tridata/tri06/pdr/SectionB.pdf (accessed September 3, 2008); U.S. Census Bureau, American FactFinder, 2006, available online at http://factfinder.census.gov/home/saff/main.html?_lang=en (accessed August 15, 2008); Enchanted Learning.com, U.S. States: Area and Ranking, 2008, available online at http://www.enchantedlearning.com/usa/states/area.shtml (accessed September 10, 2008).

TABLE 7.3 Top Fifteen States Ranked by Pounds of TRI Releases per Square Mile, with Superfund Sites and Class, Race, and Gender Composition

Geographical unit	Median household income	Non-white (%)	Female (%)	No. of Superfund sites
United States	48,451	26.1	50.8	1,270 (mean 25.4 per state)
Alaska	59,393	31.3*	48.5	5
Indiana	45,394*	14.0	50.8	14
Ohio	44,532*	16.0	51.3	30*
Delaware	40,315*	20.8	51.5	14
Pennsylvania	46,259*	16.2	51.4	94*
Tennessee	42,146*	20.8	51.1	13
Louisiana	39,337*	35.6*	51.5	10
New Jersey	64,470	30.4*	51.2	114*
North Carolina	42,645*	29.7*	51.0	31*
Alabama	38,783*	29.6*	51.5	13
Georgia	46,832*	37.9*	50.7	15
Nevada	52,998	26.4*	49.0	1
Illinois	52,006	29.3*	50.8	43*
Florida	45,495*	23.9	50.9	48*
Utah	51,309	10.9	49.7	15

*Indicator of environmental injustices: higher pounds per square mile than U.S. average, lower median household income than U.S. average, higher percentage non-white than U.S. average, more Superfund sites than U.S. average.

Sources: U.S. Environmental Protection Agency, 2006 report, available online at http://www.epa.gov/tri/tridata/tri06/pdr/SectionB.pdf (accessed September 3, 2008); U.S. Census Bureau, American FactFinder, 2006, available online at http://factfinder.census.gov/home/saff/main.html?_lang=en (accessed August 15, 2008); U.S. Environmental Protection Agency, Final National Priority List Sites by State, 2008, available online at http://www.epa.gov/superfund/sites/query/queryhtm/nplfin.htm (accessed September 5, 2008).

Florida, and Illinois moved by one rank; Indiana, Louisiana, and Alabama moved by two ranks; and Tennessee moved by four ranks. The large states Texas and Missouri dropped out of the top fifteen, and Nevada and Utah each dropped four ranks. The small states Delaware and New Jersey moved from the bottom to the top fifteen states. The regional pattern remains of southeastern states carrying the heaviest TRI poundage.

To check for disproportionate exposure to TRI chemicals by social class, race/ethnicity, and gender, I obtained census data for each state's median household income, percentage of population that is non-white, and percentage of population that is female. I added number of Superfund sites per state as another indicator of hazards. For comparison, I obtained national averages for all variables. In Table 7.3, asterisks indicate environmental injustice: higher pounds of releases per square mile, lower median household income, higher percentage of non-white population, and more Superfund sites than U.S. averages. Table 7.3 reveals the following:

- The median household incomes of 10 states are below the national average.
- The non-white percentage of the population in eight states exceeds the national average.

TABLE 7.4   Environmental Injustices by State

State	Injustice indicators
North Carolina	Superfund + Class + Race/ethnicity
Ohio	Superfund + Class
Pennsylvania	Superfund + Class
Florida	Superfund + Class
Illinois	Superfund + Race/ethnicity
New Jersey	Superfund + Race/ethnicity
Alabama	Class + Race/ethnicity
Georgia	Class + Race/ethnicity
Louisiana	Class + Race/ethnicity
Indiana	Class
Delaware	Class
Tennessee	Class
Alaska	Race/ethnicity
Nevada	Race/ethnicity
Utah	—

- The share of the population that is female ranges from 48.5 percent to 51.5 percent, demonstrating no pattern of gender bias.
- Six states contain more than the average number of Superfund sites.

Table 7.4 ranks states by number of environmental injustice indicators. North Carolina's toxic burden is unjust on the basis of class, race, and number of Superfund sites. Alabama, Georgia, and Louisiana are disproportionately toxic by class and race. The non-white populations in these southeastern states are primarily African American. Alaska's and Nevada's ethnically disproportionate burden falls on the Inupiat and Native Americans. Class-based environmental injustice is borne by Indiana, Delaware, and Tennessee. Ohio, Pennsylvania, and Florida are disproportionately burdened on the basis of class and number of Superfund sites, and Illinois and New Jersey are disproportionately burdened on the basis of race/ethnicity and number of Superfund sites. Only Utah has no indicators of environmental injustice in the toxic burden.

Narratives of Environmental Injustice Communities

Examination of TRI data demonstrates environmental injustice based on class and race. But neither tables representing TRI releases by state nor statistical analyses of communities that host hazardous waste facilities adequately depict the plight of victims of environmental injustice. To add rich description to numerical accounts, I present narratives of three communities whose residents are compelled to carry an unfair burden of contaminated workplaces and homes.

Workers at the Oak Ridge Nuclear Reservation

In 1942, the army eliminated several small towns in eastern Tennessee to construct a secret installation, one of three Manhattan Project sites created to develop the first atomic bomb. Workers were required to obtain security clearances that prohibited them from talking about their jobs, and each knew only the requirements of his own task. Workers suspected of inappropriate behavior, such as talking about the job, were denied due process. Conviction could bring a prison sentence or execution. Wartime secrecy was infused with patriotism, creating a rigid code of silence that permeated the local culture. In August 1945, the B-29 bomber *Enola Gay* dropped the "Little Boy" atomic bomb on Hiroshima. The bomb's enriched uranium was produced at the Oak Ridge facility. After a second bomb was dropped on Nagasaki, World War II ended. Oak Ridge residents were only then informed of their part in the secret war.

The Oak Ridge Nuclear Reservation participated in Cold War efforts to develop a hydrogen bomb. The government kept secret the enormous amounts of mercury required for production so the Soviets would not guess the status of U.S. progress on the bomb. In 1983, rumors of a secret government study of mercury contamination at the Y-12 plant led a local journalist to file a Freedom of Information Act request for the report. Release of the government study from 1977 forced U.S. Department of Energy (DOE) officials to acknowledge that 2.4 million pounds of mercury had been "lost"—unintentionally released—from the Y-12 plant between 1950 and 1977.

A congressional investigation criticized the DOE for publicizing misleading information about mercury losses and using national security to hide them. The reservation was placed on Superfund's National Priority List in 1989. More than 700 separate sites were listed, including 247 buildings, some as large as auto plants, contaminated with radiation and other hazardous substances; 56 waste burial grounds contaminated with solvents, lubricants, chemicals, uranium, mercury, strontium, thorium, tritium, and contaminants still classified as secret; and 52 settlement ponds with chemicals, metals, and polychlorinated biphenyls (PCBs). Contaminated sites cover 5,000 acres; about 1,400 are so radioactive that they must be guarded in perpetuity.

Today, the Reservation, the largest of the nation's seventeen nuclear weapons sites, employs approximately 12,000 workers. The community remains economically dependent on the Reservation—the only new enterprise to develop is the environmental cleanup industry. Officials find themselves in a predicament: despite public confessions of massive contamination that warrants the entrance of a new industry, they insist that few people have been sickened by the contamination.

Throughout five decades of weapons production, Reservation workers were exposed mostly to mercury, cyanide, uranium, and beryllium—substances with known associations with illnesses. Mercury exposures are linked to tremors, respiratory problems, emotional instability, sleeplessness, memory loss, muscle weakness, headaches, slow reflexes, and numbness. Acute and chronic cyanide exposure is related to headache, heart palpitations, convulsions, skin disorders, nasal irritation and drainage, and tremors. Exposure to radioactivity is associated with malignant effects, such as cancers of the bone, liver, thyroid, and lung, and nonmalignant effects, such as degenerative changes and impaired function of bone marrow, kidneys, lungs, and the eyeball lens. Beryllium can instigate life-threatening respiratory problems, including berylliosis and lung cancer.

Interviews indicate that workers were always aware of exposure to hazardous production materials (Cable, Shriver, and Mix 2008). Several described exposure at the "salvage yard," a notorious storage area for hazardous waste where numerous pallets of 55 gallon drums—some whose lids had rusted and fallen into the drums' contents—emitted sharp chemical odors. A worker splashed by a vapor cloud was immediately summoned to the Reservation's medical center for tests. He was informed of neither the reason for nor the results of the tests.

Workers described a range of symptoms they attributed to occupational exposure: thyroid problems, chronic fatigue, rashes, memory loss, headaches, dizziness, respiratory problems, and vision and hearing loss. Officials not only denied but also harassed ill workers. They denied workers' illness claims by insisting that no records documented their exposure. A worker who recognized her symptoms in an account of cyanide poisoning expected cooperation from her supervisor, who instead denied that cyanide was present in her work environment. "I write monthly reports to DOE, and I've got at least three or four projects that have got 'cyanide' in the title!" she said. "Don't tell *me* there is no cyanide out there!" (Cable, Shriver, and Mix 2008: 393).

Officials frequently harassed complaining workers by reassigning them to undesirable tasks. A worker described these punitive reassignments: "They would move you to the dirty jobs, if you questioned that something wasn't being done right . . . maybe down at the scrap yard in the middle of summer by yourself, surveying pipes—with swarms of bees and wasps around you" (Cable, Shriver, and Mix 2008: 393). The best-documented account is a whistleblower case from 1991. After a worker publicized safety violations in handling nuclear materials, he was reassigned to an office containing radioactive wastes. When he complained, he was reassigned to conduct an inventory of chemical wastes in a former mercury reclamation room. He filed a whistleblower case and was recommended for $30,000 in damages. But the U.S. Labor Secretary dismissed the case because it had not been filed within the statute's required thirty days of the alleged acts.

Workers' illness claims were also contested by physicians employed at the Reservation who refused to inform workers of medical test results. Most workers who *were* informed were told that the results were normal. Local private care physicians contested workers' illness claims by discrediting more open-minded peer physicians and by harassing workers. The oncologist Bill Reid suspected that high incidences of unusual symptoms among his patients were related to occupational exposure. After he diagnosed several patients with heavy metal poisoning, his peers publicly vilified him as a drug addict and medical incompetent, subjected him to a punitive peer review, suspended his hospital privileges, and warned at least one staff member that if she continued to work for Reid, she would not find other employment in the county. Private care physicians also harassed ill workers. Many workers reported that their physicians dismissed their questions about possible links between their illnesses and occupational exposures and instead treated them for depression and similar emotional disorders.

Racism and Environmental Injustice in Oak Ridge

Nearly all studies of environmental injustice examine either of two cases: a hazardous facility is proposed for construction in an established low-income or minority community, or low property values attract a low-income or minority community in close proximity to an existing hazardous facility. I describe a unique case in which a minority population was deliberately collected and placed in a community built specifically for it in close proximity to a hazardous facility.

During World War II, the U.S. Army recruited black laborers from throughout the Southeast for the wartime project at the Oak Ridge Nuclear Reservation. Black men were recruited to fill manual labor jobs as janitors and in construction. Unlike whites, black men initially could not bring spouses. Spouses were permitted later if employed by the government, but no children were allowed until after the war. Most black men worked in positions that exposed them to hazardous substances: treating chemical spills, disposing of leftover chemicals, and cleaning up contaminated areas at day's end. Black women worked as domestics in white soldiers' barracks and white scientists' homes.

Housing during the war was allocated by occupational rank. The families of white scientists lived in relatively spacious three-bedroom houses with indoor plumbing, fireplaces, hardwood floors, fully equipped kitchens, and coal furnaces. White male and female laborers lived in dormitories, trailer camps, and prefabricated houses or duplexes. All black workers lived in hutments—16-by-16 foot single-room dwellings with plywood walls, coal-burning potbellied stoves, and one door. The hutments lacked insulation, plumbing, interior finishes, and glass windows. All black laborers shared common bathhouses. Black women, including employees' spouses, lived in "the Pen," hutments separated from men's hutments by a five-foot fence topped by barbed wire and patrolled nightly by security guards to ensure the women's compliance with their 10 P.M. curfew. With the initial postwar drop in population, the Army allowed married black employees to live together, and spouses living elsewhere were permitted to move to the Reservation. Children remained banned until the black community was relocated.

In 1949, the Atomic Energy Commission (AEC) consolidated the scattered black communities into one segregated and gated area, known as Scarboro. Beyond the gate, two miles and a highway separated blacks' homes from the nearest whites' homes. Two 300 foot ridges formed two of Scarboro's boundaries. Just beyond a ridge lay the massive Y-12 plant. Who decided to site the black community so close to a hazardous facility?

My colleague, Tamara Mix, and I could not uncover a definitive answer. Pressing interviewees, scouring government documents, and even filing a Freedom of Information Act request did not reveal the decision-making process. We report here the story from unclassified and declassified government documents and the recollections of black and white wartime residents of Oak Ridge.

In 1948, the AEC began planning the relocation of all black residents. Commission documents report that the AEC formed a committee to help plan the new community, temporarily called the Negro Village or Neighborhood 10. The AEC sent letters to black community leaders requesting their participation. Those leaders brought in others. Two potential sites were identified: East Village and Gamble Valley. No documents we obtained referred to a decisive committee meeting or the committee's recommendation.

The following are typical recollections of relocation by *white* residents:

> Actually, the Atomic Energy Commission, when it first came here, began plans almost immediately to build new housing for black residents. That was what was said—that this would be a new black housing area for residents. The concerns and the talk wasn't so much about the segregation [as] about the quality of the housing. Would they have obviously separate but more nearly equal housing facilities?

> Those considered leaders of the black community were called together by the AEC, and out of these conferences came the choice of the location for the new homes for blacks. Gamble Valley, the pre–Oak Ridge name for the area, had been a large trailer park for whites during the war.

Recollections of the relocation by *black* residents differed from those by whites. Some recalled that black pastors were involved in the siting decision but differed on their role:

> They were going to move the blacks to a different area, on the other end of town, but a group protested, led by a couple of black pastors who didn't want to be that far away. So they moved them into what is now Scarboro.

> There was Reverend Simms, Reverend Fuller, and a Reverend Johnson, and Johnson lived in Knoxville, and Fuller and Simms lived here. But they just had to go along with the program. That was it—they went along with the program.

> They talked to some black ministers that were here that came in and did not have any knowledge about what was going on and [went] through a kind of a—I don't want to say brainwash—a kind of, maybe a little coercion.

Many participants attributed the decision to prevailing segregation norms, without reference to Y-12:

> At one point, they were going to put the black folks in the eastern part of the town. But there were so many white folks that came in that they needed that land over there for them. So they decided to put the black folks over here.

> I think it just fit into the norm throughout the country. In most other cities, minority communities are strategically located in certain parts of the city. I expect [it's] no different than other parts of the country.

> To me, there is a lot of hidden racism. Sure, racism exists—is it blatant? You can't necessarily say it's blatant.

They were not *forced* to live in Gamble Valley, but it was a take-it-or-leave-it situation. If they wanted to live here, that was the only place black people could live.

You know, my gut feeling is that it was not necessarily intentionally put there. I think maybe the land was cheaper and that kind of thing—it was not prime land. I think it was more an attempt to keep the races separated. That's what I really think the purpose of putting it there was.

They wanted to keep the race separate. They didn't want integrated housing. In order to do that, they were going to build the blacks in one area and the whites all around everywhere else.

A small number believed that black residents were deliberately placed near Y-12:

Everybody felt like they put us here in this valley, which was right under Y-12. When they was choosing the area, they had this place here, which was Gamble Valley, and they had a place down the turnpike, which was East Village. So they put the black people over here in Gamble Valley. It was right up under the plant there and, anything happened, it would get them first. That was the way that we felt about it, though maybe that wasn't [the case]. . . . [S]ince I've gotten older, I try not to be critical. . . . But that was the way that it looked.

I have a feeling that they may have [chosen Gamble Valley] because of the proximity to the plant. My property butts up to the security fence in the backyard there. It probably goes 10 feet to the 10 to 11 foot high security fence that goes around the property. Y-12 is directly over the hill. My feeling is—it was chosen because it was kind of isolated. Maybe [Gamble Valley was intended as] a longtime guinea pig. It was isolated—out of sight, out of mind.

I am convinced that this was one reason they was made to choose—the site was chosen because of the proximity. The things that are going to happen with all the stuff they're doing at the plant—they're testing uranium and mercury and everything else—that [blacks] be the one at risk. Anything that happens, they'll get it first—I'm convinced of that.

The mercury losses from Y-12 acknowledged in 1983 concerned Scarboro residents. East Fork Poplar Creek runs through Y-12 and was known to be contaminated; the creek also winds around Scarboro. Residents were advised not to eat fish caught from the stream, and some concern was expressed about vegetables grown near the creek. Both the fish and the vegetables were diet supplements for many Scarboro residents. In 1997, a regional newspaper published a series on health problems in Oak Ridge and focused specifically on heightened incidence of respiratory illnesses among Scarboro's children. Emissions from Y-12 were suspected. The CDC partnered with the Tennessee Department of Health to investigate. Researchers found that Scarboro's 13 percent prevalence rate of asthma was higher than national rates of 7 percent in all children and 9 percent among black children, and the 35 percent prevalence rate of wheezing was higher than most national and international rates, which ranged from 1.6 percent to 36.8 percent.

Regardless of who made the decision to locate the black population in Y-12's hazardous shadows, still-segregated Scarboro residents declare themselves victims of environmental racism.

Native American "Chat Rats"

In the early 1900s, rich lead and zinc deposits were found in Ottowa County, Oklahoma. The region is inhabited by the remainder of the Quapaws, a nearly extinct tribe that was once one of the largest in the lower Mississippi. The Quapaws owned a substantial portion of the resource-rich land near the town of Picher, but the U.S. Department of the Interior managed it for them. The official story, recorded in EPA documents, is that the federal government acted on the tribe's behalf to negotiate profitable leases with private mining corporations. The unofficial story, told by many Picher residents, is that the federal government catered to mining corporations and effectively robbed the tribe of land and the revenues it generated. Picher was the center of the nation's largest lead and zinc mining area, producing 60 percent of the nation's minerals between 1919 and 1929. But the center shifted away, and by 1954 Picher mines produced only 28 percent of the nation's total (Rosner and Markowitz 1991).

Mining operations stopped in 1970, prior to passage of the Surface Mining Control and Reclamation Act of 1977. Mine owners were not required to reclaim the landscape; they simply walked away. Residents lost their economic base and were stuck with approximately 100 miles of underground tunnels, 1,000 mineshafts, tens of thousands of boreholes, enormous underground caverns with ceilings up to 100 feet high, 500 open mine shafts, and 800 acres of flotation pond sediments (Shriver, Cable, and Kennedy 2008). Seventy-five million tons of tailings containing lead, zinc, cadmium, and arsenic were heaped around the community in 75–200 foot mounds of "chat piles" called the "Picher Mountains."

Chronic low-dose exposure to lead is dangerous because the body cannot metabolize it. Instead, lead accumulates in the body, causing problems with kidney function, the immune system, and memory; hypertension; hearing loss; balance problems; anemia; and muscle paralysis. Children are particularly susceptible because of their greater capacity for absorbing lead and their greater likelihood of ingesting or inhaling it from playing on the floor and ground. The Agency for Toxic Substances and Disease Registry finds that blood-lead levels (BLLs) as low as 10 micrograms per deciliter in children are associated with decreased cognitive function, decreased IQ, delayed motor development, mental retardation, compromised growth, attention deficits, and behavior problems. The effects of lead exposure are irreversible.

With no warnings of potential danger, residents' actions increased lead exposure. The Picher Mountains served as picnic grounds, ski slopes, and sledding and biking trails. Flotation ponds were treated as swimming holes. Chat removed from the piles was used for small children's sandboxes, liners on ball field base paths, road-building material, foundation filler for construction, and fill-in for mine shafts and cave-ins. Children grew up playing in the chat piles, referring to themselves as "chat rats."

In 1979, heavy rains filled mineshafts, creating acid mine water that discharged into streams and aquifers. Residents' complaints and urging by the governor of Oklahoma resulted in EPA studies finding that surface water contained lead, zinc, and cadmium in concentrations that greatly exceeded drinking water standards and that the main drinking water source was threatened with contamination from the downward migration of acid mine water through abandoned mining wells. The Picher area was designated a Superfund site in 1983 on the basis of water problems, not the towering chat piles. The EPA began a water remediation project, installing dikes, plugging abandoned wells, and diverting the path of Tar Creek (Shriver, Cable, and Kennedy 2008). The project was completed in December 1986. The EPA's five-year progress report concluded that the water remediation project was largely unsuccessful, but because surface water conditions were deemed irreversible, the agency took no further action.

A routine health study of 192 Quapaw children participating in the local Women, Infants, and Children program was conducted by Indian Health Services in 1994. The study found that 34 percent of the children had BLLs exceeding the recommended limit (Shriver, Cable, and Kennedy 2008). EPA officials analyzed soil samples from residences, day-care centers, playgrounds, and schoolyards. Ninety-seven percent of the homes in Picher contained lead, the majority exceeding the recommended limit by a factor of 10. Subsequent studies by various citizens' groups revealed similar findings.

In 1997, the EPA began remediating lead-contaminated soil, initially targeting 16 city parks and 300 residences with either high concentrations of lead in the soil or with preschool children whose BLLs exceeded 10 micrograms per deciliter. The remediation process removed up to 18 inches of contaminated soil, backfilled with clean topsoil, and replanted grass. The excavated soil was dumped in dried-up flotation ponds.

Chat piles were not targeted because none of them were on residential property or public property.

In 2000, the EPA announced that children's BLLs had been reduced by half. But a study by a citizens' group found that 12 percent of the children in Picher still showed elevated BLLs and that most of them lived in homes that had already been remediated. Residents blamed the chat piles as a perpetual source of re-contamination, arguing that steady Oklahoma winds continually blew dust from the chat piles into yards and homes. Studies by the University of Oklahoma and a citizens' group found that remediated homes were re-contaminated beyond acceptable levels within nine months, that thirty-six of forty-three homes tested were re-contaminated in an average of 160 days, and that several homes were re-contaminated in only eleven days (Shriver, Cable, and Kennedy 2008).

Concern about the consequences of children's exposure to lead was publicly voiced at a town meeting in 2003 (Shriver, Cable, and Kennedy 2008). An elementary school principal described students' reading disabilities as evidence of lead toxicity, asserting that about half of the students required 75–100 repetitions to learn a reading lesson, compared with the average of 25 repetitions. She said that the students "hit a wall" in their learning by age 12. A school superintendent reported on a study of 28 students from kindergarten to third grade: half had BLLs lower than the recommended level yet averaged more than nine months behind normal expectations for their age cohorts.

Numerous residents were persuaded that children's elevated BLLs caused the reported learning disabilities and wanted access to special educational programs and compensation for services that the children would likely require as adults (Shriver, Cable, and Kennedy 2008). They were surprised to discover that, despite scientific evidence establishing the link between lead exposure and neurological damage in children, the federal government was not obligated to aid or compensate victims in any way.

The government is absolved of such responsibilities because of the nature of environmental policies. Policy instruments include regulations, which are enforceable, and recommendations, which are not. Regulations limit toxic *emissions at the facility level* by establishing emissions standards, enforceable by law. The EPA regulates facilities' lead emissions through the Clean Air Act, requiring that concentration of lead in air breathed by the public not exceed 1.5 micrograms per cubic meter, averaged over three months. The Occupational Safety and Health Administration regulates facilities' lead emissions in the workplace, requiring that lead concentration in workroom airspace not exceed 50 micrograms per cubic meter in an eight-hour workday.

But enforceable regulations cannot limit the *level of toxic material in an individual's body*. The government offers only unenforceable recommendations for individual levels, which merely provide guidelines on threshold levels at which adverse effects might be expected. Children with BLLs that exceed recommended limits are simply advised to undergo medical evaluation.

When regulations are properly enforced, toxic emissions and public exposure remain within standards. As a consequence, individual body loads do not exceed recommended limits, and policy recommendations for individual toxic levels are irrelevant. But when regulations are not properly enforced, standards for toxic emissions and public exposure are exceeded. Inevitably, individual body loads increase and may exceed recommended limits. But the ill have no recourse for compensation.

A study by the EPA in 2003 advocated a voluntary relocation of Picher residents. In 2004, the state legislature funded the buyout of residents with preschool children, and fifty-two families relocated before the funds expired. A study of the potential for subsidence of areas overlying mine tunnels by the U.S. Army Corps of Engineers in 2004 found that one-third of Picher's 400 homes were in imminent threat of subsidence. The federal government initiated a $20 million voluntary buyout program, and many families relocated.

Many members of the dwindling Quapaw tribe do not want to leave their tribal lands. They remain in Picher—with the chat piles. Tribal teens, many of them high school dropouts because they could not keep up with their peers, continue to ride their four-wheelers up the slopes of the Picher Mountains.

Failed Petro-dependent Environmental Policies

Substantial resource depletion and pollution testify that petro-dependent policies do not acknowledge ecological principles. We violate the first principle by altering nearly the entire biosphere; the second, by operating an economic system that contradicts ecosystems; the third, with our manipulation of nature's processes to manufacture materials that are incompatible with ecosystems; and the fourth, with our biological hubris. Violation of ecological principles has ruptured the material fabric of life.

Authorities' and the public's routine tolerance of violations of environmental policy in favor of expanding production attest to petro-dependent policies' denial of a link between economic activities and the environment. Instead, we sever economic policies from environmental policies and adopt the dangerous belief that economy and ecology are unrelated spheres. It is a delusion in the strictest sense of the word: a mental state "marked by loss of or greatly lessened ability to test whether what one is thinking and feeling about the real world is actually true" (Merriam-Webster Dictionary 1995: 421).

Statistical analyses of contaminated sites; cursory examinations of TRI releases; case studies of workers, African Americans, and Native Americans; and even an elementary understanding of human societies reveal that environmental policies do not enact democratic principles of fairness and justice. Instead, policies that permit environmental inequalities persist because they ensure that the privileged remain privileged—free to make decisions about environmental use that benefits them without input from those who suffer the consequences.

Environmental policies fail to erect a regulatory system that sustainably and equitably maintains citizens' survival, not because of inherent complexities in the biosphere, but because of human power relationships. C. S. Lewis (1947: 17) wrote, "What we call Man's power over Nature turns out to be a power exercised by some men over other men with Nature as the instrument." In the next chapter, I analyze the social mechanisms and institutions through which petro-dependent power operates to shape policymakers' formulations.

8

Petro-dependent Obstacles to Sustainable Policies

The Corporate State and Its Institutional and Cultural Reflections

Environmental policy should maintain human life at the most fundamental level—the material fabric of life. But even ramped-up conservation and pollution abatement policies formulated by environmentally concerned legislators and implemented on scientific grounds by concerned individual employees of coordinated bureaucracies fall short. The gap between petro-dependency's environmental impacts and environmental policies is a yawning chasm, enlarging as we continue to poison the material fabric of life. Through what mechanisms is power exercised in ways that keep us on the path of least resistance? Why is petro-dependency the path of least resistance?

The economic institution is society's dominant institution because of our primary goal of survival. Corporations are the driving organizations of petro-dependency's economic system. Corporate dominance is backed by the power of the political institution. So inextricably tied are the two institutions that Martin Marger (1987: 115) describes the state's framework as "essentially determined by the needs of the society's economic system." Kenneth Dolbeare (1974: 26) asserts that the state's "priorities, its personnel, and its policies are either those of the economic system or ones consistent with the imperatives of that system." Analysts, then, refer to the intertwined institutions of corporation and state as a "corporate state," whose officials are guided above all by economic imperatives. The operations of social institutions necessarily overlap to maintain coordination and stability throughout the social system. As a consequence, the economic imperatives of the corporate state find expression in scientific and judicial institutions. Institutional actions are further coordinated and reinforced through the cultural system.

In this chapter, I analyze factors underlying petro-dependent policymaking. I examine the corporate state in some detail before turning to its reflections in science, the judicial system, and mainstream culture.

The Corporate State

As I recounted in the Preface, twenty-some years ago I was conducting research in a community contaminated by tannery wastes and in which residents had mobilized to protest the contamination. I interviewed an activist at the kitchen table in his mountaintop cabin as he ticked off the high personal costs of the battle he and others were waging: excessive mileage on his truck, workdays missed to attend meetings and hearings, and enormous phone bills from calling state and federal officials. When I asked what kept him going, the gentle family man gazed thoughtfully out the window to the peaceful valley below, then suddenly banged his work-worn fist on the kitchen table and bellowed, "Them Big Boys ought to have to obey the laws same as I do."

The man had a point. Laws prohibit the release of contaminating substances into communities. Residents had repeatedly notified local, state, and federal Environmental Protection Agency (EPA) officials of the contamination, wary of its potentially harmful effects on livestock and people. But no criminal investigation occurred; no one was arrested; no one was jailed. Activists learned—and taught me—that our lives are shaped, and our environmental decisions are fashioned, by the economic imperatives of the corporate state.

The Corporation

The corporation is the principal institution of the past one hundred years. Corporations determine much of reality for most of the planet's people. Corporations were initially developed in the fifteenth century as state-chartered agents to serve the public good. Over the centuries, corporate power grew, and corporations became less accountable to the public. The sole objective of contemporary corporations is to earn profits for shareholders. I examine the corporation's development, power, and influence in environmental policymaking.

Development of the Corporation

The modern corporation evolved from fifteenth-century British and Dutch merchant companies. Mercantilist monarchs granted to limited liability joint stock companies the power to act as nation-states within foreign territories. Charters established corporate rights and obligations, including the share of profits due to the crown in exchange for privileges. Corporate–state relations since then have featured continual pressure by corporations to expand their rights and limit their obligations (Korten 2001: 61).

In the mercantilist United States, individual states chartered corporations as public entities (Derber 1998; Hertz 2001; Korten 2001). Corporations were fully accountable to the public, chartered only to serve specific public purposes such as canal and bridge construction and toll road management. Charters were valid for a specified duration, typically twenty years, and could be revoked for failing to serve the public interest. They contained specific provisions limiting

the accumulation of personal power. Corporations were prohibited from own-
ing other corporations, and limits were placed on borrowing capacity, landownership, and profits. Individual corporate members were personally liable
for all debts incurred by the corporation. By 1800, states had granted about 200
corporate charters (Korten 2001: 63).

The state's right to revoke or amend corporate charters was challenged in
1819 when the State of New Hampshire moved to revoke Dartmouth College's
charter, granted by King George III before U.S. independence. The college
opposed the state's action, and the U.S. Supreme Court ruled in favor of Dartmouth College, arguing that the charter contained no revocation clause (Korten
2001).

Industrialists took advantage of the political disorder from the Civil War, the
assassination of President Abraham Lincoln, and economic recession to enlarge
corporate power. They used profits from military procurement contracts to buy
legislation that granted them considerable funds and land to expand the western
railway system. They secured favorable legislation in the banking and railroad
industries, establishment of tariffs, control of labor, and disposition of public
land (Korten 2001).

The powerful modern corporation was formed in the United States between
1886 and 1919. The shift began with a U.S. Supreme Court ruling in 1886 in which
corporations' public accountability was removed in a perversion of the Fourteenth Amendment. Attorneys in multiple cases argued that the amendment
entitled corporations to the same status and rights as individuals and that corporate money was protected by the amendment's due process clause. Between 1868
and 1911, 576 of the 604 U.S. Supreme Court decisions involving the Fourteenth
Amendment dealt with corporate rights rather than individual civil rights
(McAdam 1982). These precedents established the protection of corporations
and corporate property as a centerpiece of constitutional law.

State laws limiting the size of corporations were evaded through corporations' formation of "trusts"—conglomerates designed to appear as independent
operators—such as John D. Rockefeller's Standard Oil. Strong public opposition
pressured Congress to pass the Sherman Antitrust Act in 1890, and several large
corporations, including Standard Oil, were broken up. But corporations continued to grow by pitting states against each other. In 1889, New Jersey passed the
first law allowing a corporation to own equity in other corporations, and corporations flocked to establish headquarters there. Other states began to compete in
wooing corporations by removing restrictions such as limitations on size and
mergers. Lawrence Mitchell (2007: ix) describes this formative era of corporate
capitalism: "Industrialism transformed from independent factories owned by
entrepreneur industrialists, their families, and some business associates to giant
combinations of industrial plants owned directly and indirectly by widely dispersed shareholders."

Corporate power increased further when high unemployment and inflation
in the late 1970s resisted the Keynesian economic cure of government intervention. Corporate actors mobilized political resources to regain control of the politi-

cal agenda and the court system. The administrations of Ronald Reagan in the United States and of Margaret Thatcher in the United Kingdom adopted a neoliberal agenda featuring global advancement of corporate power. Neoliberal policies reduced taxes on the rich and removed restraints on corporate mergers and acquisitions. Advocates of neoliberal policy weakly enforced environmental and labor standards, broke unions, reduced wages and benefits, downsized corporate workforces, and shifted manufacturing operations abroad to benefit from cheap labor and lax regulation.

The most recent court-endowed corporate civil right is the right to free speech. In *Citizens United v. Federal Election Commission 2010*, the U.S. Supreme Court struck down the provision of the McCain-Feingold Act prohibiting corporations from broadcasting electioneering communications and ruled that corporate funding of independent political broadcasts in elections cannot be limited under the First Amendment (Vicini 2010).

Corporations have utterly transformed from the early public organizations charged by political leaders to fulfill a public good. The contemporary corporate charter establishes private organizations with the rights of individuals whose members marshal enormous economic and political resources to advance narrow private agendas while protecting themselves from legal liability for the public consequences of their actions.

Corporate Power

The modern corporation has three defining characteristics:

- The vast bulk of national wealth is privately owned and controlled.
- Profits are the motivational underpinning of the corporation. Ownership of private property ensures that all profits are private profits. Even public investment in social programs reaps private profits, because the government, constitutionally prohibited from competing with the private sector, is obliged to depend on private firms, such as those in the defense industry, for materials and services.
- Corporations exacerbate the unequal distribution of wealth because the means by which wealth is accumulated—ownership of factories, machines, real estate, and financial capital—are unequally distributed.

Corporate wealth is the most important form of privilege in modern societies. Concentration of power within a few giant corporations in almost every economic sector creates a system in which decisions about production and distribution are seldom made in the marketplace. With nearly monopolistic powers, corporations set prices and determine the quantities of goods produced and marketed. Kerbo (2009) describes corporate concentration by focusing on market dominance, concentration of stock control, and interlocking directorates.

Although 200,000 industrial corporations operate nationally, 75 percent of total industrial assets are controlled by only one hundred corporations (Dye 1995; Kerbo 2009). Banks possess the largest group of corporate assets and the greatest power because they control the crucial commodity for expansion and investment: money. In *Forbes* magazine's list of the top twenty-five corporations in 2007, the top two were financial institutions: Citibank and Bank of America. Three oil companies ranked in the top ten. Auto companies dropped from the top twenty-five. Market concentration and size have significantly reduced national competition. Between two and five corporations dominate business in nearly every industry, wielding enormous influence through their decisions: "Their performance as corporations, their profits, losses, and layoffs, affect the lives and well-being of millions of people" (Kerbo 2009: 190).

Corporate concentration appears in the concentration of control over stock. Until recently, stock was controlled by individual families, granting them substantial influence in corporate decision making. But the proportion of total family-owned stock has declined to 50 percent, replaced with stocks controlled by institutions whose actors invest in workers' pension programs and other large trust holdings such as banks and insurance companies (O'Sullivan 2000). For example, large banks are the principal stock owners in other large banks. Institutional investors do not own the stocks but exercise considerable control through voting rights, contributing to the concentration of economic power (O'Sullivan 2000).

Interlocking corporate directorates further concentrate corporate power. The board of directors is the highest authority in the corporate hierarchy, with the mandate to hire and fire and to set broad policy. Board members are drawn from the corporation's president and vice presidents and from top executives of other corporations. Board members' responsibility is to represent stockholders' interests, but stockholders are often institutional investors—other corporations. Through interlocking directorates, two or more corporations are linked through at least one board member. Although direct interlocking directorates between competing corporations are illegal, competing companies may legally establish extensive indirect interlocking directorates, with two corporations linked by board members through a third corporation.

G. William Domhoff (2002) examined interlocking directorates among 1,029 corporations and found that twenty-eight corporations had twenty-eight to forty-five ties with others, sixty-five corporations had twenty to twenty-seven such ties, and 248 companies had ten to nineteen ties. Val Burris (2005) examined more than 700 corporate board members from more than 1,000 large corporations to assess whether interlocking directorates are associated with common political attitudes and behavior. He found that interlocked directorates are more strongly associated with cohesion and shared political behavior than other factors, such as type of industry.

Interlocking directorates create another layer of economic concentration by reducing competition among corporations, providing opportunities to share information about plans and operations and fostering unity among top corporate officials that aids them in persuading government officials to consider corporate interests in economic and environmental policies.

Corporate Influence in Environmental Policymaking

Since 1970, corporations have "played a uniquely important role in environmental policymaking" and have been "among the most significant policy actors at all levels of government" (Kraft and Kamieniecki 2007: 3). Corporate officials deploy their power through two tactics: lobbying at each stage of the policymaking process and mobilizing anti-environmentalists.

Corporations influence policy proactively by making contributions to the campaigns of candidates and political parties that express views sympathetic to corporate interests, with the expectation that their policy decisions will favor business (Duffy 2007). When an issue is placed on the legislative agenda, corporate advocates attempt to frame environmental issues and shape public attitudes via media and mass-mobilization strategies (Guber and Bosso 2007). Corporate lobbyists seek out congressional committee members to advocate their views, engage in public confrontations with environmentalist opponents, and challenge environmentalists' scientific evidence (Layzer 2007). They schmooze agency officials to gain influence in rulemaking and implementation processes (Coglianese 2007; Furlong 2007).

Kay Lehman Schlozman and John Tierney (1986) found that 75 percent of nongovernmental organizations in Washington, D.C., represented business interests, and they concluded that the lobbying community is more weighted in corporations' favor than ever. Michael Kraft and Sheldon Kamieniecki (2007: 6) observe that, although corporations have been ineffective in repealing the major environmental laws, they have been successful in "modifying their implementation in the executive agencies. . . . [B]usiness groups appear to be highly successful in getting what they want from policymakers."

A second corporate tactic to influence policymaking is the mobilization of anti-environmentalists. The anti-environmental countermovement emerged in the early 1970s (Athanasiou 1996; Austin 2002; Burke 1994; Foster 1996; Helvarg 1997; Menon and Menon 1997; Rowell 1996; Smith 1991; Stefancic and Delgado 1996; Tokar 1997). It is led by people in powerful positions and consists of think tanks, science "mills" (Austin 2002: 78), and so-called astroturf groups.

Politically conservative, pro-business think tanks were organized after corporate leaders recognized their shared problem of "an ideological imbalance in scientific production" (Austin 2002: 79). The Heritage Foundation, the think tank most often cited by the media (Austin 2002), is funded by wealthy people and led by corporate officials who recruit writers and politicians to conservative causes. The American Enterprise Institute, funded by corporations such as Standard Oil, routinely publishes antiregulatory literature. Similar think tanks are the Washington Institute for Values in Public Policy, the Cato Institute, and the Environmental Policy Project.

Other anti-environmental countermovement organizations produce scientific literature with a conservative bent. The Science and Environmental Policy Project is funded by corporations such as Monsanto, Texaco, and Exxon. The

American Council on Science and Health, funded by Exxon, Ford, and Mobil, has produced a documentary featuring antiregulatory scientists who minimize the danger of pesticides (Austin 2002). Similar organizations are the 21st Century Science Associates, the U.S. Council on Energy Awareness, and the Committee for a Constructive Tomorrow. Such think tanks and scientific organizations produce anti-environmental literature in the form of books, websites, and pamphlets, denying global climate change, arguing that environmental regulation adversely affects the poor, and criticizing environmentalists as idealists, opportunists, and Luddites.

Astroturf groups are seemingly grassroots citizen organizations that are conceived, created, or funded by corporations, industry trade associations, political interest groups, or public relations firms. These synthetic grassroots movements are manufactured for a fee by companies such as Bonner and Associates (Greider 1992). Andrew Austin (2002: 88) argues that these faux activists "present themselves to the public as ordinary citizens: the logger, the farmer, and the hunter—in short, the common man."

The wise use movement is at the vanguard of astroturf organizing (Rowell 1996). Formed in 1988 (Layzer 2007), the wise use movement advocated the development of oil and gas reserves in the Arctic National Wildlife Refuge; the elimination of development restrictions on wetlands; unlimited mineral and energy production on public land; the re-designation of nearly all of the National Wilderness Preservation System for motorized trail travel, commercial development, and commodity use; the institution of civil penalties against those who mount legal challenges to development on federal land; and the recognition of private rights to mining claims, water, grazing, and timber on federal land. Some wise use organizations were industry fronts, such as the Marine Preservation Association, whose members defined preservation as the promotion of the interest of petroleum and energy companies. Others were funded by companies such as Nerco Minerals, Cyprus Minerals, Chevron, and Heclo Mining.

Simultaneously, the property rights movement emerged and advocated the rights of people who own land within national park boundaries, claiming that the guarantee of compensation for property taken by eminent domain under the Fifth Amendment makes property rights paramount and property owners should be compensated when government regulation devalues their property. In 1991, wise use and property rights groups joined to form the Alliance for America, aiming to dismantle environmental regulations that affect private and public land. Activists used dual messages—one for hardcore activists and the other for mainstream support—filed lawsuits and occasionally engaged in violence and intimidation against researchers, environmental activists, and federal officials.

Austin (2002) identifies ties between anti-environmentalists and political-power holders. For example, the National Wildlife Institute appears to be a pro-environment organization yet was founded by the Hardwood Manufacturers Association, and timber harvesters lobby through the institute. The former secretary of natural resources of the Commonwealth of Virginia and former assistant secretaries of the U.S. Department of the Interior and U.S. Department of Agriculture served on the advisory board (Austin 2002). The general council included a former energy secretary, a former interior secretary, a former employee of the Bureau of Land Management, a former secretary-general of the UN Convention on International Trade in Endangered Species of Wild Flora and Fauna, and four members of Congress.

The Petro-dependent State

The petro-dependent state sustains corporate power and facilitates economic imperatives because of its assigned functions of accumulation and legitimacy. The accumulation function, established by liberal ideology and updated by neoliberalism, obliges the state to promote and maintain social conditions that facilitate capital accumulation and economic growth. The legitimacy function, founded on democratic ideology, requires the state to maintain citizens' participation in government decisions that affect them. As long as citizens believe that they are free to participate—whether or not they actually do so—they view the state as legitimate and do not challenge power arrangements.

The accumulation function serves the corporate class, and the legitimacy function serves the lower classes. Because they serve different classes, they occasionally contradict each other. Serving the corporate class's facilitation of capital accumulation by not enforcing environmental laws violates the lower classes' legitimacy function because the public is not protected from the externalization of the environmental costs of production. When the functions conflict, the state faces a crisis. Historically, it resolves such crises by continuing to facilitate accumulation while taking actions that at least appear to support democratic reform. For example, contamination in Love Canal instigated the passage of the Comprehensive Environmental Response, Compensation, and Liability Act (CERCLA), which addressed residents' demands to have a voice in the cleanup because they mistrusted the government. CERCLA requires public meetings and citizens' input to environmental remediation processes and appears to protect the state's legitimacy, even if citizens complain that their input is typically rejected on scientific or bureaucratic grounds (Cable, Shriver, and Hastings 1999).

The state facilitates capital accumulation through four mechanisms: corporate taxation and subsidies, government consumption of goods and services, foreign policy management, and business regulation.

A complex system of corporate tax laws erected over fifty years yields corporations lower percentages of tax payments and, occasionally, enormous tax refunds (Marger 1987). Related mechanisms are tax credits, exemptions, deferrals, and deductions. Capital accumulation is also fostered through subsidies—direct and indirect federal payments to support the economic well-being of selected industries or corporations. The airlines, defense contractors, and commercial agriculture receive substantial direct subsidies. Indirect subsidies are granted through, for example, the federal postal service's subsidizing of mail-order merchandising, federal highway construction's subsidizing of the trucking industry, and federal airport and harbor construction's subsidizing of airlines and shipping companies.

Donald Barlett and James Steele (1998) refer to such subsidies as corporate welfare: any action by local, state, or federal government that gives a corporation or industry a benefit not offered to others. In 1998, the government spent $125 billion in corporate welfare, while corporate profits totaled $4.5 trillion (Barlett and Steele 1998). Corporations receive federal money to build new plants, offices, and stores; to advertise; and to train workers. They sell their products to foreign buyers who pay with U.S. government–supplied dollars. Corporations' foreign transactions are insured by the government. Corporations receive federal contracts for ordinary business operations and federal grants for research into improving profit margins. State officials justify corporate welfare by claiming that subsidies create jobs, but no records empirically demonstrate such a tradeoff (Barlett and Steele 1998).

The government also facilitates capital accumulation by consuming goods and services. Legally prohibited from competing with private enterprise, the state must purchase goods and services from private vendors. Large corporations provide office supplies, such as pencils, computers, desks, office space, and paper. Private firms supply public services such as construction of subsidized housing, mass transportation, and public education. The largest consumption area is national defense—the provision of military personnel with uniforms, medical care, housing, food, and transportation. The enormous military-industrial complex reaps huge profits for manufacturing weapons and weapons carriers and for on-site management of weapons facilities.

The state also facilitates capital accumulation through foreign policy management. Successful foreign policy protects and promotes a vital, stable economic climate through corporate support. Foreign policies protect corporate interests abroad to ensure a favorable investment climate, stimulate new corporate markets, and ensure uninterrupted flows of natural resources from less-developed to developed countries. "National security, then, becomes synonymous with corporate security" (Marger 1987: 135). Since the 1960s, foreign policy frequently has been aimed at less-developed countries because political and economic instability is perceived as endangering the global market. Not infrequently, the state uses covert intelligence and military actions to strengthen or restore regimes receptive to U.S. corporations—particularly, governments that oppose industrial nationalization. Examples include covert actions in Cuba in 1962, in Iran in 1953, in Guatemala in 1954, and in Chile in 1973.

The state facilitates capital accumulation through the regulation of business. Congress passes legislation that is implemented and enforced through rules established by regulatory agencies. Although agencies are presumed to be politically neutral because they implement, rather than create, environmental laws, Hays (2000) contends that environmental politicking really begins after a law is passed. Legislative statutes leave substantial choices to regulatory agencies that are manifested in rulemaking and permitting processes. Regulators devise specific rules for executing legislative intent. Permitting involves specific applications of law under precise circumstances to a limited clientele. Both processes take place inside regulatory agencies and away from the public eye, with the result that rulemaking and permitting are determined in "face-to-face relationships between the regulated industry and administrators" (Hays 2000: 130).

Institutional and Cultural Reflections of Economic Imperatives

Because social institutions inevitably overlap—as they must, to ensure societal coordination and reduce conflict—corporate states' worldviews leach into other institutions to reinforce the prioritization of economic imperatives over the protection of biospheric resources. The scientific community and the judiciary are particularly influential institutions in the making of unsustainable policies. Science is held hostage to the corporate state; corporate interests are aided and abetted by the judicial institution; and culture binds the components together. I discuss the shaping of the scientific and judicial institutions as reflections of the corporate state's economic imperatives and examine these institutional influences in the common cultural perspective of the human–environment relationship: the Dominant Social Paradigm.

Science: Corporate Captive

The essential nature of science combines with the social history of its development in a way that deeply enmeshes science in social, economic, and political relationships with the corporate state. Consequently, substantial scientific research is directed toward improving production technology to enlarge surplus rather than with investigating the biospheric impact of technology.

The Nature of Science

Cultural conceptions of science endow it with the power to reveal certainties. Science is popularly perceived as a source of authority based on a process that yields an objective, rational, and politically neutral body of unambiguous knowledge. Scientific norms for validating facts and the rigor of the scientific method persuade many that science is "a depersonalized and selfless quest for truth" (Ozawa 2005: 329). The cultural mystique surrounding science is so pervasive that the scientific community has been called a priesthood (Lapp 1965), an estate (Polanyi 1972), and a republic (Price 1965).

In reality, scientific findings are inherently ambiguous because science is based on falsification, not certainty: hypotheses are *dis*proved rather than proved (Popper 1959). Even the process of falsification tends to be probabilistic rather than deterministic: the testing of hypotheses yields answers of "yes," "no," and "maybe" (Freudenburg, Gramling, and Davidson 2008). The essential core of science is not a body of well-ordered facts and findings with clear meanings but, rather, an institutionalized skepticism and tolerance of uncertainty.

Researchers routinely make a range of discretionary judgments during a scientific investigation (Ozawa 2005: 333). The array of choices in assumptions, boundaries, and variable definitions imposes methodological uncertainties and indeterminacy (Klapp 1992; Wynne 1992). Contrary to the popular belief that scientific knowledge and method recognize and reduce uncertainties, the actuality is that "scientific knowledge gives prominence to a restricted agenda of defined uncertainties—ones that are tractable—leaving invisible a range of other uncertainties" (Wynne 1992: 115).

Charles Harper (2004) identifies two sources of scientific uncertainty: data and theory and multiple paradigms. First, uncertainty occurs because scientists are unable to obtain either enough or the right kind of data and consequently cannot test theories to rule out the weakest ones. The result is equally plausible competing theories. For example, toxicologists cannot know with certainty the precise exposure levels of pollutants that cause death because they are ethically barred from performing controlled human experiments to determine lethal exposure. Second, scientific uncertainty derives from the multiple paradigms that characterize the scientific division of labor. Scientists in different disciplines operate from different paradigms that render communication among them difficult. Knowledge becomes fragmented and compartmentalized, each nugget bounded by a disciplinary lingo.

Scientific conclusions are always tentative, conditional, and hedged. Inquiry creates consensus, but it does not eliminate uncertainty. As a result, dispute and contention are normal, healthy processes that animate science. Toleration of uncertainty is normal for scientists, but not for policymakers, who seek scientific certainty to make environmental decisions.

Laws require quantitative risk assessments to gauge "the risks of each substance it proposes to regulate and then either to protect the public with 'adequate margins of safety' against 'unreasonable risks' or to make choices that would balance those risks against economic benefits" (Andrews 2006: 217). But if risks are calculated on the basis of our knowledge and our knowledge is uncertain, risks cannot be adequately estimated. Despite uncertainty and the frustration it engenders, science is a dominant ideology of the modern era (Habermas 1970).

The Social History of Science

Prior to industrialization, science was an avocation only loosely related to production processes or the state (Foster 2005). Industrialization changed the direction of science. Industrial elites financially supported scientific studies to develop technology to expand production and increase profits. Recognizing the critical role of science in economic development, state officials expanded technological and scientific educational institutions, such as land grant agricultural and mining schools. The infusion of capital both stimulated and responded to new scientific inventions and generated investment in the chemical and electrical industries (Schnaiberg 1980).

Individual inventors such as Thomas Edison, who in 1876 established the first research laboratory for invention, dominated early production science. The "lone inventor" form of science quickly morphed into corporate research laboratories, emerging concomitantly with monopoly capitalism. At first, large corporations such as B. F. Goodrich, General Electric, and Bell Telephone established scientific research organizations, but by 1920, 300 corporate laboratories had become intensely involved in expanding production through scientific advances (Foster 2005).

Science was bound more tightly to production through Frederick Winslow Taylor's approach to improving labor productivity, known as scientific management. It set formal divisions between workers and managers and divided tasks between them. Managers analyzed workflow processes to discover the most scientifically efficient way to perform tasks, then provided workers with detailed instructions and supervision to ensure job performance and increased profits. The power of labor diminished as the worker was reduced to "an instrument of production" (Foster 2005: 5). Harry Braverman (1998: 166–167) refers to this trend as "the transformation of science itself into capital." But linkages between capital and science were still relatively weak (Schnaiberg 1980: 123–124).

The government mobilized and concentrated scientific and corporate efforts in military production for World War II, promoting science as the avenue to economic growth and social progress. This state-endorsed promotion reinforced the cultural conception of science as a bastion of certainty. When the productive capacity of wartime was transferred smoothly to a peacetime economy, academic science transformed into industrialized science. Keynesian economic principles justified state subsidization of science that produced a new organizational form in corporations—the research and development (R&D) laboratory. Applied science became the basis for production (Schnaiberg 1980). The government routinely measured R&D expenditures as a business barometer and supplemented areas that had insufficient private capital. Other state subsidies for industrialized science were tax-supported education in science and technology, the creation of research institutes, and the provision of grants to corporate researchers.

The state responded to the economic recession of the 1980s with renewed emphasis on science's contributions to the competitive strength of industry and military technology (Dickson 1988: 17). Since then, the state has continued to increase research budgets for universities, particularly in the physical sciences and engineering. Production sciences are given the highest priority and funding, while impact sciences that focus on the environmental consequences of production technology are assigned the lowest priority (Schnaiberg 1980: 281).

State-supported corporate research has converted scientists into "scientific laborers" (Schnaiberg 1980: 289) who develop technology to expand production and enlarge the surplus. The technology typically replaces humans with machines, exposes remaining workers to hazardous substances, consumes vast amounts of mineral energy resources, and severely degrades the environment.

"Political" Science

The quintessential nature of science is uncertainty—precisely the opposite of popular conceptions. What scientists view as competing plausible theories are perceived by non-scientists as multiple interpretations. Which interpretations find their way into policy?

Braverman (1998: 156) describes contemporary science as "the last—and after labor the most important—social property to be turned into an adjunct of capital." No longer independent, contemporary science serves as a corporate appendage directed by economic imperatives. The boundaries between science and economy have dissolved (Dickson 1988).

Science's crucial economic importance gives it *political* significance, which is often lost in debates (Dickson 1988: 5). Pressured to represent corporate interests, scientists frequently are channeled into political roles. Researchers have found that institutional affiliation is a powerful determinant of a scientist's position on an issue: industrial scientists are more politically and socially conservative than are those in universities, government, or environmental interest groups. A study of 136 scientists assessing risks associated with carcinogenic substances found that industry scientists were more likely than other scientists to favor research designs that made the regulation of a substance less likely (Lynn 1986). Thomas Dietz and Robert Rycroft (1987: 17) found that scientists' *scientific* perspective weakened noticeably, and their *ideological* perspectives strengthened when they were involved in policy issues; as advisers to government agencies and in congressional testimony, they behaved "more as politicians or political activists than as scientists."

Corporate advocates may use inherently ambiguous and probabilistic scientific findings to press policymakers to delay the implementation of policies. William Freudenburg, Robert Gramling, and Debra Davidson (2008) examined environmental controversies over the past century and found that industrial interests have often managed to delay or prevent legislative and regulatory actions even in cases in which the preponderance of scientific evidence indicated significant reasons for concern.

Science is a corporate captive because of its intrinsic uncertainty and the corporate state's manipulation of its development. The bias in contemporary science—"political" science—has several critical outcomes for environmental policymaking:

- Environmental "facts" and "solutions" are subject to nearly infinite deniability. Environmental issues frequently place scientists at the center of tense political controversies. Disagreements among scientific experts reinforce the polarization of political views. Walter Rosenbaum (2002: 126) contends, "One's data become a weapon, and science a bastion against one's critics." With polarized views and forced division over an issue, a scientist may intentionally or inadvertently shape his or her opinions to fit a preferred position or manipulate materials to fit a simplistic policy position.
- "Political" science becomes "advocacy" science, deliberately using science to shape policy formulation. The corporate state uses advocacy science to legitimize opposition to environmental regulations.
- Scientists who speak in favor of strict regulation are frequently suppressed. Brian Martin (1999) examined suppression against scientists in three con-

tentious areas: pesticides, fluoridation, and nuclear power. He found that corporate advocates undermined the scientists' dissent through censorship, denial of access to research facilities, the withdrawal of funding, reprimands, dismissals, demotions, and blacklists.

The Judiciary and Activist Judges

The politics of environmental policymaking has moved toward embroiling federal judges "in resolving legal issues that have important policy consequences" (Rosenbaum 2002: 77). The judicial system's legal responsibilities in environmental policy are to interpret environmental laws, to ensure laws' compliance with constitutional standards, and to verify that regulatory agencies discharge their responsibilities in compliance with administrative obligations (Rosenbaum 2002). The judiciary shapes environmental policy through the following mechanisms (O'Leary 2006):

- Courts are powerful gatekeepers. Prior to statutory interpretation, courts decide whether an actual controversy exists—the alleged wrong must be more than merely anticipated.
- Courts determine standing to sue, or who has the right to sue. Plaintiffs must demonstrate actual injury, but because injury from environmental exposure is seldom clearly established on scientific grounds, judges *interpret* the evidence for injury.
- Courts' statutory interpretation is often tantamount to policymaking because federal judges interpret often ambiguous statutes, administrative rules, executive orders, treaties, and prior court decisions. The judicial system is structured around setting precedents: today's statutory interpretation determines tomorrow's environmental policy.
- Courts' choice of penalties for policy violations substantially influences corporate compliance; fines constitute a weaker deterrent to violation than criminal prosecution.
- The U.S. Supreme Court, in particular, shapes policy through the selection of cases to hear and through limitations on other branches of government and states.

Federal court systems and judges cannot be entirely objective. Biases are embedded in courts' interpretations of injury and statutes and in courts' selection of cases to hear and penalties to apply. Both the historical record since the passage of the National Environmental Protection Act (NEPA) in 1970 and current judicial trends provide empirical evidence that these biases tend to support the corporate state's economic imperatives.

The Historical Record since NEPA

After decades of court decisions favoring corporate interests, the NEPA's passage in 1970 brought a temporary change: decisions in both substantive and procedural issues generally favored environmental protection (Rosenbaum 2002). Environmental organizations used NEPA as a statutory base to sue for federal enforcement of new regulatory programs. Nonprofit public-interest legal foundations won federal suits to expand criteria for standing to sue government agencies. The enhanced right to sue over the enforcement of environmental regulations granted ordinary citizens some power to take on corporate polluters in their communities without supportive actions by the EPA.

The judicial pendulum swung back to favor corporations in the mid-1980s. Corporate advocates imitated environmentalists and established public-interest legal foundations to represent corporate interests. These foundations were financed principally by corporate organizations such as the Adolph Coors Company and the Scaife Foundation, both of which opposed most major environmental regulatory programs (Rosenbaum 2002: 76).

By the 1990s, federal judges appointed by the neoliberal presidents Ronald Reagan and George H. W. Bush tended to favor economic imperatives over environmental protection. Those administrations restricted regulatory actions with substantial, targeted budget cuts. With limited resources, EPA officials chose among competing priorities. A study in 1993 examining the impact of more than 2,000 federal court decisions on the EPA's administration found that a top priority at the agency was compliance with court orders (O'Leary 1993). As a result, courts dictate which issues gain the EPA's attention.

A relatively new legal weapon in the corporate arsenal is tagged by George Pring and Penelope Canan (1993: 380) as "strategic lawsuits against public participation," or SLAPP. Corporate advocates file these multimillion-dollar civil damages cases against individuals and groups for acts such as circulating petitions, writing to public officials, speaking at and attending public meetings, mobilizing boycotts, and peacefully protesting policy violations. SLAPP suits claim harm or injury from environmentalists' efforts to garner public support and influence agency actions. Corporations need not win lawsuits to benefit: SLAPP suits delay policy enforcement, often for years, and compel environmental groups to expend scarce resources in protracted legal battles. For corporations, the legal costs are merely part of business costs, but the costs often force individuals and organizations to abandon their opposition.

Current Judicial Trend: Activist Judges

Litigation is a tactical weapon deployed in policy conflicts by all sides as a bargaining chip to gain concessions. Most environmental litigation is initiated by three sources: major environmental organizations, such as the Sierra Club and the Environmental Defense Fund; corporate and property interests; and agencies with major environmental responsibilities, such as the EPA and the U.S. Department of the Interior (Rosenbaum 2002). Several studies document state and federal judges' bias in such environmental suits (O'Leary 2006).

Researchers for the Alliance for Justice, Community Rights Counsel, and Natural Resources Defense Council examined federal rulings on environmental cases between 1990 and 2000. Their report concludes that a group of highly ideological and activist sitting judges are already threatening the very core of environmental law. In the last decade, judges have imposed a gauntlet of new hurdles in the path of environmental regulators, slammed the courthouse doors in the face of citizens seeking to protect the environment, and sketched the outline of a jurisprudence of "economic liberties" under the Takings and Commerce Clauses of the U.S. Constitution that would frustrate or repeal most federal environmental statutes. (Natural Resources Defense Council 2001)

The report documents rulings by the U.S. Supreme Court and by lower federal courts that have weakened environmental protection in favor of economic imperatives through judicial reinterpretations of the Commerce Clause, the Takings Clause, and the Eleventh Amendment.

The Commerce Clause, the statutory basis for federal environmental regulation, authorizes the federal government to regulate commerce among the states. The Natural Resources Defense Council report documents a U.S. Supreme Court ruling in 2001 that the Army Corps of Engineers had no authority to prevent the construction of a landfill in a wetlands area that sustained migratory birds. Although the birds also drew tourists who spent $1 billion annually and protected crops and forests by maintaining insect populations, the court decided that migratory birds have no connection to interstate commerce. In a second case from the report, a federal judge in Alabama reinterpreted the Commerce Clause to rule that the Superfund law did not apply to *closed* chemical waste landfills because, with no current economic activity, the matter was a local real estate issue beyond federal jurisdiction. Although the decision was overturned on appeal, it suggested a trend in reinterpreting the Commerce Clause.

The Takings Clause mandates that private property cannot be taken by the federal government for public use without compensating the property holder. The clause is typically interpreted to mean that a landowner must be compensated if the entire use of his property is destroyed by a federal action. Compensation is not required if the property can still support some use. The Natural Resources Defense Council report found multiple judicial reinterpretations of the Takings Clause that reduced environmental protection. For example, a corporation was denied a permit to mine limestone from corporate-owned land in the Florida Everglades. The corporation sued for compensation, arguing that even without the permit, the land could be sold for twice the amount the corporation had initially paid to buy it. A federal judge overturned one hundred years of precedent to award the corporation compensation for the "taking" of its mining rights. In another case, protection of an endangered salmon species reduced a landowner's water rights 8–22 percent. Although a 100 percent use reduction is required for compensation, a federal judge ruled that the federal government had to pay for the water required to preserve the fish.

The Eleventh Amendment prevents federal courts from hearing lawsuits brought against a state government by citizens of another state. The Natural Resources Defense Council report found that the U.S. Supreme Court had reinterpreted the amendment by eliminating the word "another." The Surface Mining Control and Reclamation Act designates that no mining can occur within 100 feet of a stream unless the mining company demonstrates that no adverse effects to the stream will occur. Environmental officials in West Virginia frequently issue permits for mountaintop removal, a coal-mining technique that removes thousands of tons of rock and soil from mountaintops and simply dumps it into nearby valleys and streams. When a citizen sued the state to force compliance with federal law by denying permits, a federal Appeals Court ruled that the Eleventh Amendment prohibited him from suing his own state.

Cultural Legitimation, the Dominant
Social Paradigm, and Corporate Rationalization

Petro-dependency emerged in the postwar United States and produced tremendous wealth that increased literacy, diminished suffering, provided high standards of living for large numbers of citizens, and launched thousands of scientific and technological marvels. But petro-dependency is destroying the material base of the nation's wealth. Environmental rules are broken as casually and frequently as the Tenth Commandment, with the consequences of conflict, contamination, and injustices. Yet few challenge petro-dependent institutional arrangements. What holds those arrangements together?

The social institutions that reflect economic imperatives are bound, chicken-and-egg–style, with culture: the patterns of beliefs, values, ideologies, and norms that dominate in a society. Culture normalizes and legitimates social institutions. Our beliefs about the relationship between humans and nature shape our behavior toward the biosphere. Dominant cultural perceptions of the relationship between humans and the biosphere shifted with the change from hunting and gathering to the agricultural mode of subsistence.

Hunters and gatherers were acutely aware of their dependence on biospheric resources, because if they weren't, they quickly perished—likely, before reproducing. Their dependence necessitated a comprehensive understanding of ecological operations that included respect for, and minimal intervention with, natural processes. The archaeological evidence demonstrates that their spiritual beliefs and rituals featured human dependence on nature and nature's superior capacity to punish individuals and societies (Hughes 1994; Ponting 1991).

Agriculturalists used their growing understanding of natural processes to transform the biosphere, molding it to their own purposes. As fewer hands could feed more mouths, many people no longer sought ecological knowledge. Humans' ability to replace natural selection processes transformed beliefs about the relationship between humans and the biosphere, elevating humans above natural processes. Industrialized agriculture transformed the biosphere more easily and quickly, continually reducing the proportion of the population needed to labor in producing food. Many people lived entire lives without gaining an awareness of their dependence on biospheric resources. By the twentieth century, J. R. McNeill (2000) argues, cultural worldviews of the relationship between humans and nature that were grounded in religion and other traditional sources gave way to worldviews influenced by economics and politics. The predominant cultural perspective adopted was that humans are exempt from the rules that govern the biosphere.

Petro-dependent societies monumentally amplify and extend the traditional belief that the human species is exempt from the laws of nature. The modern version of this notion hinges on development of technology to manipulate nature beyond all previous boundaries, creating unnatural chemicals, unnatural organisms, and unnatural elements. Cultural beliefs "become orthodoxies, enmeshed in social and political systems, and difficult to dislodge even if they become costly" (McNeill 2000: 326).

The widespread cultural perspective of the relationship between humans and nature weaves together human superiority and economic imperatives in a worldview that excuses—in fact, justifies—environmental degradation. Dennis Pirages and Paul Ehrlich (1974) coined the term "Dominant Social Paradigm" (DSP) to describe this view, and many other scholars have since written about it. Harper (2004: 47) summarizes the common themes found in those writings:

- *A low evaluation of "nature" for its own sake:* The environment is valued as a resource for the production of goods. Humans dominate nature, and economic growth is more important than environmental protection.
- *A compassion mainly for those near and dear:* Other species are exploited for human needs, and "other people" (non-white, non-rich) are accorded less concern. Other generations—the future—are not taken into account.
- *The assumption that maximizing wealth is important:* The value of consumerism elevates the consumption of goods into a defining feature of the good life. The ability to consume more is taken as a measure of growth, progress, and social status.
- *The belief that risks are acceptable in maximizing wealth:* Markets are preferred to regulation for the allocation of individually borne risks. Acceptance of risks is based on faith in science.
- *The assumption that there are no physical limits to growth:* All problems associated with resource depletion and pollution are temporary and can be resolved with human inventiveness.
- *The assumption that society, culture, and politics are basically OK:* Humans have caused no serious damage to nature.

The cultural value of private property ownership is a fundamental and crucial tenet of the DSP. The larger the accumulation of property, the greater is the owner's right to restrict the material liberty and political power of others, even to the point of shaping political and social institutions to his or her advantage. In the past one hundred years, and especially since 1945, private property ownership has been used to the advantage of corporate actors to acquire substantial proportions of the nation's resources. The cultural belief in private property rights results in decisions about production that are made privately, without public input and despite public consequences.

The DSP is part of a more comprehensive cultural orientation that has adverse implications for democracy. Several analysts have examined corporations' role in shaping this orientation. David Allen (2005: 2) analyzes the vital role the professionalization of the press and the law have played in the "corporate rationalization of the public sphere"—that is, the propagation of the corporate values of efficiency, profit maximization, scientific reasoning, and winning among the public. Corporate values undermine democracy by devaluing public discourse. Allen (2005: 1) uses corporate rights to free speech to illustrate how corporate values distort conceptions of democracy and citizenship: "Corporations have altered the culture of democracy by changing the language and logic that we use to evaluate public life. . . . [C]orporate ideology has become public ideology."

Alex Carey (1997: xi) describes corporations' promotion of a "propaganda-managed democracy" by deploying their public relations arms in campaigns to reduce the risks of democracy, undermining democracy by minimizing public resistance. Corporate interests are fused with national interests in patriotic strategies that project unions, welfare programs, and environmental policies, among others, as risks to democracy. A relatively small group of business interests has "sold [its] values and perspectives to the rest of society" (Carey 1997: 6) and sown widespread cynicism about government's capacity to represent, protect, and enhance the public interest.

The common argument of these and similar analyses is that corporations design and direct strategies specifically to induce the public to adopt an ideology that not only supports corporate profits but also tethers public hopes for prosperity to corporate success. With the public inculcation of corporate ideology, corporate values and democratic values are conflated in an insidious form of social control: social control by stealth. We are sold the ideology like brand-new, pre-washed, already torn blue jeans. Corporations downsize democracy and score a "twofer": management of public attitudes plus legitimation of the corporate state.

III

Environmental Policy in the Petro-dependent Empire

9

International Environmental Policymaking

The petro-dependent mode of subsistence spread through the world with the global integration of economic markets. Petro-dependency's environmental impact has likewise spread: the exacerbation of agriculturalism's impact and the novel impact of synthetic materials. Global petro-dependency has added unprecedented global impact: depletion of the stratospheric ozone layer and, more ominously, global climate changes. Under the petro-dependent flag, international environmental policymaking has fared no better than U.S. policies in approaching sustainability.

After an introduction to the chief players in the international environmental policymaking process, I offer summaries of thirty major international environmental treaties that feature several in-depth case studies for a more nuanced understanding of the dynamics underlying global policy processes.

Processes and Players in International Policymaking

International environmental treaties are formulated and implemented by the United Nations Environmental Programme (UNEP) through negotiations among UN member states. Created in 1972 as an integrated coordinating mechanism for global environmental concerns, UNEP is premised on a concept of economic development that acknowledges the environmental roots of economic problems. UNEP is *not* authorized to enforce policies. Individual member states decide whether to adopt and enforce UNEP's recommendations.

International environmental policies are designated through treaties and the laws drawn from them, known as conventions (Buck 1996). Treaties are negotiated in formal, two-week conferences of member states to foster consensus on the issues to pursue. The resultant framework convention describes the basic architecture for international remedial efforts. Between major conferences, multiple

Conferences of the Parties (COPs) convene, in which member states negotiate protocols for achieving environmental objectives and clarify implementation rules. Ratification of the protocol signifies a member state's commitment to the implementation rules.

Representatives of accredited nongovernmental organizations (NGOs) are permitted to attend conferences. The UN website defines "NGO" as "a not-for-profit, voluntary citizens group organized on a local, national, or international level to address issues in support of the public good." NGOs raise concerns to governments, monitor the implementation of programs, and provide analysis and expertise. Accredited NGOs must support UN principles, enjoy national or international standing, receive tax-exempt status, provide annual financial statements, publicize their efforts, feature a transparent decision-making process, and represent constituencies bound by interests rather than nationality (Starkey, Boyer, and Wilkenfeld 2005).

NGOs participate only as observers rather than negotiators in formal conferences. But "negotiation processes and outcomes are shaped by more than just what happens during isolated, two-week formal negotiating sessions" (Betsill and Corell 2008: 6). NGO representatives engage in pre-conference negotiating to influence the definition of problems and setting of agendas. NGOs often initiate and formulate environmental proposals through domestic channels or more informal settings (Betsill and Corell 2008). Multiple studies show the increasingly significant role of NGOs in negotiations (Betsill and Corell 2008). Only 250 NGOs participated in the Stockholm Conference in 1972, compared with 1,400 in the Rio Conference in 1992 and 3,200 in the Johannesburg conference in 2002. Agenda 21 (Betsill and Corell 2008) officially recognized accredited NGOs as partners in promoting sustainable development.

UNEP's Medium-Term Strategy for 2010–2013 identifies six priorities for environmental action: climate change, disasters and conflicts, ecosystem management, environmental governance, hazardous substances, and resource efficiency.

International Environmental Treaties

UNEP's *Register of International Treaties and Other Agreements in the Field of the Environment* (UNEP 2005) lists 272 international environmental treaties and related instruments. My intent is not to enumerate all environmental treaties but to describe their basic statutory structures. I eliminated bilateral agreements, superseded conventions, items with regional rather than global fields of application, items dealing with occupations and the military, and items prior to 1945. Thirty multilateral, global treaties constitute the main body of current international environmental policy.

I examine the laws grouped by targeted environmental sector (see Table 9.1), noting their relation to petro-dependency's environmental problems: resource depletion and pollution of biological resources, oceans, land, and air and the unprecedented global problems of climate change and depletion of the stratospheric ozone layer.

TABLE 9.1 Objectives of UN Environmental Conventions

Adopted	Convention title	Entry into force; amendments	Objective
		Biological Resources	
1951	International Plant Protection Convention	1952	To protect plant species through inspection, disinfection, and the issuing of certificates.
1958	Convention on Fishing and Conservation of the Living Resources of the High Seas	1966	Through international cooperation, to solve the problems involved in the conservation of the living resources of the high seas, considering that through the development of modern techniques, some of these resources are in danger of being overexploited.
1971	Convention on Wetlands of International Importance Especially as Waterfowl Habitat	1975	To stem the progressive encroachment on and loss of wetlands.
1973	Convention on International Trade in Endangered Species of Wild Fauna and Flora	1975; amended 1979, 1983	To protect certain endangered species from overexploitation by means of a system of import and export permits.
1979	Convention on the Conservation of Migratory Species of Wild Animals	1983; amended 1986, 1988, 1991, 1994, 1997	To protect those species of wild animals that migrate across or outside national boundaries.
1991	Convention for the Protection of New Varieties of Plants	1998	To recognize and protect the rights of breeders of new varieties of plants and their successors in title and to do so in a harmonized way.

(continued on next page)

TABLE 9.1 Continued

Adopted	Convention title	Entry into force; amendments	Objective
1992	Convention on Biological Diversity	1993	To conserve biological diversity, promote the sustainable use of its components, and encourage equitable sharing of the benefits arising out of the utilization of genetic resources. Such equitable sharing includes appropriate access to genetic resources, as well as appropriate transfer of technology, taking into account existing rights to such resources and such technology.
2001	Agreement on the Conservation of Albatrosses and Petrels	2004	To achieve and maintain a favorable conservation status for albatrosses and petrels.
2001	International Treaty on Plant Genetic Resources for Food and Agriculture	2004	To conserve and use sustainably plant genetic resources for food and agriculture and share equitably the benefits arising out of their use, in harmony with the Convention on Biological Diversity.
2006	Tropical Timber Agreement	Not in force	Successor agreement to the International Tropical Agreement of 1994. To provide a framework for consultation, international cooperation, and policy development with regard to all relevant aspects of the world timber economy and provide a forum for consultation to promote nondiscriminatory timber trade practices.
		Oceans	
1954	Convention for Prevention of Pollution of the Sea by Oil	1958; amended 1962, 1969	To take action to prevent pollution of the sea by oil discharged from ships.
1969	Convention Relating to Intervention on the High Seas in Cases of Oil Pollution Casualties	1975; amended 1983 to update substances besides oil	To enable countries to take action on the high seas in cases of a maritime casualty resulting in danger of oil pollution of the sea and coastlines while ensuring that such action does not affect the principle of freedom of the high seas.

Year	Convention	Objective
1969	Convention on Civil Liability for Bunker Oil Pollution Damage	To adopt uniform international rules and procedures for determining questions of liability and providing adequate, prompt and effective compensation in cases of damage caused by pollution resulting from the escape or discharge of bunker oil from ships.
1971	Convention Relating to Civil Liability in the Field of Maritime Carriage of Nuclear Material	To ensure that the operator of a nuclear installation will be exclusively liable for damage caused by a nuclear incident occurring in the course of maritime carriage of nuclear material.
1972	Convention on the Prevention of Marine Pollution by Dumping of Wastes and Other Matter	To control pollution of the sea by dumping.
	(dates:) 1975; amended 1978, 1980, 1984, 1985, 1987, 1989, 1990, 1991, 1992, 1993, 1994, 1995, 1996, 1997, March 2000, October 2000, 2006, 2008	
1973	Convention on the Law of the Sea	To codify the rules of international law relating to the high seas.
1990	Convention on Oil Pollution Preparedness, Response, and Cooperation	To strengthen the legal framework for the control of environmental pollution by oil, in general, and marine pollution by oil in particular.
1996	Convention on Liability and Compensation for Damage in Connection with the Carriage of Hazardous and Noxious Substances by Sea	To adopt uniform international rules and procedures for determining liability and compensation in respect of damage caused by incidents in connection with the carriage by sea of hazardous and noxious substances.
2001	Convention on the Control of Harmful Anti-fouling Systems on Ships	To reduce or eliminate adverse effects on the marine environment and human health caused by anti-fouling systems.

Note: The "year in force / date" column values are: 1969 — 2001; amended 2008. 1971 — 1975. 1972 — 1975; amended 1978, 1980, 1984, 1985, 1987, 1989, 1990, 1991, 1992, 1993, 1994, 1995, 1996, 1997, March 2000, October 2000, 2006, 2008. 1973 — 1994. 1990 — 1995. 1996 — Not in force. 2001 — 2008.

(continued on next page)

TABLE 9.1 Continued

Adopted	Convention title	Entry into force; amendments	Objective
		Land	
1963	Convention on Civil Liability for Nuclear Damage	1977	To establish minimum standards to provide financial protection against damage resulting from peaceful uses of nuclear energy.
1989	Basel Convention on the Control of Transboundary Movements of Hazardous Wastes and Their Disposal	1992	To reduce transboundary movements of certain wastes to a minimum consistent with the environmentally sound and efficient management of such wastes, to minimize the amount and toxicity of hazardous wastes generated and ensure the environmentally sound management of the hazardous and other wastes they generate.
1997	Joint Convention on the Safety of Spent Fuel Management and on the Safety of Radioactive Waste Management	2001	To achieve and maintain a high level of safety in spent fuel and radioactive waste management and to ensure that during all stages of these processes there are effective defenses against potential hazards so that individual, society and the environment are protected from harmful effects of ionizing radiation.
1998	Rotterdam Convention on the Prior Informed Consent Procedure for Certain Hazardous Chemicals and Pesticides in International Trade	2004	To promote shared responsibility and cooperative efforts among Parties in the international trade of certain hazardous chemicals in order to protect human health and the environment from potential harm; to contribute to the environmentally sound use of those hazardous chemicals, by facilitating information exchange about their characteristics, by providing for a national decision making process on their import and export and by disseminating these decisions to parties.
2001	Stockholm Convention on Persistent Organic Pollution (POP)	2004	To protect human health and the environment from chemicals that remain intact in the environment for long periods, become widely distributed geographically and accumulate in the fatty tissue of humans and wildlife through measures to eliminate or reduce the release of POPs into the environment.

1979	Convention on Long-Range Transboundary Air Pollution	1983	To reduce releases to the air of pollutants such as sulfur, nitrogen oxides, volatile organic compounds, heavy metals, and persistent organic pollutants.
1985	Vienna Convention for the Protection of the Ozone Layer	1988	To protect human health and the environment against adverse effects resulting from modifications of the ozone layer.
1986	Convention on Assistance in the Case of a Nuclear Accident or Radiological Emergency	1987	To facilitate the prompt provision of assistance in the event of a nuclear accident or radiological emergency.
1986	Convention on Early Notification of a Nuclear Accident	1987	To provide relevant information about nuclear accidents as early as possible in order that transboundary radiological consequences can be minimized.
1992	United Nations Framework Convention on Climate Change	1994	To regulate levels of greenhouse gas concentration in the atmosphere, so as to avoid the occurrence of climate change on a level that would impede sustainable economic development or compromise initiatives in food production.
1997	Convention on Supplementary Compensation for Nuclear Damage	Not in force	To create a global legal framework for allocating responsibility for compensating for nuclear damage resulting from a nuclear incident and for assuring, in the unlikely event of such an incident, the prompt availability of meaningful compensation with a minimum of litigation and other burdens while reaffirming the principle that jurisdiction over a nuclear incident lies only with the courts of the country where the incident occurs.

Regulation of Biological Resources

Only three of ten conventions on biological resources refer to conservation. The Convention on Wetlands of International Importance, Especially as Waterfowl Habitat (1971) obligates contracting parties to designate at least one national wetland for inclusion on a List of Wetlands of International Importance. Parties agree to establish nature reserves for wetlands and waterfowl conservation management. Parties to the Convention on the Conservation of Migratory Species of Wild Animals (1979) acknowledge the need to avoid endangerment of migratory species. The Agreement on the Conservation of Albatrosses and Petrels (2001) calls for parties to apply a precautionary approach in conservation measures.

Two biological resources conventions specify permits to implement laws related to trade. Signers of the Institutional Plant Protection Convention (1951) must establish a plant protection organization to ensure the inspection and disinfection of plants and to issue permits for plant exports. The Convention on International Trade in Endangered Species of Wild Fauna and Flora (1973) specifies permits to regulate international trade in wild animals and plants. The law lists species in three appendixes. Appendix 1 lists all species threatened with extinction that are or may be affected by trade, Appendix 2 lists species that may become threatened unless trade is regulated, and Appendix 3 lists species identified by individual parties as requiring cooperation from other parties to control trade. Permits for trade in these species mandate that export and import will not be detrimental to species' survival.

Four biological resources conventions concern sovereignty and contain provisions for dispute settlements. The Convention on Fishing and Conservation of the Living Resources of the High Seas (1958) acknowledges that new technology allows ships to go further into waters than before, leading to conflicts over sovereignty issues. The law establishes procedures for settling disputes. The Convention for the Protection of New Varieties of Plants (1991) protects breeders' rights for specified production and commercial marketing of new varieties of plants, stipulating that rights be restricted only for reasons of public interest and that breeders be compensated. The Convention on Biological Diversity (1992) retains the principle of national sovereignty over domestic natural resources but obligates parties to provide for research, training, education, and awareness for conserving biological diversity. Parties are required to conduct environmental impact assessments of projects that are likely to have significant adverse effects. The law carries provisions for technology transfer to maintain equity and establishes procedures for settling disputes. The International Treaty on Plant Genetic Resources for Food and Agriculture (2001) obligates parties to conserve, explore, collect, and document plant genetic resources for food and agriculture and to facilitate access to those resources for equitably shared benefits.

Case Study: Tropical Timber Policy. A brief case history of the International Tropical Timber Agreement (2006) offers insights into the policymaking process. Under the auspices of the United Nations, negotiations on international regulation of tropical forests occurred between 1976 and 1983. Although many people worldwide expressed concern about tropical deforestation, the view persisted that the tropical timber trade was crucial to economic development in tropical nations. These contradictory views were reconciled in the International Tropical Timber Agreement of 1983, which accorded equal importance to conservation and trade on the premise that a flourishing trade in tropical timber based on principles of sustainability would provide valuable foreign exchange and employment while protecting forests.

In 1986, the United Nations established the International Tropical Timber Organization (ITTO), an intergovernmental organization to promote conservation, sustainable management, use, and trade of tropical forest resources. David Humphreys (2008) reports that NGOs exercised considerable influence on the agreement. ITTO develops internationally agreed-on policies to promote sustainable forest management and assists tropical member states in adapting policies to local circumstances. ITTO members agreed to grant observer status to NGOs and timber trade organizations that attend semiannual meetings.

The European environmental NGO network Ecoropa launched a petition and lobbying campaign in 1987 highlighting tropical forest destruction by forest-based industrial development and urging the UN General Assembly to call an emergency special session (Humphreys 2008). Activists believed it urgent to halt and reverse deforestation and biodiversity loss in all forested regions, insisting that reforestation reproduce the original natural forest conditions as closely as possible. Attributing deforestation to powerful political and economic interests, they advocated the redistribution of power from global and national to local levels to address underlying causes of deforestation, including the International Monetary Fund's structural adjustment programs, external debt, and large-scale development projects.

At the Rio Conference in 1992, delegates from the Northern Hemisphere and Southern Hemisphere were polarized. Delegates from the developed North framed deforestation narrowly as a global conservation issue. Delegates of southern developing countries framed it as a national economic issue, claiming sovereignty over forest resources, asserting their rights to forest development, and resisting northern interference. Deadlocked, member states left Rio with only the non-legally binding Statement of Forest Principles. Despite internal squabbling, lobbying by NGOs was partially successful: the statement advocated wider participation in discussion, recognition of indigenous knowledge, promotion of women's participation, and benefit sharing.

The North–South stalemate was broken in 1994. The Canadian and Malaysian governments co-sponsored an intergovernmental working group that established an international agenda for forestry. The Tropical Timber Agreement (1994) was adopted in modified form by the Commission on Sustainable Development (Humphreys 2008). The commission created a temporary subgroup, the Intergovernmental Panel on Forests, that managed negotiations from 1995 to 1997, when it was succeeded by the Intergovernmental Forum on Forests. The first subgroup focused on financial and technology transfers from North to South and the relationship between trade and the environment. The second subgroup, which managed negotiations from 1997 to 2000, identified underlying causes of deforestation. NGOs offered to contribute research on the causes of deforestation and arranged regional workshops with indigenous peoples' organizations (Humphreys 2008).

The second subgroup was dissolved in 2000 and replaced with the UN Forum on Forests, which reported to the UN Economic and Social Council and was given the task of designing mechanisms for reporting on the implementation of the 1994 agreement. Many NGO representatives advocated a bottom-up approach, based on monitoring and reporting by NGOs, indigenous people's organizations, and civil society, but they had little influence (Humphreys 2008). Australia favored compulsory national reporting, while the United States and some developing countries preferred voluntary reporting. The United States opposed collectively defined targets and timetables for implementation, insisting that nations should set their own. The United States won the issue (Humphreys 2008).

The International Tropical Timber Agreement of 2006 builds on and extends the foundations of the previous agreements, focusing on the world tropical timber economy and the sustainable management of the resource base—simultaneously encouraging the timber trade and improving forest management.

Regulation of the Oceans

Eight of nine conventions related to oceans concern pollution: four aim solely at oil pollution, one at nuclear pollution, and three at other substances. The ninth convention is concerned with international law as it relates to the high seas.

The foundational international ocean oil pollution law is the Convention for Prevention of Pollution of the Sea by Oil (1954). It prohibits ships and tankers from discharging materials containing oil at sea but allows exemptions for tankers of under 150 tons gross tonnage, other ships of under 500 tons gross tonnage, naval ships, and whaling ships. Certain circumstances are also exempted—for example, if the instantaneous rate of discharge does not exceed 60 liters per mile, if the oil content of discharge is less than 100 parts per million, if discharge is made as far as practicable from land, if the tanker is more than 50 miles from land, or if leakage is unavoidable and measures are taken to minimize it.

Other conventions authorize interventions in cases of oil pollution, assign liability, and require emergency plans. The Convention Relating to Intervention on the High Seas in Cases of Oil Pollution Casualties (1969) authorizes parties to act to prevent, mitigate, or eliminate grave and imminent danger when oil pollution threatens the sea, coastlines, or related interests. Such measures may be taken only *after* notifying the flag state of the ship, consulting independent experts, and notifying those whose interests might be affected by the measures. The Convention on Civil Liability for Bunker Oil Pollution Damage (1969) places liability on a ship's owner for pollution damage caused by bunker oil on board or originating from the ship, unless exonerated under certain conditions. Registered owners of ships with gross tonnage over 1,000 tons are required to buy insurance to cover liability for pollution damage. The Convention on Oil Pollution Preparedness, Response, and Cooperation (1990) obligates parties to ensure that all ships flying their flags have oil pollution emergency plans based on the convention's prescriptions and to report all incidences of oil discharge.

The Convention Relating to Civil Liability in the Field of Maritime Carriage of Nuclear Material (1971) addresses pollution from nuclear substances, holding the operators of nuclear installations liable for damage sustained in a nuclear incident during maritime transport of the materials.

Three conventions address other ocean contaminants. The Convention on the Prevention of Marine Pollution by Dumping of Wastes and Other Matter (1972) covers oil and hazardous substances. The law specifies substances prohibited from being dumped and substances requiring permits to be dumped in the ocean. Prohibited substances include organohalogen compounds, mercury, cadmium, crude oil, fuel oil, heavy diesel oil, lubricating oil, hydraulic fluids, high-level radioactive matter, materials produced for biological and chemical warfare, and persistent plastics and other synthetic materials that might float or be suspended in the sea, interfering with fishing, navigation, and other legitimate sea uses. Substances requiring permits for dumping in the ocean are wastes containing significant amounts of arsenic, lead, copper, zinc, organosilicon compounds, cyanides, fluorides, and pesticides and pesticide byproducts.

The second convention addressing non-oil, non-nuclear ocean pollution is the Convention on Liability and Compensation for Damage in Connection with the Carriage of Hazardous and Noxious Substances by Sea (1996). It requires ships' owners to maintain liability insurance and to obtain an insurance certificate for trading under the flag of a party. In addition, ships' owners must contribute to a Hazardous and Noxious Substances Fund to compensate people for damage when ships' owners do not. The Convention on the Control of Harmful and Anti-fouling Systems on Ships (2001) prohibits or restricts the use of certain anti-fouling systems; certain coatings on the undersides of vessels to prevent biological fouling; and the accumulation of microorganisms, plants, algae, and animals. The materials in many anti-fouling systems were found to be toxic to marine life.

The Law of the Sea (1973) does not regulate pollution. Instead, it attempts to codify the rules of international laws relating to territorial waters and ocean resources. The law defines nations' rights and responsibilities in using oceans and establishes guidelines for managing marine natural resources. In the seventeenth century, ocean use was ruled by the freedom-of-the-seas doctrine, which limited national rights and jurisdiction over the oceans to a three-mile belt of sea on a nation's coastline. The rest, the high seas, were proclaimed free to all. But by the end of World War II, conditions threatened to transform the seas into an arena for conflict.

Case Study: The Law of the Sea. Ocean resources are vast—fish, petroleum, natural gas, and minerals. As technology was developed to exploit resources more fully, nations extended their claims on territorial waters beyond three miles. U.S.

actions in 1945 posed the first major challenge to the freedom-of-the-seas doctrine. President Harry Truman, responding to pressure from domestic oil corporations, unilaterally extended U.S. jurisdiction to all natural resources on the U.S. continental shelf.

Other nations quickly followed this lead. Argentina claimed its continental shelf in 1946. Chile and Peru claimed their continental shelves in 1947, and in 1950 Ecuador asserted sovereign rights over a 200 mile zone to limit access by foreign fishing fleets and control fish stocks. Egypt, Ethiopia, Saudi Arabia, Libya, Venezuela, and some eastern European countries claimed a 12 mile territorial sea. Indonesia and the Philippines asserted sovereignty over all waters separating their islands. By the 1950s, large fishing vessels that could remain at sea for several months roamed the oceans far from their native shores. Conflicts frequently erupted as nations poached the richest fishing waters beyond the limits set by the nation claiming sovereign rights to the waters. I illustrate such conflict with an account of the "Cod Wars" of 1958–1975.

The Cod Wars were a series of three confrontations between Iceland and the United Kingdom over fishing rights in the North Atlantic. In 1958, Icelandic law extended Iceland's territorial waters 4–12 miles from its coastline. But the British continued to fish for cod. A patrol vessel from the Icelandic Coast Guard attempted to overtake a British trawler but was thwarted when another British ship intervened. The two vessels collided, and gunshots were exchanged. The conflict led the two nations to a settlement stipulating that any future disagreement over fishery zones would be referred to the International Court of Justice in The Hague.

In 1972, Iceland again expanded its territorial waters, to 50 miles. British and West German trawlers continued fishing in the zone. When the Icelandic Coast Guard cut trawlers' fishing nets, the British government dispatched a fleet of Royal Naval warships and tugboats to protect British crews. The battle featured several cases of vessels deliberately ramming each other. Meetings sponsored by the North Atlantic Treaty Organization (NATO) resulted in an agreement that permitted British fishing in certain areas inside the 50 mile zone but limiting the annual cod catch to 130,000 tons.

When the agreement expired in November 1975, Iceland claimed 200 miles of territorial seas, triggering the third Cod War. British trawlers continued to fish in the claimed waters; the Icelandic Coast Guard cut more nets; and several incidents of ramming occurred between Icelandic ships and British trawlers, frigates, and tugboats. In 1976, Iceland threatened retaliation by closing a NATO base, which would have impaired NATO's ability to defend the Atlantic Ocean from the Soviet Union. A compromise between the two states allowed a maximum of twenty-four British trawlers access to the disputed 200 nautical mile limit.

In addition to codfish, the desire to control petroleum resources presented a challenge to the freedom-of-the-seas doctrine. Offshore oil production expanded from modest beginnings in 1947 to nearly 400 million tons in the mid-1960s. Oil explorations occurred farther from land and more deeply into the bedrock of continental margins, as far as 4,000 meters below the ocean surface. Supertankers ferried oil from the Middle East to European and other ports, passing through congested straits and leaving a trail of oil spills. Tension between nations heightened over conflicting claims to ocean space and resources.

In 1967, Malta's ambassador to the United Nations spoke before the General Assembly to call for a new international regime over the seabed and the ocean floor that transcended national jurisdictions. Many recognized that tension could be reduced by updating the freedom-of-the-seas doctrine. The ambassador's speech generated a fifteen-year global diplomatic process to negotiate a constitution for the seas.

The UN Conference on the Law of the Sea convened in New York in 1973. Representatives of more than 160 nations negotiated for nine years before adopting the Convention on the Law of the Sea of 1982. It was adopted as a "package deal," to be accepted as a whole without reservation on any parts. Among the convention's provisions are international recognition of each nation's 200 mile exclusive economic zone, stipulations granting landlocked countries the right of access to the sea, principles describing the right to conduct marine scientific research, navigational rights, the legal status of resources on the seabed beyond the limits of national jurisdiction, passage of ships through narrow straits, conservation and management of marine resources, protection of the marine environment, and a binding procedure for settling disputes.

The United Nations has no direct operational role in the convention's implementation. The International Seabed Authority, which was established by the United Nations, organizes and regulates the exploitation of deep seabed resources beyond national jurisdictions. The International Tribunal for the Law of the Sea is authorized to settle ocean-related disputes over interpretations of the convention. Implementation is monitored by organizations such as the International Maritime Organization and the International Whaling Commission.

Land

Five conventions address hazardous land pollution. Two aim specifically at nuclear pollution. The Convention on Civil Liability for Nuclear Damage (1963) requires operators of nuclear installations to maintain liability insurance and assigns to operators all liability for nuclear damage caused by incidents within installations or involving nuclear material originating from or sent to installations. Liability is not imposed if an incident results from a conflict, civil war, insurrection, or grave natural disaster.

The Joint Convention on the Safety of Spent Fuel Management and on the Safety of Radioactive Waste Management (1997) requires parties to take appropriate steps to ensure that individuals, society, and the environment are adequately protected against radiological hazards from civilian nuclear reactors. Proposed sites for installations must be evaluated for safety impact; the plans must include reactor decommissioning; and all information must be publicly available.

The Basel Convention on the Control of Transboundary Movements of Hazardous Wastes and Their Disposal (1989) emphasizes land pollution by hazardous wastes. Parties that prohibit the importing of hazardous and other wastes must inform other parties of their decision, and those other parties are required to comply. If the nation intended to receive the import does not provide prior written informed consent, the import is prohibited. Only authorized people may transport or dispose of the wastes.

The Rotterdam Convention on the Prior Informed Consent Procedure for Certain Hazardous Chemicals and Pesticides in International Trade (1998) regulates trade in petrochemicals. The convention identified forty chemicals that are banned or severely restricted in many nations: eleven are industrial chemicals and twenty-nine are pesticides. UNEP then provided parties with decision-guidance documents for the chemicals, requesting parties' decisions on allowing imports. Parties' decisions are published by the Secretariat and publicized every six months. Parties are required to ensure that their exports do not violate the decisions.

The Stockholm Convention on Persistent Organic Pollutants (2001) is aimed specifically at petrochemicals, including polychlorinated dibenzo-p-dioxins, dibenzofurans, hexachlorobenzene, and polychlorinated biphenyls (PCBs). The convention requires parties to reduce or eliminate releases.

Air

The Convention on Long-Range Transboundary Air Pollution of 1979 requires parties to reduce annual emissions of sulfur, nitrogen oxide, ammonia, and volatile organic compounds.

Three conventions address nuclear pollution. Two were instigated by the explosion and fire at the Chernobyl nuclear power plant in 1986. The Convention on Assistance in the Case of a Nuclear Accident or Radiological Emergency of 1986 facilitates prompt assistance in those events. Parties may call for assistance from any other party, either directly or through the International Atomic Energy Agency. The Convention on Early Notification of a Nuclear Accident of 1986 requires the party undergoing a nuclear accident to notify states that are or may be affected that an accident has occurred and about its nature and time and location of occurrence. The party must provide information for minimizing consequences. The Convention on Supplementary Compensation for Nuclear Damage of 1997 includes ecological harm as nuclear damage and provides compensation funds.

Two conventions address the first global-scale environmental problems: ozone depletion and global climate change. The first discovery of a hole in the ozone over Antarctica instigated the Vienna Convention for the Protection of the Ozone Layer (1985). It established mechanisms for international cooperation in research on the ozone layer and the effects of ozone-depleting chemicals.

After a series of negotiations, the Montreal Protocol on Substances that Deplete the Ozone Layer (1987) was signed by twenty-four countries and the European Economic Community. It stipulated that the production and consumption of compounds that deplete stratospheric ozone—chlorofluorocarbons (CFCs), halons, carbon tetrachloride, and methyl chloroform—be phased out by 2000.

The Montreal Protocol was one of the first international environmental agreements to include trade sanctions to achieve treaty goals, justified on the grounds that ozone-layer depletion was most effectively addressed at the global level.

UNEP and the World Meteorological Organization established the Intergovernmental Panel on Climate Change (IPCC) in 1988 to review regularly all scientific, technical, and socioeconomic information about global climate change, its potential effects, and options for adaptation and mitigation. The panel's First Assessment Report, in 1990, stated with certainty that emissions from human activities were substantially increasing atmospheric concentrations of greenhouse gases, resulting in warming of the Earth's surface, and that carbon dioxide is responsible for more than half of the enhanced greenhouse effect.

The IPCC's report prompted the UN Framework Convention on Climate Change in 1992. Signed at the Rio Conference, the framework created the architecture for international negotiations and established the objective as stabilization of atmospheric concentrations of greenhouse gas at a level that would prevent anthropogenic interference with the climate system.

The Kyoto Protocol of 1997 required signatories of developed countries to reduce their greenhouse gas emissions substantially by 2012. Negotiations between 1998 and 2000 aimed at ratification failed to produce agreement. Member states began a second round of negotiations that culminated in the Bonn Agreement and Marrakesh Accords of 2001, which finalized implementation rules. The conference of the parties held in Copenhagen in December 2009 failed to negotiate a legally binding text with emissions limits, instead suggesting a deadline of the end of 2010 for the text.

Global Ecological Disruption

Petro-dependent agriculture and manufacturing have been globally expanded with international environmental policies that have failed. I substantiate this assertion with an examination of biospheric disruptions, relying on two reports: the Millennium Ecosystems Assessment released in 2005, which evaluates changes in global ecosystems and their consequences for human well-being, and the *Living Planet Report 2006,* issued by the World Wildlife Fund. The *Living Planet Report 2006* uses two indices: the Living Planet Index, which measures the state of global ecosystems, and the Ecological Footprint, which measures the human demand placed on ecosystems.

Millennium Ecosystems Assessment

The Millennium Ecosystems Assessment examines linkages between changes in ecosystem services and human well-being. Approximately 1,360 experts from ninety-five countries wrote the report, which synthesizes information from the scientific literature and peer-reviewed datasets and models, incorporating knowledge held by the private sector, practitioners, local communities, and indigenous peoples.

Ecosystem services are benefits people obtain from ecosystems. They include provisioning services, such as food, water, timber, and fiber; regulating services, which affect climate, floods, disease, waste, and water quality; cultural services, which provide recreational, aesthetic, and spiritual benefits; and supporting services, such as soil formation, photosynthesis, and nutrient cycling.

The most important direct drivers of changes in ecosystem services are habitat change, invasive species, overexploitation of resources, climate change, and excessive nutrient loading. The first three drivers are unlikely to diminish soon; climate change and excessive nutrient loading will likely become more severe. Rural poor people are most directly reliant on ecosystem services and are most vulnerable to changes. Significant progress toward the eradication of poverty, improved health, and environmental sustainability is unlikely if ecosystem services continue to be degraded. I discuss two major findings of the Millennium Ecosystems Assessment.

Finding 1

Over the past fifty years, humans have extensively changed ecosystems. Some changes were inadvertent results of unrelated activities, such as the construction of roads, ports, and cities, and pollution discharges. But most were deliberately undertaken to meet a growing global population's increased demands for food, fresh water, timber, fiber, and fuel. Between 1960 and 2000, the demand for ecosystem services grew as the global population doubled to 6 billion and the economy increased more than sixfold. Food production increased two and a half times; water use doubled; wood harvests for pulp and paper production tripled; hydropower capacity doubled; and timber production increased by more than half.

Ecosystem structure and functioning changed more rapidly in the second half of the twentieth century than at any time in human history. More land was converted to cropland between 1950 and 1980 than between 1700 and 1850. Cultivated systems now cover one-quarter of the Earth's terrestrial surface. In the last decades of the twentieth century, 20 percent of the world's coral reefs were degraded, and another 20 percent were lost. Thirty-five percent of mangroves were lost in the same period. The volume of water impounded behind dams has quadrupled since 1960, and between three and six times as much water is held in reservoirs than in natural rivers. Water withdrawals from rivers and lakes have doubled since 1960. Seventy percent of worldwide water use is absorbed in agriculture. Atmospheric carbon dioxide has increased by 32 percent since 1750, but about 60 percent of that increase has taken place since 1959.

Human activities are having a fundamental and irreversible impact on biodiversity. More than two-thirds of the area of two out of the fourteen major terrestrial biomes, and more than half of the area of four other biomes, had been changed by 1990, primarily by agriculture. Over a wide range of taxonomic groups, population size, range, or both is declining for the majority of species. Species distribution is becoming homogeneous: the set of species in any region of the world is similar to the set in other regions, primarily as a result of intentional and inadvertent introductions of species from increased travel and shipping. The total number of species is declining. Over the past few hundred years, humans have accelerated the species extinction rate 1,000 times over background rates across the Earth's history. Between 10 percent and 30 percent of mammal, bird, and amphibian species are threatened with extinction; freshwater ecosystems have the highest proportion of threatened species. Genetic diversity has declined globally, particularly among cultivated species.

Finding 2

Approximately 60 percent of ecosystem services are being degraded or used unsustainably, including capture fisheries, water supply, waste treatment and de-toxification, water purification, natural hazard protection, air quality regulation, regional and local climate regulation, and erosion regulation. Actions to increase one ecosystem service often cause the degradation of other services. For example, increasing food production with additional water and fertilizers and expanded cultivation degrades water quality, reduces biodiversity, and decreases forest cover. Ecosystem changes increase the likelihood of nonlinear and potentially abrupt changes when a threshold is reached. Many such changes—the emergence of disease, eutrophication and hypoxia, the collapse of fisheries, the introduction and loss of species, and regional climate change—are difficult, expensive, or impossible to reverse. The Millennium Ecosystems Assessment predicts that the harmful consequences of ecosystem degradation are likely to grow significantly worse in the next fifty years. Consumption of ecosystem services, which are often unsustainable, will grow because of a likely three- to sixfold increase in global gross domestic product by 2050.

The *Living Planet Report 2006*

The *Living Planet Report 2006* uses three measures of changes in global biodiversity and human consumption: the Living Planet Index, which tracks the populations of 1,686 vertebrate species across all regions of the world; the Ecological Footprint, which measures changes in humanity's demand on the area of productive land and sea for resource extraction and waste absorption; and the Water Footprint, which measures human demand on national, regional, and global water resources.

The Living Planet Index

The Living Planet Index tracks nearly 5,000 populations of 1,686 vertebrate species of mammal, bird, reptile, amphibian, and fish. Direct anthropogenic threats to biodiversity are habitat loss, fragmentation, or change, especially due to agriculture; overexploitation of species, especially due to fishing and hunting; pollution; the spread of invasive species or genes; and climate change.

Natural habitats are lost, altered, or fragmented through conversion for cultivation, grazing, aquaculture, and industrial or urban use. River systems are dammed and altered for irrigation, hydropower, and flow regulation. Marine ecosystems, particularly the seabed, are physically degraded by trawling, construction, and extractive industries.

Overexploitation of wild species populations results from harvesting or kill-ing animals or plants for food, materials, or medicine at rates that exceed the population's reproductive capacity. Overexploitation is the dominant threat to marine biodiversity and a serious threat to terrestrial species, particularly tropi-cal forest mammals hunted for food. Overharvesting of timber depletes forests and associated plant and animal populations.

Invasive species are the main threat to endemic species on islands and in freshwater ecosystems because they become competitors, predators, or parasites of indigenous species, causing declines of native species populations.

Pollution causes biodiversity loss, particularly in aquatic systems. Nitrogen and phosphorus fertilizers pollute with excess nutrient loading that causes eutro-phication and oxygen depletion. Hazardous chemical pollution is a product of pesticide use, industry, and mining. Increased concentrations of carbon dioxide in the atmosphere cause acidification of the oceans, which particularly affects shell- and reef-building organisms.

Climate change is potentially the greatest threat to biodiversity. Early effects of climate change are observed in polar, mountain, and marine ecosystems.

Overall biodiversity declined nearly 30 percent from 1970 to 2005, varying by climate zone, biographic realm, and biome. While the temperate climate zone showed relatively little change, tropical biodiversity plunged by 50 percent. The statistics do not *necessarily* mean that biodiversity loss in tropical zones is worse than that in temperate zones. An index covering centuries instead of decades might indicate an equal or larger decline among temperate species populations.

Biographic realms include terrestrial, marine, and freshwater ecosystems. In the terrestrial realm, biodiversity has consistently declined since 1970, with a 33 percent average decline in terrestrial vertebrate populations between 1970 and 2005. Most of the decline occurred in the tropics because of deforestation and other habitat destruction driven by agricultural conversion and overexploitation. In the marine realm, overall biodiversity declined by an average 14 percent due to rising sea temperatures, destructive fishing methods, and pollution. With less than 1 percent of the world's oceans designated as marine protected areas, 40 percent are severely affected by human activities. Overfishing is a major driver: most of the world's commercial marine fisheries are either fully exploited or over-exploited. Biodiversity in the freshwater realm averaged declines of 35 percent between 1970 and 2005. Wetland areas decreased by 50 percent, attributable to overfishing, invasive species, pollution, creation of dams, and water diversion.

The world's biomes are tropical forest, dry land, and grasslands systems. Deforestation is a severe problem in tropical biomes. Primary forests disappear in Brazil at a rate of almost 3.5 million hectares per year and in Indonesia, at 1.5 million hectares per year. Habitat destruction contributed to a loss of more than 60 percent in 503 populations of 186 animal species. Dry land biomes make up more than 40 percent of the Earth's terrestrial system, including such diverse ecosystems as deserts, savannahs, and tropical dry woodlands. Biodiversity in dry lands has declined by about 44 percent since 1970. Grassland biomes are found on all continents except Antarctica. Since 1970, biodiversity has declined

36 percent among grassland vertebrate populations due to high rates of conversion to agriculture.

The Ecological Footprint

The Ecological Footprint represents humanity's demand on the biosphere. The supply side of the equation is biocapacity, the world's total productive area of cropland, grazing land, forests, and fishing grounds. It is measured in global hectares, or hectares that have a world-average ability to produce resources and absorb wastes. In 2005, global biocapacity was 13.6 billion global hectares, averaging 2.1 global hectares per person. Biocapacity is not evenly distributed. Nations with the most biocapacity are the United States, Brazil, Russia, China, Canada, India, Argentina, and Australia, together containing 50 percent of total global biocapacity.

The demand side of the equation is a country's total ecological footprint, determined by population size and residents' average footprint. It is the sum of cropland, grazing land, forests, and fishing grounds required to produce the food, fiber, and timber required for consumption, waste absorption, and space for infrastructure.

Humanity's ecological footprint first exceeded total biocapacity in the 1980s and has continued to increase. In 2005, the global ecological footprint was 17.5 billion global hectares, or 2.7 global hectares per person, exceeding the planet's regenerative capacity by 30 percent. The single largest human demand on the biosphere is its carbon footprint, which grew more than tenfold after 1961.

In 2005, the United States and China had the largest national ecological footprints, each using 21 percent of the planet's biocapacity. China has a substantially smaller per person footprint but a population more than four times larger than that of the United States. India's footprint was the third largest, using 7 percent of the total biocapacity. Nations also draw on other nations' ecological capacities. For example, when China imports wood from Tanzania or Europe imports beef from cattle raised on Brazilian soy, these countries depend on biocapacity outside their borders to provide the resources consumed by their populations.

Three of the eight countries with the largest biocapacities—the United States, China, and India—are ecological debtors: their footprints exceed their biocapacities. The remaining five are creditor countries. Of the three countries with the highest biocapacity per person—Gabon, Canada, and Bolivia—only Canada's per person footprint is higher than the global average, but it is still lower than the nation's biocapacity. Congo has the seventh highest average biocapacity, at 13.9 global hectares per person, but an average footprint of only .5 global hectares per person, the fourth smallest per person footprint of all nations with populations of more than 1 million.

The number of debtor countries is growing. In 1961, most countries' biocapacity exceeded their ecological footprint, leaving a net ecological reserve. By 2005, humanity as a whole and many individual countries had become ecological debtors, with footprints greater than their biocapacities. Ecological debtor countries can maintain their level of consumption only through a combination of harvesting their own resources faster than they can be replaced, importing resources from other nations, and using the global atmosphere as a dumping ground for greenhouse gases. Overexploitation and depletion of natural resources may result in permanent loss of ecosystem services, increasing the likelihood of a country's dependence on imports.

Trends in International Environmental Policymaking

Table 9.2 lists international environmental conventions in chronological order, revealing broad trends in environmental policymaking. From 1951 to 1985, international laws concerned the depletion of biological resources, the emerging commercial nuclear power industry, ocean pollution specifically from petroleum, and air pollution. International policymakers in 1985 responded to evidence of the global-scale environmental problem of depletion of the stratospheric ozone layer. Three laws between 1986 and 1990 aimed at environmental disasters: two in response to the Chernobyl explosion and one in the wake of the *Exxon Valdez* oil spill. A treaty negotiated in 1989 addressed the management of petrochemicals and other hazardous substances. Global climate change gained international policymakers' sustained attention in 1992. Of nine laws negotiated between 1996 and 2006, five deal with the management of radioactive materials, petrochemicals, and other hazardous substances.

Environmental policies are conventionally perceived to aim at resource conservation and pollution abatement. But analysis of international statutes demonstrates that nearly half of them address *conflict resolution*. Table 9.3 identifies statutes grouped by policy type, and Table 9.4 shows the distribution of statutes by policy type and resource. Of thirty laws, only five (17%) concern conservation and eleven (37%) concern pollution. Fourteen statutes (47%) relate to the resolution or avoidance of conflicts among nations over environmental issues. Together, the tables indicate the following trends in international policymaking:

- Sources of conflict addressed in statutes are access to biological resources and liability for pollution.
- International pollution laws aim at ocean pollution by oil, radioactive materials, heavy metals, and petrochemicals; at land pollution by radioactive materials, heavy metals, and petrochemicals; and at air pollution by radioactive materials. Only two statutes emphasize pollution prevention; the remainder emphasize pollution abatement. Pollution statutes concern the petro-dependent society's fundamental production base: oil, radioactive materials, heavy metals, and petrochemicals.
- Conservation statutes address only biological resources, and two laws relate more to trading than to conservation by establishing permit criteria for commerce in biological resources.

How do trends in international environmental statutes compare with policy trends in the world's first petro-dependent society? My earlier examination of

U.S. laws revealed a bias toward economic growth over environmental protection, with substantial responsibility for implementation and enforcement placed on individual states. This bias is more pronounced in international laws but is tempered with greater recognition of the link between economic development and ecological stability. Both national and international laws rely on self-reports to

TABLE 9.2   Chronological List of UN Environmental Conventions

1951	International Plant Protection Convention
1954	Convention for Prevention of Pollution of the Sea by Oil
1958	Convention on Fishing and Conservation of the Living Resources of the High Seas
1963	Convention on Civil Liability for Nuclear Damage
1969	Convention on Civil Liability for Bunker Oil Pollution Damage
1969	Convention Relating to Intervention on the High Seas in Cases of Oil Pollution Casualties
1971	Convention on Wetlands of International Importance Especially as Waterfowl Habitat
1971	Convention Relating to Civil Liability in the Field of Maritime Carriage of Nuclear Material
1972	Convention on the Prevention of Marine Pollution by Dumping of Wastes and Other Matter
1973	Convention on International Trade in Endangered Species of Wild Fauna and Flora
1973	Convention on the Law of the Sea
1979	Convention on Long-Range Transboundary Air Pollution
1979	Convention on the Conservation of Migratory Species of Wild Animals
1985	Vienna Convention for the Protection of the Ozone Layer
1986	Convention on Assistance in the Case of a Nuclear Accident or Radiological Emergency
1986	Convention on Early Notification of a Nuclear Accident
1989	Basel Convention on the Control of Transboundary Movements of Hazardous Wastes and Their Disposal
1990	Convention on Oil Pollution Preparedness, Response, and Cooperation
1991	Convention for the Protection of New Varieties of Plants
1992	Convention on Biological Diversity
1992	United Nations Framework Convention on Climate Change
1996	Convention on Liability and Compensation for Damage in Connection with the Carriage of Hazardous and Noxious Substances by Sea
1997	Convention on Supplementary Compensation for Nuclear Damage
1997	Joint Convention on the Safety of Spent Fuel Management and on the Safety of Radioactive Waste Management
1998	Rotterdam Convention on the Prior Informed Consent Procedure for Certain Hazardous Chemicals and Pesticides in International Trade
2001	Agreement on the Conservation of Albatrosses and Petrels
2001	International Convention on the Control of Harmful Anti-fouling Systems on Ships
2001	International Treaty on Plant Genetic Resources for Food and Agriculture
2001	Stockholm Convention on Persistent Organic Pollution
2006	Tropical Timber Agreement

TABLE 9.3   International Statutes Grouped by Policy Type

Conservation Statutes (5/30, 17%)

Biological Resources (5/5, 100%)

1951	International Plant Protection Convention—trade permits
1971	Convention on Wetlands of International Importance Especially as Waterfowl Habitat
1973	Convention in International Trade in Endangered Species of Wild Fauna and Flora— trade permits
1979	Convention on the Conservation of Migratory Species of Wild Animals
2001	Agreement on the Conservation of Albatrosses and Petrels

Pollution Statutes (11/30, 37%)

Oceans (5/11, 45%)

1954	Convention for Prevention of Pollution of the Sea by Oil
1969	Convention Relating to Intervention on the High Seas in Cases of Oil Pollution Casualties
1972	Convention on the Prevention of Marine Pollution by Dumping of Wastes and Other Matter
1990	Convention on Oil Pollution Preparedness, Response and Cooperation
2001	Convention on the Control of Harmful Anti-fouling Systems on Ships

Land (1/11, 9%)

2001	Stockholm Convention on Persistent Organic Pollution

Air (5/11, 45%)

1979	Convention on Long-Range Transboundary Air Pollution
1985	Vienna Convention for the Protection of the Ozone Layer
1986	Convention on Assistance in the Case of a Nuclear Accident or Radiological Emergency
1986	Convention on Early Notification of a Nuclear Accident
1992	United Nations Framework Convention on Climate Change

monitor compliance. I found that U.S. resource management policies emphasize *controlling* resources rather than conserving them. At the international level, only biological resources are addressed with conservation laws, but half of the biological resources statutes address conflicts over access—similar to control. U.S. pollution policies emphasize abatement over prevention, favoring the regulation of production's waste byproducts rather than the regulation of production technology. This trend is more evident in international law because the dictation of national production processes by the United Nations would violate sovereignty. Decisions about U.S. production technology are made privately by corporations rather than through democratic participation by the public. This trend is equally true of international laws because of sovereignty issues.

The trends indicate that international environmental regulation largely concerns conflicts over access to the resources that underlie petro-dependent wealth and pollution associated with production expansion. International laws inevitably fail for two reasons. First, the United Nations only formulates and implements

TABLE 9.3   Continued

<u>Conflict Resolution Statutes (14/30, 47%)</u>

Biological Resources (5/14, 36%)

1958	Convention on Fishing and Conservation of the Living Resources of the High Seas
1991	Convention for the Protection of New Varieties of Plants
1992	Convention on Biological Diversity
2001	International Treaty on Plant Genetic Resources for Food and Agriculture
2006	Tropical Timber Agreement

Oceans (4/14, 29%)

1969	Convention on Civil Liability for Bunker Oil Pollution Damage
1971	Convention Relating to Civil Liability in the Field of Maritime Carriage of Nuclear Material
1973	Convention on the Law of the Sea
1996	Convention on Liability and Compensation for Damage in Connection with the Carriage of Hazardous and Noxious Substances by Sea

Land (4/14, 29%)

1963	Convention on Civil Liability for Nuclear Damage
1989	Basel Convention on the Control of Transboundary Movements of Hazardous Wastes and Their Disposal
1997	Convention on Supplementary Compensation for Nuclear Damage
1998	Rotterdam Convention on the Prior Informed Consent Procedure for Certain Hazardous Chemicals and Pesticides in International Trade

Air (1/14, 7%)

1997	Joint Convention on the Safety of Spent Fuel Management and on the Safety of Radioactive Waste

TABLE 9.4   Distribution of Statutes by Policy Type and Resource

Resource	Conflict statutes	Pollution statutes	Conservation statutes	Total
Biological	5	0	5	10
Oceans	4	5	0	9
Land	4	1	0	5
Air	1	5	0	6
Total	14	11	5	30

environmental policies, lacking the crucial bite of enforcement. Second, compliance with environmental laws is merely voluntary because member states choose whether to enter into agreements.

Failed national and international environmental policies leave us with the global environmental problems of overpopulation, the approaching peak in oil production, and climate change.

10

Global Environmental Problems

Overpopulation, Peak Oil,
and Climate Change

Humans developed modes of subsistence to increase the availability of resources for the provision of food, clothing, and shelter. Global population growth is the inevitable consequence of increased resources. Equally inevitably, larger populations exploit more resources and produce more pollution.

The petro-dependent mode of subsistence, the mother of all modes, monumentally increases resources preferred by humans and produces a population explosion. Without adequate international environmental policies, larger populations deplete more resources and pollute more densely and at unprecedented global levels. The world's most pressing resource depletion problem is the approaching peak in oil production, and our most threatening pollution problem is global climate change.

Overpopulation

Ecologists maintain that all species populations undergo three phases of existence: growth, stability, and decline. Population growth is the natural consequence of surplus food resources. Populations with unlimited resources grow exponentially if left unchecked by other factors, because individuals usually produce more than one offspring. In the growth phase, ecosystems entirely absorb the surplus through population growth, particularly among species higher in the food chain. When the surplus is eliminated, growth rates level off, and the population enters the stability phase. Stability is typically preceded by a population crash—a sizable die-off—because the rapidly growing population abruptly exceeds resources. Stability is the longest population phase, but it inescapably yields to decline and is eventually followed by the extinction of all populations of the species.

Agriculture, industrialized agriculture, and petro-agriculture have produced ever larger surpluses of food resources. Although humans, unlike ecosystems, divert a large portion of the surplus to the accumulation of even larger future ones, some surplus is inevitably expended in population growth. As a consequence of continually increased surpluses, the human species remains in the exponential growth phase.

A major feature of the twenty-first century is the crowding of this exploding population into large cities. The number of cities has grown since the 1960s as petro-dependency has spread across Africa, Asia, and Latin America, driving subsistence farmers off the land. While eighty-six cities had populations of more than 1 million in 1950, today 400 cities have populations that large. Demographers predict that by 2015, 550 cities will have 1 million or more inhabitants. Two-thirds of global population growth since 1950 has occurred in urban areas. By 2008, and for the first time in human history, more people lived in urban centers than in rural areas.

A related and striking feature is that 1 billion of the world's 3 billion urban dwellers live in slums, leading the social analyst Mike Davis to refer to the Earth as the Planet of the Slums. But the planet's Southern Hemisphere holds most of the slum population: 6 percent of urban populations in developed countries are slum residents, compared with 78 percent of urban populations in less developed countries. Slum growth has outpaced urbanization in the Southern Hemisphere.

The dynamics of this demographic shift differ from the urbanization and slum development of Europe and North America in the nineteenth century and early twentieth century. In areas that industrialized first, slum dwellers lived in inner cities in hand-me-down housing, such as the brownstones of Harlem, government-subsidized tenements, or church flophouses. Since the worldwide debt crisis of the 1970s, in contrast, a major share of urban population growth worldwide has been absorbed by slum communities on cities' peripheries.

Urbanization in developing countries differs from the developed world's process in that it frequently takes place *without* economic growth—the two processes are decoupled (Davis 2007). The debt crisis and economic recession of the 1970s manifested in plant closures and deindustrialization that eliminated jobs in the great industrial cities of the Southern Hemisphere—Bombay, Johannesburg, Buenos Aires, and São Paulo. The International Monetary Fund and the World Bank directed economic restructuring in Africa, Latin America, the Middle East, and much of South Asia. These "structural adjustment" programs and agricultural deregulation shredded social safety nets and left farmers increasingly vulnerable to drought, inflation, high interest rates, and low commodity prices (Davis 2006). The consequence was the mass exodus of surplus rural labor to urban areas at the moment that cities lost job opportunities. From necessity, migrants resorted to flimsy, self-built shanties for shelter in unplanned and underserved settlements on the urban fringe.

Mike Davis (2007: 16) explains that cities such as Kinshasa, Luanda, Khartoum, Guayaquil, and Lima continue to grow rapidly

> despite ruined import-substitution industries, shrunken public sectors, and downwardly mobile middle classes. The global forces "pushing" people from the countryside—mechanization of agriculture in Java and India, food

imports in Mexico, Haiti, and Kenya, civil war and drought throughout Africa, and everywhere the consolidation of small holdings into large ones and the competition of industrial-scale agribusiness—seem to sustain urbanization even when the "pull" of the city is drastically weakened by debt and economic depression. As a result, rapid urban growth in the context of structural adjustment, currency devaluation, and state retrenchment has been an inevitable recipe for the mass production of slums.

The slum population in São Paulo grew from 1.2 percent of Brazil's total population in 1973 to 19.8 percent in 1993. Eighty-five percent of Kenya's total population growth from 1989 to 1999 occurred in urban slums. Eighty percent of urban growth in the Amazon is in shantytowns on the outskirts of cities. India's slum population grows 250 percent faster than the overall population (Davis 2006).

Slum settlements are located on devalued and often hazardous land, such as floodplains, hillsides, swamps, and brownfields—land previously used for industrial purposes and in locations adjacent to hazardous industries such as metal plating, dyeing, tanning, battery recycling, and chemical manufacturing. Slum residents are seldom served by municipal water, sewage, and garbage utilities or by municipal transportation systems. A UN study in 2009 linked the growth of global urban slums to weather extremes caused by climate change, arguing that the resultant risks from "megadisasters" such as devastating floods and cyclones have substantially increased (Murphy 2009).

Jonathan Harris and Neva Goodwin (2003) estimate that the global population will swell by more than 70 million people per year between 2000 and 2020. As the population rises, so does the threat of food insecurity. Petro-dependent agriculture, typically called the Green Revolution, has fed the burgeoning population for fifty years, but some analysts believe it is near collapse.

For example, the Indian government paid farmers to shift from old-fashioned crops of grains, beans, and vegetables to new, high-yield varieties of wheat, rice, and cotton. Farmers applied low-cost petrochemical fertilizers instead of cow dung, erected large-scale irrigation systems rather than relying on rainfall, and plowed with gasoline-powered tractors instead of bulls. The technology substantially contributed to India's transformation into a superpower and prominent grain exporter, but it now appears to be failing. Daniel Zwerdling (2009) reports on the rise and fall of petro-agriculture in the village of Chotia Khurd, in India's breadbasket Punjab region. With the adoption of petro-agriculture, farmers in Chotia Khurd increased grain harvest per acre by three to four times (Zwerdling 2009). Prosperity allowed them to pave roads, build brick and cement houses, and buy consumer goods, from tractors to cell phones.

Prosperity in Chotia Khurd is now fading (Zwerdling 2009). Farmers apply three times the fertilizers they did thirty years ago to get the same crop yield. Insects are now so resistant to pesticides that damage often forces farmers to destroy large portions of their crops. Groundwater levels have sunk at a rate of 3 feet per year, pressuring farmers continually to deepen their wells as the water table recedes. They often tap salty water that kills crops and strips soil of nutrients such as nitrogen, phosphorus, iron, and manganese. Already in debt for their houses, farmers pay for wells by borrowing from non-bank lenders who charge high interest rates. A study by the Punjab State Council for Science and Technology in 2009 concluded that regional agriculture was unsustainable and nonprofitable. Analysts fear that, without substantial changes, the heartland of India's agriculture could be barren in 10–15 years (Zwerdling 2009).

Food insecurity continually climbs in developing countries because population growth, surging costs, drought, and climate change pressure world food supplies (Associated Press 2008c). The United Nations estimates that 923 million people are hungry today and expects the number to increase by 461 million by 2030. Food insecurity pushes some governments to introduce genetic engineering to protect crops from insect damage and to boost harvests. China has significantly increased its percentage of genetically modified crops. Some European, African, and Asian governments that previously banned the growth and import of genetically modified foods are loosening restrictions and accelerating research (Associated Press 2008c).

Peak Oil Production

Petroleum is the core of the petro-dependent mode of subsistence, the petro-dependent world's source of food, clothing, and shelter.

Oil is used in every phase of agricultural production and distribution. Petro-agriculture depends on oil for the fertilizers, pesticides, farm machines, and irrigation pumps used to grow food. Oil underlies the transport, processing, packaging, marketing, and kitchen preparation of food. Lester Brown (2006: 28–29) writes, "The oil-intensive modern food system that evolved when oil was cheap will not survive as it is now structured with higher energy prices."

Clothing and other consumer goods rely on petroleum for manufacturing and transportation. They are made from oil-based synthetic fibers and plastics. Machines fueled and lubricated by oil manufacture the products and transport them to consumers via trucks, trains, ships, and airplanes. The spread of shopping malls and discount chains is based on subsidies of cheap oil.

Human shelter requires petroleum. Construction depends fundamentally on oil: "Modern cities are a product of the oil age" (Brown 2006: 36). Based on oil, cities concentrate vast amounts of food and material and dispose of mountains of garbage and human wastes. With urban growth, landfills reach capacity, and garbage is transported to more remote disposal sites. Geographically isolated suburbs rely on oil to obtain all human needs.

Rising standards of living and development in the Southern Hemisphere continue to escalate global rates of oil consumption, which are currently estimated at 84 million gallons per day. But petroleum is a nonrenewable resource, and eventually demand will exceed supply. We will reach global peak oil production. In the 1950s, M. King Hubbert, an oil geologist with the U.S. Geological Survey, developed a method for predicting a nation's peak in oil production by calculating the time lag between the peaking of new discoveries and the peaking of production. Using the established U.S. peak oil discovery date of 1930, Hubbert successfully predicted in the 1950s that U.S. oil production would peak in 1970. After the peak, oil production inevitably declines. When the global peak point is reached, oil prices will skyrocket. Petro-dependency makes the approaching peak in oil production the world's most pressing resource depletion problem. "When production turns downward, it will be a seismic economic event, creating a world unlike any we have known during our lifetimes. Indeed, when historians write about this period in history, they may well distinguish between before peak oil (BPO) and after peak oil (APO)" (Brown 2006: 21).

Discoveries of new oilfields worldwide peaked in the 1960s (Foster 2008). Oil production peaked in Austria in 1955; in Germany in 1967; in the continental United States in 1970; in Romania in 1976; in Indonesia in 1977; in Alaska in 1989; in Egypt in 1993; in India in 1995; in Syria in 1995; in Gabon and Malaysia in 1997; in Argentina and Venezuela in 1998; in Colombia and Ecuador in 1999; in the United Kingdom in 1999; in Australia in 2000; in Oman, Norway, and Yemen in 2001; and in Denmark and Mexico in 2004 (Energy Watch Group 2007). In 2004, world oil production averaged 30.5 million barrels per day. But oil discoveries amounted to only 7.5 million barrels per day (Brown 2006: 24). Petroleum geologists estimate that 95 percent of the world's oil reserves have been discovered, and that the oil reserves of the world's major countries are shrinking yearly. Investments in oil extraction from shale and tar sands are unlikely to do more than slow the decline in world oil production (Foster 2008).

Estimates of energy supplies are regularly publicized by the International Energy Agency (IEA). The IEA was established following the oil crisis in 1973 in a treaty signed in 1974 by twenty-eight members of the Organisation for Economic Co-operation and Development. In 2009, IEA economists reported that oil was running out far faster than previously predicted and that global production was likely to peak by 2019—a decade earlier than most predictions (Connor 2009). The agency's assessment of more than 800 global oil fields covering 75 percent of global reserves found that most of the biggest fields had already peaked and that the decline in oil production was 6.7 percent per year, substantially higher than the 3.7 percent decline predicted in 2007 (Connor 2009). The report estimated that if the demand for oil remained steady, the world would have to find the equivalent of four Saudi Arabias to maintain production levels and that six Saudi Arabias would be required to keep pace with anticipated increases in demand by 2030. IEA economists indicated that chronic underinvestment by oil-producing countries was likely to generate an oil crunch by 2013 that would jeopardize recovery from the global economic recession (Connor 2009). They predicted that the market power of Middle Eastern oil-producing countries with substantial reserves would increase rapidly as an oil crisis emerged after 2010.

The IEA's estimates have been criticized for being too optimistic. In late 2009, whistleblowers at the agency publicly expressed misgivings about the methods by which the IEA collected and interpreted energy statistics (Macalister 2009). The whistleblowers hypothesized that U.S. influence and fears of stock market panic encouraged IEA officials to minimize the potential for future oil scarcity. The IEA report has also been criticized by researchers from Uppsala University in Switzerland, the University of Liverpool, and other institutions, which claim that some of the IEA's assumptions drastically underplay the scale of future oil shortages (Macalister 2009). They charge that IEA economists unjustifiably assumed that oil would be extracted at an unprecedented pace, failing to provide adequate information about their figures on high future production rates from unconventional sources such as tar sands. The researchers claim that oil production is likely to be 75 million barrels per day by 2030, instead of the 105 million barrels cited by the IEA assessment, which is significantly lower than the world's oil consumption of 84 million gallons per day in 2005.

The immediate impact of peak oil production will be uneven. Certain global economic sectors—particularly, the food and automobile industries—will be affected first. Rising oil prices will draw agricultural resources into the production of fuel crops, instigating a competition for food resources between "affluent motorists and low-income food consumers" (Brown 2006: 39).

The earliest and worst human suffering will occur in developing countries, as population growth collides with shrinking oil supplies and living standards plummet. The world after peak oil is likely to be marked by continual conflict. James Howard Kunstler (2005: 68) describes this clash: "The lack of a moderating market mechanism, such as surplus supply, to influence price will, by default, lead to allocation-by-politics. The politics of jihad (them) and blood-for-oil (us) will prove to be a very unfavorable basis for allocating scarce-but-indispensable commodities."

Some analysts argue that Middle Eastern oil is a crucial strategic factor in the post-peak crisis (Foster 2008; Klare 2004; Phillips 2008). John Bellamy Foster asserts that the early twenty-first century is characterized by a rise in militarism from global economic elites' attempts to gain control over diminishing oil supplies. He cites the invasion of Iraq and the occupation of Afghanistan, the gateway to the Caspian Sea basin's oil and natural gas.

Foster (2008) and Michael Klare (2004) contend that key figures in the administration of President George W. Bush advocated an invasion of Iraq even before the attacks in the United States on September 11, 2001. Foster holds that by early 2001, the Bush administration, energy corporations, and U.S. national security and energy analysts believed that the world's light oil capacity threatened a series of oil-price shocks. The officials advocated military action to increase oil production in the Persian Gulf enough to avert the growth of a gap between oil production and demand over the following two decades. Increased oil production required a regime change in Iraq. Foster (2008: 1) warns of "a dangerous new era of energy imperialism."

Global Climate Change

The Intergovernmental Panel on Climate Change (IPCC) was established to assess scientific, technical, and socioeconomic information relevant to the potential impact of climate change and options for adaptation and mitigation. The

IPCC issued four assessment reports, in 1990, 1995, 2001, and 2007. The Synthesis Report summarizes the key findings of the Fourth Assessment Report (IPCC 2007a, 2007b).

The IPCC panelists found that, since 1970, the Earth's average temperature had risen by .8 degrees Celsius. In each decade since 1970, the rise in temperature was greater than the preceding one. Since recordkeeping began in 1880, the twenty-two warmest years have been since 1980, and the top warmest came after 1998 (IPCC 2007a). The evidence they assessed included observations of increases in global average air and ocean temperatures, the widespread melting of snow and ice, rising global average sea level, and surface ocean acidity. Calling the evidence for global warming unequivocal, the panelists concluded that a higher than 90 percent probability exists that increases in anthropogenic greenhouse gas emissions, led by fossil fuel combustion, explain most of the global warming of the past fifty years.

Greenhouse gas emissions have grown significantly above levels of 35,000 megatons (carbon dioxide equivalents) in 1990 to 45,000 megatons in 2004 (Netherlands Environmental Assessment Agency 2006). The output of carbon dioxide, the chief greenhouse gas, increased 3 percent between 2006 and 2007— higher even than the highest growth predicted in the IPCC's Fourth Assessment Report (Associated Press 2008e; IPCC 2007a).

Greenhouse gas emissions at or above current rates would induce larger climate changes during the twenty-first century than documented in the twentieth century (IPCC 2007a). The IPCC report estimates temperature increases by 1.8–4 degrees Celsius and a sea level rise of 18–59 centimeters. If continental ice sheets melt, the sea level will rise much higher.

The severity of climate change depends not only on the magnitude of the temperature increase but also on the potential for irreversibility. Susan Solomon and her colleagues (2009) show that climate change due to increases in the concentration of carbon dioxide will be largely irreversible for at least 1,000 years after the emissions entirely stop. They reason that, although halting greenhouse gas emissions would decrease radiative forces, the reduction would be largely canceled out by the slower loss of heat in the oceans. If atmospheric concentrations of carbon dioxide are increased instead of halted, irreversible reductions in rainfall in the dry seasons of several regions are likely to rival the "Dust Bowl" conditions in the United States in the 1930s. Thermal expansion of the ocean and melting glaciers and ice sheets could raise sea levels several meters over the next millennium.

The effects of higher global temperatures include diminished crop yields, melting snow and ice and rising seas, weather extremes, and wildlife loss. Higher temperatures diminish crop yields by reducing photosynthesis, preventing pollination, and dehydrating crops, particularly rice, wheat, corn, and soybeans. During the growing season, a temperature increase of 1–2 degrees Celsius shrinks the grain harvest in major food-producing regions. For example, record-high temperatures and drought in 2002 substantially reduced harvests in the major grain-producing nations of India, the United States, and Canada. World grain harvests that year consequently dropped by 90 million tons—5 percent below consumption (U.S. Department of Agriculture 2005).

Mountain snow and ice masses are nature's freshwater reservoirs, feeding rivers during summer dry seasons (Brown 2006: 66). A rise in temperature of 1 degree Celsius in mountainous regions reduces the portion of precipitation falling as snow and increases rainfall, causing flooding in rainy seasons and less snowmelt to feed rivers. Mountain reservoirs are frequently the primary source of irrigation and drinking water. Global climate models project a 70 percent reduction in the amount of snow pack for the western United States by midcentury (Brown 2006). The Himalayan snow-ice mass feeds all of the major rivers in Asia—the Indus, Ganges, Mekong, Yangtze, and Yellow—where half the world's people live. Increased rainfall and reduced snowfall in the Himalayas could affect the water supply of hundreds of millions of people (Yohe 2004).

Warmer temperatures would melt glaciers and continental ice sheets, contributing to sea level rise. Satellite data show accelerated melting of glaciers in the South American Andes, the Swiss Alps, and the French and Spanish Pyrenees (American Institute of Physics 2001). The Quelccaya ice cap in the Peruvian Andes is projected to disappear between 2010 and 2020. Eighty percent of South American glaciers are estimated to disappear within fifteen years (Hansen 2002). Kilimanjaro, Africa's tallest mountain, lost 33 percent of its ice field between 1989 and 2000 (The peak of Mt. Kilimanjaro 2005). The Arctic tundra, a carbon sink that holds an estimated 350 billion–450 billion tons of carbon dioxide, is warming twice as fast as the rest of the planet, releasing carbon dioxide and methane as it melts (Stokstad 2004). From 2005 to 2008, surface air temperatures in the central Arctic were more than 5 degrees Celsius above normal. Arctic sea ice is melting so rapidly that it is now estimated to disappear in thirty years, far earlier than the previously predicted end of the twenty-first century (Schmid 2009).

The continental Antarctic ice sheet covers an area twice the size of Australia and contains 70 percent of the world's freshwater resources. Ice shelves extend from the continent, formed by the flow of glacial ice to lower levels in the surrounding sea. The breakup of the outer fringe of ice shelves is a natural process that forms icebergs, but that process is now accelerated by warmer temperatures. Three enormous icebergs, one as large as Rhode Island, broke off from ice shelves in 1995, 2000, and 2002 (Shepherd 2003). Without ice shelves to slow glacial ice flow, accelerated flow could thin the edges of the continental ice sheet and contribute to sea level rise. The melting of the Greenland ice sheet could increase sea levels by 23 feet (Dahl-Jensen 2000; Harris and Goodwin 2003). Melting would also disrupt ocean circulation—particularly that of the Gulf Stream, which moderates the climate in western Europe, the northeastern United States, and eastern Canada (Harris and Goodwin 2003).

The IPCC (2007a) reported that, between 1961 and 2003, the global average sea level rose by 1.8 millimeters per year. Indicating the acceleration of the effects of higher temperatures on sea level, the rate of sea level rise between 1993 and

2003 was 3.1 millimeters per year (IPCC 2007a). Brown (2006) estimates that each 1 meter rise in sea level would reduce shorelines by nearly a mile. Half of Bangladesh's rice acreage would be inundated, forcing migration that would impose even greater hardships on that impoverished nation. More than a third of the city of Shanghai would be under water, and the United States would lose about 14,000 square miles of land in the Mid-Atlantic and Mississippi Gulf states (Gaffin 1997).

Global warming causes more frequent weather extremes, such as tropical storms, drought, and wildfires. Warmer surface water temperatures in tropical oceans radiate more energy into the atmosphere, causing more frequent and destructive tropical storm systems. The most vulnerable regions for extreme storms are the U.S. Atlantic and Gulf coasts, the Caribbean, and eastern and southeastern Asia (Harris and Goodwin 2003). In 1998, Hurricane Mitch struck the eastern coast of Central America, killing at least 11,000 people, demolishing infrastructure, and destroying 70 percent of the crops in Honduras (Brown 2006; Roberts and Parks 2007). Japan suffered a record ten typhoons in 2004, and four of the ten costliest hurricanes in U.S. history struck Florida in the same year (Roberts and Parks 2007). In 2005, Hurricane Katrina carried a storm surge of more than 20 feet that destroyed coastal towns, flooded New Orleans, and required thousands to evacuate. Droughts have worsened. The proportion of land surface experiencing very dry conditions expanded from less than 15 percent of the Earth's total land area in the 1970s to 30 percent in 2002 (National Center for Atmospheric Research 2005). The U.S. Forest Service estimates that an increase in summer temperatures by 1.6 degrees Celsius could double the area of wildfires in eleven western states (Brown 2006).

These conditions increase habitat destruction and endanger wildlife. A megastudy of forty scientific reports linking high temperatures and ecosystem changes found that spring began nearly two weeks early in the United States, tree swallows nested nine days earlier than they did forty years ago, red foxes encroached on the Arctic fox's range, and robins sang in Alaska (Parmesan and Galbraith 2004). The researchers estimate that continued climate change could extinguish more than 25 percent of all land animals and plants (Parmesan and Galbraith 2004).

Human health is directly affected by climate change. Heat waves killed 700 Chicagoans in 1995 (Klinenberg 2003), 1,000 residents of a single Indian state in 2002 (CNN 2002), and 49,000 Europeans in eight countries in 2003 (Larsen 2003). Disease will increase with warmer temperatures. As ground-level ozone increases, pulmonary and cardiovascular problems will rise. Worsened depletion of the stratospheric ozone will increase skin cancer, cataracts, and immune deficiencies. Disease-carrying insects forced to alter their ranges will appear where people have not developed immunity. Higher water temperatures and more frequent floods will cause sanitation facilities to fail more frequently, increasing the spread of infectious diseases such as cholera and diarrhea. Health problems will have a disproportionate impact on poor citizens of wealthy countries and on all citizens of poor countries.

Global Environmental Inequalities
and Government Corruption

International environmental treaties do not acknowledge ecological principles. Although they are more likely than U.S. policies to recognize the link between economic activities and the environment, they consistently defer to economic development, particularly in developing countries. Such deference sinks democratic aspirations. The consequence for developing nations is an unequal share of global environmental problems and associated illnesses, persistent underdevelopment, and a trend toward corrupt political systems.

Western Europeans and their descendants have dominated the world economy since the 1500s. Jared Diamond (1999) documents the environmental and random conditions that have favored Europeans over Asian, African, and South American civilizations. Western European dominance and wealth were achieved through the exploitation of other civilizations, generating a global stratification system that persists today—that is, countries of the Northern Hemisphere continue to exploit countries of the Southern Hemisphere. The South bears ecological scars from the North's ransacking, including depleted forests, soil, and fresh water and polluted land and water from organisms, military waste, hazardous waste received from developed countries, pesticides, and acid rain.

The disproportionate share of global environmental degradation borne by developing countries is reflected in an unequal burden of global environmental illnesses. A World Health Organization (WHO) study conducted in 2006 estimates the global burden of disease caused by environmental degradation (Prüss-Üstün and Corvalán 2006). It provides quantitative estimates of the effects of environmental factors on 102 major categories of disease and injury. Researchers quantified the deaths and diseases caused by conditions that can be rectified with technology and policies that are already available.

In southern countries, 25 percent of all deaths were attributed to environmental causes, compared with 17 percent in northern countries. Diseases with the largest burden attributable to rectifiable conditions were the following:

- *Diarrhea:* 94 percent of the diarrheal burden of disease was associated with unsafe drinking water, poor sanitation, and hygiene.
- *Lower respiratory infections:* 42 percent of infections in southern countries, compared with 20 percent in northern countries, were attributable to environmental factors such as outdoor and indoor air pollution, largely related to household solid fuel use and second-hand tobacco smoke.
- *Malaria:* 42 percent of malaria cases were attributable to environmental factors related to land use, deforestation, and water resource management.

The total number of healthy life years lost per capita due to rectifiable conditions was fifteen times higher in southern countries than in northern countries. The environmental burden per capita of diarrheal diseases and lower respiratory infections was 120–150 times greater in southern countries than in northern countries.

Children in southern countries lose eight times more healthy life years per capita than their counterparts in northern countries. In the most impoverished nations, the number of healthy life years lost to childhood lower respiratory infections is 800 times greater than in other areas, and for diarrheal diseases, the number is 140 times greater.

Northern countries urge southern countries to lift themselves out of such poverty and misery by following the same path to progress that secured the North's dominance. The gospel according to modernization theory holds that economic development produces democratic political systems and that industrialization inevitably brings prosperity; rational-legal administrative structures; and a democratic, pluralist-representative political system. Economic development is based on neoliberal principles of liberalizing trade and investment rules and privatizing public goods and services.

But practice proves the opposite. Neither development nor democracy has arrived. No opportunities remain for southern nations to use imperial expansion and colonization to gain wealth, as northern nations did. Southern nations are further hampered by the unequal interdependencies structured by colonial relationships, particularly the global division of labor. Northern nations retain decisive economic dominance because they control finance capital and terms of trade. They use the modernization model as justification for directing southern economic development in ways that further their own development at the cost of southern underdevelopment. The North distorts southern development by gearing it to meet northern needs for raw material and new markets. Rather than promoting reinvestment in domestic development, the specialization in raw material exports makes southern countries' economies responsive to global market demands. Wealth continues to flow from South to North, as in colonial times. Class formation in the South yields a small group of elites whose wealth is linked to northern foreign investors. The majority of the population remains land poor, uneducated, and impoverished.

Government corruption is perceived as such a barrier to economic growth in developing nations that in 2003 the United Nations adopted the Convention against Corruption, obliging its 148 signatories to implement anti-corruption measures (UN Convention against Corruption 2003: iii). As conditions that facilitate corruption, analysts identify extensive economic intervention by the government, governmental structures that are permeable to influence by economic elites, weak competition for political office, public officials' power to allocate resources, and substantial government control of information (Denoeux 2007; Heywood 1997; Jain 2001; Kaufmann 1998; Montinola and Jackman 2002; Morris 1991; Rose-Ackerman 2001; Shleifer and Vishny 1993; Wade 1985).

In a recent study of corruption in the Egyptian government, Hussein Soliman and I found that neoliberal reform in developing nations actually nurtures the conditions associated with high-level corruption (Soliman and Cable 2011). Neoliberal reform involves economic restructuring that alters the power relationship between state and corporation, reduces economic regulation by the government, increases privatization and foreign investment, and increases the size of the private sector. It forces the state to pursue economic growth, with the consequence that oppositional political candidates seldom win office. Captured by corporate interests, the state deregulates the economy, weakening, if not removing, mechanisms of political accountability. Diminished political accountability allows high-level corruption because citizens can neither obtain accurate information about elites' actions nor vote the rascals out.

The theme of the United Nations' celebration of International Anti-Corruption Day in 2009 was "Don't let corruption kill development" (UN Convention against Corruption 2009). In a press release in 2010, Secretary-General Ban Ki-moon said that corruption "distorts markets, curbs economic growth and discourages foreign investment." He urged global business leaders to denounce corruption, saying, "Preventing corruption makes good business sense."

The social institutions behind developing nations' unequal share of global environmental problems and associated illnesses, persistent underdevelopment, and corrupt political systems are transnational corporations, firms with central offices in one country and subsidiaries in other countries. Taken together, these corporations form a distinct, transnational economy that operates beyond public regulation or international rules. They pursue their own global strategic interests in search of profit, oblivious to the domestic goals of individual nations. Northern countries direct southern economic development through transnational corporations.

11

Sustaining Unsustainability

The Transnational Corporate State

Major obstacles to sustainable international environmental policies are transnational corporate power and deficiencies in the organizational infrastructure for international policymaking. In this chapter, I discuss each and then illustrate them with the example of policy efforts to address climate change.

Transnational Corporations:
Kings of the Petro-dependent Empire

The United States is the world's premier petro-dependent society, and its most significant export is the petro-dependent mode of subsistence, transmitted through corporations. With petro-dependency's globalization, corporate operations increasingly cross political boundaries to become transnational corporations (TNCs).

Transnational corporations are chartered in one nation with branch offices, operating divisions, and subsidiary companies conducting business throughout the globe. Global mobility allows them to move factories, sales rooms, and offices to any country without regard for domestic impacts. Mobility liberates corporations from governments' efforts to provide for the public good; releases corporations from pressure by unions for higher wages and safer working conditions; and empowers corporations to pursue the narrow goal of short-term financial gain. In a "market tyranny" (Korten 2001: 22) dominated by neoliberal tenets, TNCs reap unprecedented profits by locating production where wages and benefits are the lowest, labor unions are the most suppressed, and environmental regulations are the weakest.

The TNC is the organizational juggernaut directing the accelerated integration of global markets. Although globalization began with the fifteenth-century trading activities of corporations chartered by the crown, post–World War II globalization is a scheme designed by the war's victors to maintain power and avoid another Great Depression. Representatives of TNCs and powerful politicians have collaborated to erect an international governance system that values commercialism, corporate rights, and free trade.

The Petro-dependent Nurturing of the Transnational Corporation

At the Monetary and Financial Conference at Bretton Woods, New Hampshire, sponsored by the United Nations in 1944, leaders of forty-four nations sketched the blueprint for global economic growth, the integration of global markets, and the spread of petro-dependency. The meeting's purpose was to address the war's destruction of European economic infrastructure and the consequent rupture of stable trade arrangements. Attributing the Great Depression of the 1930s to high trade barriers and tariffs imposed by nations to protect their industries from foreign competition, the attendees identified increased trade between nations as the primary requisite of an international economy that would continue market expansion, enlarge sales and profits, and improve living standards.

Bretton Woods established the World Bank, the International Monetary Fund (IMF), and the General Agreement on Tariffs and Trade (GATT) as institutional guardians of globalization. The World Bank's purpose was to advance capital investment in the reconstruction of damaged European industries by promoting private foreign investment through guarantees and loans. The IMF's task was to promote international monetary cooperation to facilitate the expansion of international trade. GATT, an international trade organization formed to minimize barriers to international trade, was constructed as a multilateral trading system operating through a series of trade negotiations. Each round of GATT negotiations over the decades has resulted in freer flows of international trade. Although the Soviet Union sent delegates to Bretton Woods, tension between the Soviets and the Western nations heightened, and Soviet leaders withdrew from negotiations. The Bretton Woods institutions and agreements prioritized the interests of the United States and Britain over those of other nations (Korten 2001).

In 1948, confronted with western Europe's devastated economy and the Soviet-imposed isolation of communist eastern European nations, U.S. President Harry Truman signed the Economic Cooperation Act (Marshall Plan) with two purposes: to expedite European economic recovery and to stop the spread of communism. The Marshall Plan's European Recovery Program provided financial assistance to rebuild European nations, directing most of the military expenditures and funds for industrialization to Great Britain, France, Italy, and West Germany. The plan was highly profitable for the United States: an important market was restored, and international aid money purchased U.S. goods shipped to Europe in U.S. vessels.

The Marshall Plan required European nations to act as a single economic unit in the cooperative development of funding projects. To forge a "common market," leaders of Belgium, Germany, France, Italy, Luxembourg, and the Netherlands established the European Coal and Steel Community in 1951; it eliminated tariffs and trade quotas in coal and steel industries, imposed external tariffs on related imports, and placed controls on production and sales. The European Coal and Steel Community was succeeded in 1957 by the European Economic Community and in 1993 by the European Union. During these transitions, the common-market rules were increasingly extended beyond coal and steel to other economic sectors.

By the 1960s, many African, Asian, and Latin American countries had achieved independence from colonial rule. Nascent governments adopted the petro-dependent path in seeking economic growth to improve living standards. With western Europe's industrial infrastructure completely rebuilt, the World Bank moved its funding focus to newly independent nations in the global South. World Bank officers shaped the development projects, favoring large-scale, capital-intensive, and centralized projects that produced quantifiable economic returns over less quantifiable social and ecological benefits (Korten 2001).

Many nations failed to generate expected revenues, accumulating ever higher debt loads. The IMF began monitoring countries that were having difficulties with balances of payment, setting the precedent for later interventions. The OPEC nations invested their profits from the 1973–1974 oil crisis in Western banks. The World Bank and other international financial institutions used these petro-dollars to make further loans to nations whose debt loads were already high. Increasing oil prices and rising interest rates brought indebted nations closer to the brink of default. By 1982, Mexico faced defaulting on its loan payments to the IMF. World Bank officers intervened with loans.

But the money came with neoliberal strings—structural adjustment policies (SAPs). Through these programs, which demanded reduced expenditures and increased revenues, the U.S.-dominated World Bank and IMF forced debt-burdened countries to restructure their economies and open them to penetration by foreign TNCs (Korten 2001). SAPs drastically cut spending on social welfare, devalued national currencies, eliminated consumer subsidies on items such as gasoline and public transportation, eliminated barriers to imports from wealthy nations, lifted restrictions on foreign investment, and integrated southern economies more tightly into the northern-dominated world economy with a focus on export-based economic development (Shefner 2004). Commercialized agriculture imposed on debtor nations shifted production to consumable goods that could be sold on the world market. Debtor nations were frequently forced to import food that previously had been grown indigenously. Increased revenues from neoliberal changes were applied to debt payments.

Events in the late 1980s and 1990s further enhanced the economic dominance of TNCs. The disintegration of the Soviet Union and the democratic revolutions in eastern Europe secured the supremacy of neoliberal imperatives in a truly global economy (Korten 2001). Transnational corporations such as Coca-Cola, McDonald's, and Levi Strauss quickly expanded their markets into newly democratic countries.

International trade governance based on global economic expansion was embodied in the North American Free Trade Agreement (NAFTA) of 1994.

NAFTA created a trilateral trade bloc among the United States, Canada, and Mexico to eliminate barriers to trade and investment. Many tariffs were either eliminated immediately or phased out over periods of five to fifteen years. Public concern about the environmental consequences of NAFTA pushed the administration of President Bill Clinton to negotiate a side agreement with Canada and Mexico that led in 1994 to the creation of the Commission for Environmental Cooperation (CEC), whose mandate was to produce a focused and systematic body of evidence addressing environmental concerns. The CEC concluded that, although NAFTA did not present an inherent *systemic* environmental threat, *specific* threats occurred in areas where government environmental policy, infrastructure, or mechanisms were unprepared for the increased production scale of trade liberalization. The most serious increases in pollution related to NAFTA were in the base metals sector, the Mexican petroleum sector, and the transportation equipment sector in the United States and Mexico.

The World Trade Organization (WTO) replaced GATT in 1995 and remains the major multinational agreement on trade rules, policy, and dispute resolution. The WTO has 153 member countries (World Trade Organization 2012). But decision making is dominated by the United States, the European Union, Japan, and Canada (Bruno and Karliner 2002), where 75 percent of TNCs are based. Like NAFTA and GATT, the WTO is a powerful trade regime with enforceable rules. Frequently, TNCs are directly involved in writing and shaping WTO rules through national trade advisory committees (Bruno and Karliner 2002). Aided by SAPs, the WTO's rules have forced open developing nations' economies for a rapid escalation of corporate investment, particularly by oil, coal, and auto corporations.

The WTO uses economic sanctions and a secret dispute resolution process to subordinate environmental protection to corporate rights to trade and invest freely around the world (Wallach and Sforza 1999). The WTO's rules grant TNCs favored access to natural resources while weakening the abilities of national governments to protect resources (Bruno and Karliner 2002). The WTO has ruled every environmental policy it has reviewed an illegal trade barrier (Wallach and Sforza 1999).

The Power and Influence of Transnational Corporations

Corporations have mutated substantially from fifteenth-century corporate charters issued by states. They transformed from publicly accountable to unaccountable, from serving public purposes to pursuing profits for stockholders, and from being chartered by the state to directing state policies. Transnational corporations are now global enterprises, operating above national laws and affecting people from Wall Street to the poorest villages.

The power of TNCs derives from their sovereignty, prevalence, and size. Their national origins are usually obscure, resulting in less regulation and greater control. They operate as relatively independent units whose economic and political power exceeds that of many governments. Their freedom to manage cross-border flows of capital, labor, and technology renders geography and national identity practically irrelevant.

The prevalence of TNCs is demonstrated by their sheer numbers and geographic dispersion. In 1970, there were approximately 7,000 TNCs (French 2002). By 1990, 35,000 TNCs operated worldwide. The number has more than doubled since 1990, having reached 60,000 by 2002 (French 2002) and 75,000 by 2005 (Roach 2007). Firms are classified by country of the parent company, even if most business is conducted elsewhere. Approximately 73 percent have headquarters in developed economies (Roach 2007). Denmark hosts 12 percent of the world's TNCs, followed by South Korea, with 10 percent; Germany, with 8 percent; Japan, with 7 percent; and the United States, with 3 percent. Since the 1990s, the numerical growth in TNCs has been especially dramatic in developing countries, particularly in China, India, and Brazil. Between 1990 and 2005, the number of TNCs in developed countries increased by 66 percent, while the number in developing countries increased by more than 700 percent (Roach 2007).

But power remains with the petro-dependent leaders: a greater share of the largest TNCs have headquarters in the United States and Japan. Ranked by revenues in 2006, 34 percent of the world's 500 largest firms have headquarters in the United States (Roach 2007). Approximately 8 percent are located in developing countries, primarily China, Brazil, India, Malaysia, and Mexico. Transnational corporations account for more than 70 percent of world trade and at least 20 percent of total world production. In 2000, for example, the top 200 firms were equivalent to 27.5 percent of all world economic activity. Together, TNCs earn $15 trillion in annual sales (Hytrek and Zentgraf 2008).

Several approaches are used to rank TNCs by size, but the most common is by annual revenues, as is done with *Fortune* magazine's Global 500 list. In the 1990s, the ten largest firms in the world had collective revenues of $801 billion, greater than the revenues of the smallest one hundred nations taken together (Hawken 1993: 91–92). In 2005, the 500 largest firms by sales had combined revenues of about $19 trillion, amounting to more than $2,900 for every individual on the planet (Roach 2007). The world's fifty largest firms conducted one-third of the world's sales. The world's largest TNC in 2005 was Exxon Mobil, with sales of $340 billion (Roach 2007). Nine of the ten largest TNCs in the world in 2005 were either oil companies or automobile companies; Wal-Mart was the lone exception. In political and economic power, the largest TNCs resemble nations without boundaries. In fact, some advocates of world trade hail TNCs as the nations of the future.

Growth in revenue is not necessarily matched by comparable growth in employment. In the 1990s, the world's 500 largest companies controlled 25 percent of the world's gross output but employed only .05 percent of the world's population (Hawken 1993: 91–92). The top 200 TNCs in 2000 accounted for 27.5 percent of world economic activity but employed only .78 percent of the world's workforce (Hytrek and Zentgraf 2008). In 2002, TNCs on *Fortune*'s Global 500 list employed about 47 million people. But with a global labor force of more than 3 billion, that figure is only 1.6 percent of the world's labor force (Roach 2007). The world's fifty largest TNC employers collectively provide jobs for about 20 million people, less than 1 percent of the 3 billion global workforce (Roach 2007). Overall, between 1983 and 2005, the profits of the world's fifty largest TNCs increased by a factor of 11, while employment increased by a factor of 2.3 (Roach 2007).

Transnational corporations conduct lucrative business in nations with high corporate tax rates yet avoid paying taxes by maintaining headquarters in nations with low taxation. They sell products in one country that are banned in others for health or environmental reasons. Transnational corporations reduce risks and increase profits by acting as marketing companies, contracting with other companies for the actual production of goods—frequently with their own subsidiaries: "Almost half of what we call foreign trade actually involves transactions between different parts of the same company—between a domestic firm and its overseas subsidiaries or between a foreign firm and its domestic subsidiaries. In a geopolitical sense, this is foreign commerce. To the company, however, these international flows of goods and services are internal transfers" (Weidenbaum 2004: 26). Contracting for the production of goods leaves TNCs with little concern about resource extraction, workers' health and safety, and waste disposal.

Petro-dependency relies on TNCs as the tool for gaining food, clothing, and shelter from the biosphere. These private organizations with the rights of individuals marshal enormous economic and political resources to advance their narrow private agendas while protecting themselves from legal liability for the public consequences of their decisions. Petro-dependency was successfully exported to developing nations, but the benefits were not. Instead, a global stratification system emerged in which the political elites of developing countries cast their lot—and their nations' fates—with TNC elites. The consequence is an urbanized world in which production activities are shifted from industrialized, wealthy nations characterized by union labor and environmental policies to developing, impoverished nations characterized by cheap labor and few environmental protections. The world consists of two kinds of societies: those that are petro-dependent and those that have petro-dependency thrust on them.

The earlier analysis of the United States demonstrated that environmental policy is the political instrument of the corporate class and that the corporate class is no longer obliged to serve the public good. If TNCs are integral parts of a global economic and cultural system, how effective can national solutions for environmental problems be? Globalization processes have weakened environmental regulation and enforcement because they undermine the state's ability to pursue domestic economic development while restraining the state's attempts to maintain legitimacy through social programs that protect and benefit the public (Hytrek and Zentgraf 2008).

Transnational Corporation–United Nations Collaboration

Through five world conferences between 1972 and 2002, United Nations Environmental Programme (UNEP) member states negotiated 272 international environmental treaties and related instruments to produce a body of thirty multilateral global treaties that constitute current international environmental policies. But powerful TNCs countered these efforts by co-opting the concept of sustainability. The original meaning of sustainability employed by the United Nations emphasized meeting the needs of the present generation without compromising the ability of future generations to meet their needs. Distorting that meaning, TNCs propagate an interpretation of sustainability that serves their economic-expansionist interests and sucks the United Nations into collaboration.

The Hijacking of "Sustainable Development" by Transnational Corporations

Advocates of TNCs defined global corporate environmentalism through a series of strategy meetings that culminated in 1991 in the Second World Industry Conference on Environmental Management, sponsored by the International Chamber of Commerce (ICC). Attendees declared that "sustainable development" meant environmental protection through economic growth and created a Business Charter for Sustainable Development that asserted as a high corporate priority the nesting of environmental management within a free market setting. They claimed that resource conservation, pollution reduction, and elimination of poverty were possible without restricting corporations. More than 1,000 corporations signed the non-binding charter.

Transnational corporations were prominently represented at UNEP's first Earth Summit in 1992. The summit was financed by the Eco-Fund (created by the United Nations), which franchised rights to use the Earth Summit logo to TNCs such as Arco, 3M, and Mitsubishi (Harding, Kennedy, and Chatterjee 1992). UNEP leaders actively solicited advice in planning the conference from polluting corporations such as Royal Dutch Shell, Dow Chemical, Mitsubishi, Nike, Chevron, and DuPont. They declared at the summit that open markets were necessary prerequisites for achieving sustainable development and that corporations could be persuaded to comply *voluntarily* with environmental principles (Bruno and Karliner 2002: 22). The Earth Summit produced Agenda 21, a declaration stating that sustainable development is best promoted through trade liberalization. Kenny Bruno and Joshua Karliner (2002: 28) maintain that the summit "marked the coming of age of global corporate environmentalism, the melding of ecological and economic globalization into a coherent ideology that paved the way for TNCs to reconcile, in theory and rhetoric, their ubiquitous hunger for profits and growth with the stark realities of poverty and environmental destruction."

A consortium of corporate chief executives founded the World Business Council for Sustainable Development (WBCSD) and published a book in 1992 providing a global business perspective on development and the environment (Schmidheiny and World Business Council for Sustainable Development 1992). The book elaborates the conception of sustainable development promoted at the summit in 1992, stating that the fundamental prerequisite of sustainable development is freeing market forces to promote economic growth through open and competitive trade (Bruno and Karliner 2002: 26). It promotes pricing mechanisms that accurately reflect the environmental costs of production and advocates self-regulation as the most efficient method for transforming corporate practices.

The United Nations and the ICC issued a joint statement in 1998 urging increased cooperation between the United Nations and the private sector. The statement declared that the United Nations' goals of peace and development and corporate goals of creating wealth and prosperity were mutually supportive.

In 2000, UN Secretary-General Kofi Annan and the heads of fifty TNCs organized the Global Compact, in which corporate partners agreed to abide by nine environmental, labor, human rights, and anticorruption principles. Without rules for monitoring or enforcement, signees were required only to produce their own best practices case studies—their own selected, unverified examples detailing their methods for addressing one of the nine principles. The Global Compact consists of 7,700 participants: six UN agencies, representatives of 5,300 TNCs with headquarters in 130 countries, governments, labor groups, and civil society organizations.

Under Global Compact policies, participating TNCs are required to issue annual progress reports on implementation of the initiative's environmental, labor, human rights, and anticorruption principles. A de-listing policy was added in 2008, mandating that consecutive failures to submit annual progress reports result in the corporation's removal from the Global Compact database. But de-listed TNCs may rejoin the compact merely by sending a progress report and new commitment signed by the chief executive to the UN secretary-general. Between October 2009 and February 2010, 859 corporations were de-listed for failing to provide annual progress reports.

With the Global Compact, corporate accountability for the environmental consequences of production technology was ditched, and corporate responsibility was emphatically defined as *voluntary* responsibility.

Transnational Corporations in NGO Clothing

I conducted an empirical check of UN–corporate collaboration with an examination of NGO partners to a UN environmental convention. I chose a convention with a Global Plan of Action on the assumption that NGO partners would be especially active in the policy implementation stage. The Convention on the Law of the Sea has a Global Plan of Action for the Protection of the Marine Environment from Land-Based Activities. This plan obliges governments to take measures to prevent, reduce, and control pollution of the marine environment from land-based sources.

I obtained from the UN website the names of the twenty-eight NGOs listed as partners for the plan. I then searched the Internet for their websites. I could not locate sites for Foundation Hernandiana, Rio Systems, or Société pour Vaincre la Pollution/Society to Overcome Pollution (SVP/STOP). The URL for one partner, Department of Planet Earth, produced the message "Domain for sale by owner." From the websites for the remaining twenty-four NGOs, I analyzed mission statements, funding sources, and other descriptive materials to classify each one's priority as either environmental protection or industry promotion (see Appendix).

The classification of eight of thirteen NGOs that prioritize environmental protection was straightforward. The descriptive materials for four of them—the Center for International Environmental Law, Earth Action, Friends of the Earth, and the World Wide Fund for Nature—contained the words "just," "justice," or "poverty." The websites for three NGOs—the Environmental Defense Fund, the Cousteau Society, and the World Resources Institute—referred to "future generations." Greenpeace's website emphasized that funds from corporations were neither solicited nor accepted.

I classified four additional NGOs as environmental protectionist after further thought. The Advisory Committee on Protection of the Sea emphasized its nonpolitical nature. The Foundation for International Environmental Law and Development's website referred to "siding with the disadvantaged." The Woods Hole Oceanographic Institution's website described a mission of "research and higher education in ocean science to benefit society." The National Academy of Science presented strong statements on the credible scientific evidence for anthropogenic climate change, stressing that scientific understanding of anthropogenic climate change had become sufficiently clear to justify nations' taking prompt action (National Academy of Sciences 2005, 2007, 2008, 2009).

The final NGO classified as environmental protectionist is the International Union for Conservation of Nature (IUCN; formerly World Conservation Union). The IUCN works with a wide range of government, foundation, and corporate partners to "improv[e] corporate environmental performance" and "find pragmatic solutions" to environmental challenges in the areas of biodiversity, climate change, sustainable economies, and human well-being.

The classification of eight of eleven NGOs that prioritize industry promotion was also straightforward. Five NGOs—the Chlorine Institute, the European Chemical Industry Council, the European Crop Protection Association, the International Council of Chemical Associations, and the International Fertilizer Industry—claimed on their websites to represent industry. Two NGOs were self-proclaimed trade organizations: the American Crop Protection Association and the Chemical Manufacturers Association. The Chlorine Chemistry Council's website claimed to represent producers.

I classified another two NGOs as industry promoters after further thought. The website of the Environmental and Energy Study Institute referred to corporations as funders, among them Austin Energy, Coca-Cola, the Polyisocyanurate Insulation Manufacturers Association, and the American Forest and Paper Association. The website of the International Association of Ports and Harbors prominently listed the dollar amount of trade undertaken by members.

The remaining industry-promoting NGO required research. The International Council of Environmental Law (ICEL) claims to operate in the public interest to promote information exchange about the legal and policy aspects of conservation. After researching the listed funders to obtain further clues for accurate classification, I determined the ICEL to be an industry promoter.

My expectation that most NGO partners would prioritize environmental protection over industry promotion was proved wrong. NGO partners were almost evenly split on their priorities, with thirteen (54.2%) prioritizing environmental protection and eleven (45.8%) prioritizing industry promotion.

Efforts by the petrochemical industry to influence environmental policy are apparent: nine of eleven industry-promoting NGO partners are producers or major users of petrochemical products. Three NGOs represent pesticide producers; three represent pesticide and plastic producers; and two represent producers of pesticides, plastics, and chlorinated solvents. One NGO represents world ports—an enormous consumer of petrochemical products. Of the remaining two NGO industry promoters, one has ties to a large global corporation—the Tengelmann Group—and a second receives substantial corporate funding.

The language used by environmental protectors differed considerably from that used by most industry promoters. Environmental protectors employed words and phrases such as "just," "justice," "progressive," "disadvantaged," "poverty," "poor," "people of color," "public interest," "future generations," "sustainable societies," "accountability," "empower," and "equitable." In contrast, most industry promoters used the phrases "sound science," "dollar value," "number of workers," "rational laws," "sustainable development," and "voluntary mechanisms."

Direct comparisons of phrasing are particularly striking. Environmental protectors used "sustainable societies," while industry promoters used "sustainable development"; environmental protectors used "accountability," compared with industry promoters' "voluntary mechanisms"; and environmental protectors referred to "equitable" laws, while industry promoters referred to "rational" laws. The industry-promoting NGOs I had trouble classifying tended to use language that subtly suggested grassroots environmental organizations, such as "nonprofit," "democratic," "serve the public," and "education."

My analysis of NGOs' self-presentations on the Internet indicates that the United Nations Environmental Programme (UNEP) actively seeks collaboration with TNCs as well as environmental protection organizations. Consequently, UNEP is pulled by NGOs in opposite directions—toward more and toward less corporate regulation—and is pressured by the United Nations not to hinder the agency's project of promoting economic growth in developing countries. These forces likely play substantial roles in the production of treaties that defer to growth initiatives.

International Court of Justice

Analysis of obstacles to sustainable environmental policies in the United States showed that the judiciary system frequently supports corporate interests over environmental protection. Does the same hold true for international environmental policies? To address the question, I researched the International Court of Justice (ICJ), the principal judicial organ of the United Nations. Established in

1945 by the UN Charter, the ICJ is seated in The Hague, Netherlands, and is composed of fifteen judges elected for nine-year terms by the UN General Assembly and the Security Council.

The ICJ's task is to apply international laws in two types of cases. Advisory proceedings derive from requests for opinions on legal questions by five UN organs and sixteen specialized UN agencies. Unlike the ICJ's judgments, advisory proceedings have no binding effect.

Contentious cases consist of legal disputes between states that are submitted to the ICJ by one or the other party for adjudication. The ICJ's jurisdiction is mandatory under two conditions. The first is when each party files a declaration with the United Nations accepting the court's jurisdiction as compulsory in disputes in which one state challenges another state's actions as illegal. The second condition is when disputing states, unable to resolve an issue, file a Special Agreement granting the ICJ jurisdiction and requesting its resolution of the dispute. In other cases, the court decides whether its jurisdiction is justified, such as when parties have signed a bilateral treaty containing a jurisdictional provision for disagreements over the interpretation or application of the treaty.

Once jurisdiction is established, the judges determine specific international laws that are applicable in the case. They hold public hearings in which each party presents its case, deliberate, and then issue rulings.

The ICJ does not have enforcement powers. If the losing party is noncompliant, the court can recommend enforcement to the UN Security Council, whose members approve or veto resolutions on enforcement. No alternative method exists for forcing compliance with a judgment. The most prevalent form of noncompliance is refusal to participate in ICJ proceedings, which typically occurs in highly political cases (Schulte 2004).

I examined contentious cases in which the applicable international law was an environmental convention, collecting information from "Summaries of Judgments, Advisory Opinions, and Orders of the International Court of Justice" (see Table 11.1 for summaries of information and specific websites). Between 1947 and 2010, 119 contentious cases were filed with the ICJ. Ten cases (8.4%) related to environmental issues. All of the disputes focused on oil or fisheries.

In two cases, the ICJ ruled that it did not have jurisdiction because one party's declaration of acceptance of the court's compulsory jurisdiction contained a reservation limiting jurisdiction. In the *United Kingdom v. Iran* (1952), the United Kingdom acted on behalf of the Anglo-Iranian Oil Company to charge that Iran's nationalization of the oil industry in 1951 violated an agreement between the government of Iran and the Anglo-Iranian Oil Company from 1933. Both governments had filed declarations, but the ICJ ruled that Iran's reservations limited the court's jurisdiction to disputes related to treaties and conventions accepted by Iran *subsequent* to the declaration.

In *Spain v. Canada* (1998), Spain challenged Canada's seizure of a Spanish ship, charging that Canada had no right to act on the high seas against Spanish vessels and that Canadian fisheries legislation could not be invoked against Spanish vessels. Although both parties had previously filed declarations, Canada's new declaration, filed in 1994, contained a reservation excluding from ICJ jurisdiction disputes over Canadian conservation and management in the Northwest Atlantic Fisheries Organization Regulatory Area, as defined in the Convention on Future Multilateral Cooperation of 1978. In 1995, the Canadian government seized a Spanish fishing vessel on charges of violating the nation's Coastal Fisheries Protection Act by fishing for Greenland halibut. The ICJ ruled that Canada's reservation exempted the dispute from its jurisdiction.

Thus, the ICJ established jurisdiction in eight environmental cases. The basis for jurisdiction in four cases was reciprocity of declarations of acceptance of the court's compulsory jurisdiction—one party challenged another's actions as illegal. Special Agreements between the disputing parties were the basis in three cases; they were unable to resolve the dispute, and the parties requested the ICJ's intervention. In the eighth case, the basis for jurisdiction was prior agreements between the parties. The Law of the Sea was the international law applied in all eight cases.

In two cases adjudicated together in 1974, the applied laws were the Convention on the High Seas of 1958, a product of the First Conference on the Law of the Sea in the same year, and the Second Conference on the Law of the Sea of 1960. *United Kingdom v. Iceland* (1974) and *Federal Republic of Germany v. Iceland* (1974) derived from the Cod Wars. In 1972, Iceland notified the United Kingdom of its intention to extend exclusive fishing rights to 50 miles. As previously agreed between the nations, the United Kingdom referred the matter to the ICJ. The Federal Republic of Germany separately filed the same charges. Iceland contested the court's jurisdiction and did not participate in the proceedings. The ICJ applied the rules of the Convention on the High Seas of 1958, interpreting freedom of the high seas as freedom exercised by states with reasonable regard for other states' exercise of that freedom. The court observed that the Second Conference on the Law of the Sea (1960) accepted a 12 mile exclusive zone and introduced flexibility to allow preferential fishing rights for a coastal state that is especially dependent on fisheries. The ICJ ruled that Iceland was exceptionally dependent on fisheries but that Iceland's preferential fishing rights must be reconciled with the United Kingdom's and Germany's traditional fishing rights. The judges ruled that Iceland could not unilaterally extend its exclusive fishing rights and held that the parties were "under mutual obligations to undertake negotiations in good faith for an equitable solution of their differences" (International Court of Justice 1974: 92).

The aim of the Third Conference on the Law of the Sea in 1973 was to produce a comprehensive convention. Negotiations took place from 1973 to 1982, when the Convention on the Law of the Sea was concluded. It emphasized taking into account equitable principles and special circumstances. Although the convention did not come into force until 1994, the ICJ applied the new emphases in cases adjudicated in 1982, 1984, and 1985.

In the first case, *Tunisia v. Libya* (1982), Tunisia and Libya were unable to resolve a dispute over the areas of the continental shelf that belonged to each. With oil wells at stake, the parties signed a Special Agreement, requesting that the ICJ state the rules of applicable international laws and the practical methods for

TABLE 11.1 Contentious Environmental Cases before the International Court of Justice

Year	Case	Dispute	Jurisdiction	Relevant international environmental law	Judgment
1952	Anglo-Iranian Oil Company (*United Kingdom v. Iran*) http://www.icj-cij.org/docket/files/16/1999.pdf	Oil: United Kingdom challenged Iran's nationalization of oil industry	No jurisdiction; Iran's declaration contained reservation limiting court's jurisdiction	N/A	N/A
1974	Fisheries jurisdiction (*United Kingdom v. Iceland*) http://www.icj-cij.org/docket/files/55/5979.pdf	Fisheries: United Kingdom challenged Iceland's extension of fishing rights on the continental shelf as illegal	Declarations; Iceland contested jurisdiction and did not participate	1960 Second Conference on the Law of the Sea, 1958 Convention on the High Seas	Parties under mutual obligations to undertake negotiations.
1974	Fisheries jurisdiction (*Federal Republic of Germany v. Iceland*) http://www.icj-cij.org/docket/files/56/6003.pdf	Fisheries: West Germany challenged Iceland's extension of fishing rights on the continental shelf as illegal	Declarations; Iceland contested jurisdiction and did not participate	1960 Second Conference on the Law of the Sea, 1958 Convention on the High Seas	Parties under mutual obligations to undertake negotiations.
1982	The continental shelf (*Tunisia v. Libya*) http://www.icj-cij.org/docket/files/63/6269.pdf	Oil: Parties requested that court resolve dispute over territory on the continental shelf	Special Agreement between the parties	1958 Convention on the Continental Shelf; trends at the 1973 Third Conference on the Law of the Sea	Court specified laws and methods; did not set boundaries. Parties obligated to negotiate treaty.
1984	Delimitation of the maritime boundary in the Gulf of Maine area (*Canada v. United States*) http://www.icj-cij.org/docket/files/67/6371.pdf	Fish and oil: Parties requested that Court resolve dispute over territory on the continental shelf	Special Agreement between the parties	1958 Convention on the Continental Shelf; trends at the 1973 Third Conference on the Law of the Sea	Court set the boundaries.

Year	Case	Dispute	Basis of jurisdiction	Law applied	Outcome
1985	The continental shelf (*Libya v. Malta*) http://www.icj-cij.org/docket/files/68/6417.pdf	Oil: Parties requested that Court resolve dispute over territory on the continental shelf	Special Agreement between the parties	1982 Convention on the Law of the Sea	Court specified laws and methods; did not set boundaries. Parties obligated to negotiate treaty.
1998	Fisheries jurisdiction (*Spain v. Canada*) http://www.icj-cij.org/docket/files/96/7535.pdf	Fisheries: Spain challenged Canada's seizure of Spanish ship as illegal	No jurisdiction; Canada's declaration contained reservation limiting court's jurisdiction	N/A	N/A
2001	Maritime delimitation and territorial questions between Qatar and Bahrain (*Qatar v. Bahrain*) http://www.icj-cij.org/docket/files/87/7029.pdf	Oil: Qatar challenged Bahrain's claim to sovereignty over land and water as illegal	Two prior agreements between the parties	1982 Convention on the Law of the Sea	Court set the boundaries and decided sovereignty.
2007	Land and maritime boundary between Cameroon and Nigeria (*Cameroon v. Nigeria*) http://www.icj-cij.org/docket/files/120/14077.pdf	Oil: Cameroon challenged Nigeria's claim to sovereignty over land and water as illegal	Declarations	1982 Convention on the Law of the Sea	Court set the boundaries and decided sovereignty.
2007	Territorial and maritime dispute between Nicaragua and Honduras in the Caribbean Sea (*Nicaragua v. Honduras*) http://www.icj-cij.org/docket/files/120/14077.pdf	Fisheries: Nicaragua challenged Honduras's claim to sovereignty over land and water as illegal	Declarations	1982 Convention on the Law of the Sea	Court set the boundaries and decided sovereignty.

Source: International Court of Justice, Summaries of Judgments, Advisory Opinions and Orders of the International Court of Justice, available online at www.icj-cij.org.

the law's applications for delimiting each country's areas of the continental shelf. The parties did not request that the court determine the boundary line; they requested only that it clarify matters so that experts of the two countries could delimit the areas without difficulty. The ICJ declared the Convention on the Continental Shelf of 1958 as the applicable law and identified as the method for its application the conventional delimitation formula: in the absence of agreement or special circumstances, the boundary for opposite coasts is the median line, and for adjacent coasts, the boundary is the lateral equidistance line. Consistent with the newly accepted trends apparent at the Third Conference on the Law of the Sea, the ICJ indicated that delimitation should take into account equitable principles and the relevant circumstances characterizing the area. The court specified in detail the methods for setting the boundary, identified the relevant circumstances, and ruled that the parties were obligated to negotiate a treaty establishing the boundary line.

The second case in which the ICJ applied newly accepted trends was an unresolved dispute between the United States and Canada over maritime boundaries on the continental shelf in the Gulf of Maine (*Canada v. United States*[1984]), which contained fisheries and oil reserves. The parties signed a Special Agreement and requested that the ICJ determine the boundary line by deciding the laws to be applied and practical methods for the law's applications. The court declared the Convention on the Continental Shelf and the newly accepted trends as the applicable laws, identified the relevant circumstances, and determined a single maritime boundary defined by latitude and longitude, judging it equitable.

In the third case brought to the ICJ before the convention entered into force, *Libya v. Malta* (1985), the parties had signed a Special Agreement and requested that the ICJ determine the boundary line by deciding applicable laws and practical methods for the laws' applications to the delimitation of the areas of the continental shelf belonging to each country. The court cited the convention of 1982 as the applicable law because both parties were signatories. It specified in detail the methods and relevant circumstances for setting an equitable boundary and ruled that the parties were obligated to negotiate a treaty.

When the Convention on the Law of the Sea came into force in 1994, the new trends were formalized: delimitation must be in accordance with equitable principles and take into account all relevant circumstances to arrive at an equitable result. The case summary of *Qatar v. Bahrain* (2001) explained this "equidistant/special circumstances" method: "The most logical and widely practised approach is first to draw provisionally an equidistance line and then to consider whether that line must be adjusted in the light of the existence of special circumstances" (International Court of Justice 2001: 171).

Three cases came to the ICJ after the Convention on the Law of the Sea of 1982 entered into force in 1994. In *Qatar v. Bahrain* (2001), Qatar challenged as illegal Bahrain's claimed sovereignty over certain islands and shoals. The court noted the complexity of the case because of the long history of British control in the area and the presence of oil reserves. In 1946, the Bahrain Petroleum Company had sought permission to drill in certain areas of the continental shelf that

British officials thought might belong to Qatar. The officials contended that permission could not be granted until they established the seabed boundary between the two countries. The boundary and sovereign rights were established by the British in 1947. Qatar and Bahrain ceased to be British protected states in 1971 and were admitted to the United Nations. Qatar contested the boundaries set by the British. Negotiations between the parties from 1976 to 1991 failed to resolve the issue. Qatar instituted proceedings to have the ICJ decide applicable laws and practical methods for the laws' applications for the delimitation of the areas of the seabed belonging to each country. The court declared the Convention of the Law of the Sea of 1982 as the applicable law, specified in detail the methods and relevant circumstances for setting an equitable boundary, set the boundaries, and assigned sovereignty.

In *Cameroon v. Nigeria* (2007), Cameroon challenged as illegal Nigeria's placement of military and police forces in an area considered under Cameroonian sovereignty. Cameroon requested that the ICJ determine the course of the maritime boundary between the states and specify the frontier between them from Lake Chad to the sea. The court handled the land and maritime boundary disputes separately because different international laws applied. For the maritime boundary dispute, the ICJ declared as applicable the Convention of the Law of the Sea of 1982. Both parties had ratified the convention, obliging them to negotiate in good faith with a view to agreeing on an equitable delimitation of their maritime zones. In identifying relevant circumstances, the court decided that oil wells are not relevant. Its judgment fixed the maritime boundaries between the parties.

In *Nicaragua v. Honduras* (2007), Nicaragua challenged Honduras's claim to sovereignty over certain cays in the Caribbean Sea and requested that the ICJ determine the maritime boundary. In 1977, Nicaragua had initiated negotiations with Honduras on matters relating to the maritime boundary in the Caribbean. The negotiations made no progress, and relations between the countries deteriorated, with several incidents involving attacks on each other's fishing vessels. Nicaragua asked the court to determine the course of the single maritime boundary between the areas of territorial sea, continental shelf, and exclusive economic zone in the Caribbean Sea belonging to each party. The ICJ declared as applicable law the Convention on the Law of the Sea of 1982, determined that the equitable principles and relevant circumstances method of delimitation was not feasible, and justified application of the bisector method because of the geographical configuration of the coast and the area's geo-morphological features. The bisector is the line formed by bisecting the angle created by the linear approximations of coastlines. The court set the boundary and determined sovereignty.

The Transnational Corporate State

The institution that most approximates international government, the United Nations, cautiously navigates between the rock of economic development and the hard place of environmental protection.

The United States and its wartime allies orchestrated the vulnerability of the United Nations to domination by transnational corporations from its beginning. The proposal in 1944 to form the United Nations was adopted by representatives of four of the eventual five permanent members of the UN Security Council: the United States, the United Kingdom, the Republic of China, the Soviet Union, and France. The General Assembly was created on a one-country, one-vote basis. But the Security Council granted itself control of all vital international issues and halts attempted power shifts with a veto system that requires only one permanent member's veto (Bennis 2000). The World Bank and the IMF, initially designated as specialized UN agencies accountable to the General Assembly, operate without any UN oversight (Bennis 2000). The ICJ, established in 1945 by the UN Charter, lacks enforcement authority for international environmental statutes. Because enforcement power rests with the Security Council, resolutions of enforcement against one of the permanent members—and its allies du jour—are routinely vetoed.

Created in the interests of petro-dependent powers, the United Nations never gained independence in international policymaking. As corporations increasingly transcended national borders, they insinuated themselves more deeply into the United Nations, infusing the cooperative organization with the ideology of corporate environmentalism through the Global Compact and the United Nations' acceptance of industry-sponsored groups as NGO partners in policy implementation. Collaboration between TNCs and the United Nations is now so seamless that the two entities together may be treated analytically as a transnational corporate state. This de facto international government, which neither claims the title nor promotes democratic decision making (Paehlke 2004), is legitimized by the blue-and-white wrapping of the UN flag.

The Transnational Corporate State and Climate Change Politics

As an illustration, I apply the concept of the TNC state to climate change politics. I examine negotiations on climate change policy and the vitriolic responses of the naysayers—the climate change deniers. The facts illuminate the abiding split between developed and developing countries. (See Table 11.2 for a chronology of climate change politics.)

International Negotiations on Climate Change Policy

The UN Framework Convention on Climate Change (UNFCCC) of 1992 obliged developed countries to stabilize their emissions of greenhouse gas at 1990 levels by 2000. Member states debated the nature of those commitments in their negotiations. European Union member states, small island states, and environmental NGOs argued for binding targets and timetables to reduce emissions. But the United States, the top emitter in 1990 (Betsill and Corell 2008), was supported by Japan, Canada, Australia, and New Zealand in rejecting binding targets and

TABLE 11.2 Chronology of Climate Change Politics

Year	Event
1988	United Nations created International Panel on Climate Change (IPCC).
1990	First IPCC assessment report: Human activities are increasing atmospheric concentration of greenhouse gases but unequivocal evidence of global warming unlikely for a decade
1992	Member states sign UN Framework Convention on Climate Change to stabilize greenhouse gas emissions
1992	Supplementary Report of the IPCC
1995	Second IPCC assessment report: Greenhouse gas concentrations continue to increase, climate has changed in twentieth century but not since 1990
1995	COP-1 Berlin Mandate: Commitments in convention are insufficient to meet long-term goals, agree to negotiate protocol by 1997 with quantified and binding targets for reducing greenhouse gas emissions by developed nations after 2000; no such commitments for developing nations.
1997	COP-2 and COP-3: Negotiations that produce 1997 Kyoto Protocol requires developed countries to reduce their aggregate greenhouse gas emissions to 5.6 percent below 1990 levels by 2012
1998–2000	COP-4, COP-5, and COP-6: Seeking ratification of the Kyoto Protocol
2001	COP-6b and COP-7: Bonn Agreement and Marrakesh Accords finalize implementation rules of the Kyoto Protocol
2001	Third IPCC assessment report: Based on more data than previous reports, report finds that most global warming of the prior fifty years was attributable to human activities
2002–2004	COP-8, COP-9, and COP-10: Focus on ratification of Kyoto Protocol
2005	Kyoto Protocol enters into force. COP-11: Marrakesh Accords formally adopted as rulebook for Kyoto Protocol
2006	COP-12 and forty-five workshops are held on issues related to specific articles in Kyoto Protocol
2006	Fourth IPCC assessment report: Declares that evidence for global warming is now unequivocal and that continued warming will occur for more than a millennium
2007	COP-13: Attendees recognize that growth in carbon emissions in next decades will likely occur in developing countries.
	Bali Road Map: To overcome U.S. resistance, member states agree to follow two paths of negotiation simultaneously—one for the Kyoto Protocol and the second for nations not committed to mandatory emissions limits. Agree to complete negotiations by 2009, ahead of the 2012 expiration of the Kyoto Protocol
2008	COP-14: Member states commit to full negotiating mode in 2009 in preparation for COP-15
2009	COP-15: No agreement
2010	Climate change denial; "Climate-gate"
2010	COP-16 in Mexico City, November 29–December 10

timetables, arguing that they were premature because significant uncertainties remained about whether climate change was actually anthropogenic. Member states consequently requested an update from the Intergovernmental Panel on Climate Change (IPCC) on the scientific evidence of climate change. The panel's Supplementary Report of 1992 concluded that research conducted since the First Assessment Report in 1990 either confirmed the report's major conclusions or did not justify their alteration.

The final negotiated convention did not specify binding targets and timetables for stabilizing gases. It stipulated that developed countries enact national policies to limit anthropogenic greenhouse gas emissions and enhance the capacity of carbon sinks such as forests that absorb more carbon than they release. Developed countries were also obligated to provide financial support for developing countries to enable them to fulfill the terms of the convention.

The IPCC's Second Assessment Report, in 1995, stated that the balance of scientific evidence suggested a discernible human influence on global climate. The report emphasized that continued climate change is expected.

At the first Conference of the Parties (COP-1) on climate change in 1995, the majority of participants agreed that the convention's commitments were insufficient to meet long-term objectives. They adopted the Berlin Mandate, requiring parties to negotiate a protocol for implementing the convention by 1997 that contained quantified and binding targets on developed countries for reducing greenhouse gas emissions after 2000. The mandate stated that the protocol would not contain such commitments for developing nations.

The protocol was negotiated in 1997 at COP-2 in Geneva and COP-3 in Kyoto. Heated debate centered on four issues: the developed nations that would be obliged to reduce greenhouse gas emissions, developing countries' role in reducing emissions, the size of emissions reductions, and the methods for achieving reductions. Participants added an unprecedented extra day to the conference and finally reached agreement on the protocol text in the last hours.

The Kyoto Protocol required developed countries to reduce their aggregate greenhouse gas emissions to 5.2 percent below 1990 levels by 2012, when the protocol would expire. Delegates of nearly forty developed countries signed the protocol; the U.S. delegate did not sign. Each signatory agreed to an individual reduction target, ranging from an 8 percent decrease for European Union member states to a 10 percent *increase* in emissions for Australia and Iceland. The protocol established three market-based mechanisms to aid countries with emissions targets and to encourage the private sector and developing countries to contribute to reduction. The first mechanism, emissions trading, allowed countries with extra emissions units—emissions allocated but not used—to sell units to countries that exceeded their targets. Under the second mechanism, clean development, developed countries earned emissions allowances by investing in "sustainable development" projects in developing countries. Developed countries committed to fund the clean development mechanism with more than $13 million in 2006–2007. Some funds were allocated to an adjustment assistance program to support developing countries' adaptation to climate changes. The third mechanism, joint implementation, allowed a developed country to earn emissions reduction units from an emissions-reduction or removal project in a developing country. But the protocol offered neither rules nor operational details on using the mechanisms. When ratification by developed countries appeared unlikely until the rules were substantially clarified, the participants launched a second phase of negotiations.

The IPCC issued the Third Assessment Report in 2001. It cited a significantly larger data set than the second report and provided a clearer picture of warming and other climate changes. Data documented that, during the previous four decades, temperatures had risen in the atmosphere's lowest 8 kilometers and that snow cover and ice had decreased. New and more robust evidence indicated that most of the warming observed over the previous fifty years was attributable to human activities. Substantially improved computer models indicated that human activities would continue to change atmospheric composition throughout the twenty-first century and that the average global temperature and sea level would rise.

Participants negotiated implementation rules at COP-6b and COP-7, finalizing the rules in the Marrakesh Accords of 2001. Annual COPs held between 2002 and 2004 focused on ratification. The protocol entered into force in February 2005. But continued debate stalled implementation until COP-11, which attracted unprecedented corporate interest because of the emissions trading and clean development mechanisms The Marrakesh Accords were formally adopted as the rulebook for the Kyoto Protocol. COP-11 closed with the adoption of more than forty agreements to strengthen global efforts to reduce climate change. For example, the process for methodologies under the clean development mechanism was simplified and its governing body was strengthened, and a separate governing body was established for the joint implementation mechanism. A new working group was formed to discuss commitments for developed countries after 2012.

In 2006, forty-six meetings on the Kyoto Protocol were held. Besides COP-12 in Nairobi, workshops were offered on specific articles in the protocol related to land use, regional issues, and best practices. Group meetings occurred, such as the Transfer of Technology Consultative Process, the Consultative Group of Experts on National Communications, and sessions of the subsidiary bodies.

Also in 2006, the IPCC issued the Fourth Assessment Report. The panelists declared that the evidence for global warming was unequivocal and that most of the observed increase in globally averaged temperatures since the mid-twentieth century was very likely due to increased concentrations of anthropogenic greenhouse gas. They calculated the probability that warming was caused by natural climatic processes alone at less than 5 percent. They reported that anthropogenic warming and sea level rise would continue for centuries, even if greenhouse gas concentrations were immediately stabilized. The panelists predicted that world temperatures would rise by 2–11.5 degrees Fahrenheit during the twenty-first century; sea levels would rise 18–59 centimeters; and more frequent warm spells, heat waves, and heavy rainfall would be likely, with a confidence level of more than 90 percent. Increased droughts, tropical cyclones, and extreme high tides are likely, with a confidence level higher than 66 percent. Past and future anthropogenic carbon dioxide emissions will continue to contribute to warming and sea level rise for more than a millennium.

COP-13, held in Bali in 2007, proved to be a crucial conference. Observers and delegates reported more acrimony than at any other climate change conference. Continuing clashes centered on the impact of industrialization and economic growth in Asia because, although the United States and Europe are largely responsible for current concentrations of atmospheric carbon dioxide, growth in future emissions will be driven largely by developing countries. The U.S. delegate emphasized concerns about the limited steps required of emerging economic powers in Asia. Under pressure, delegates from China and other emerging powers agreed for the first time to seek ways to reduce emissions voluntarily, rejecting mandatory restrictions for the indefinite future.

The United States compromised by agreeing to pursue a new protocol to take effect in 2012 when the Kyoto Protocol expires. European Union member states proposed that negotiations proceed on two tracks: one for countries that are not committing to mandatory limits, such as the United States, and a second that builds on the Kyoto Protocol. When it appeared that talks would break down, the U.S. delegate agreed to two tracks. Participants adopted the Bali Action Plan, which did not contain the binding commitments that European nations sought and that the United States opposed. But the plan charted the course for new negotiations aimed at completing the process by 2009, and it provided a timetable for shaping the first formal addendum to the UNFCCC treaty of 1992 since the Kyoto Protocol ten years earlier.

In December 2008, COP-14 concluded in Poznań, Poland, with a commitment to shift into full negotiating mode in 2009. Progress was made on issues that are particularly important to developing countries, including finance, technology, reducing emissions from deforestation and forest degradation, and disaster management. Meetings in 2009 were based on the Bali Action Plan and aimed directly at shaping an effective international response to climate change to be agreed on at COP-15, held in Copenhagen in December 2009.

COP-15 drew representatives of 192 nations and 115 heads of government with the goal of agreement on a replacement protocol for implementation of the convention of 1992. Officials of the UN Global Compact ensured that the interests of TNCs were represented. More than 300 business representatives met in Copenhagen before COP-15 to discuss "the business role in achieving a fair, balanced and ambitious global climate treaty" (Stausberg 2009). They were welcomed with a videotaped message from former U.S. President Bill Clinton: "The business leaders brought together by the Copenhagen Climate Council and the UN Global Compact are key to whether we actually solve this crisis. There can be no effective response to the climate problem without business innovation, investment, and low-carbon technology and processes" (quoted in Stausberg 2009).

On December 14, negotiations were delayed for five hours by African delegates' accusations that rich countries were doing too little to cut greenhouse gas emissions. The protests ended, but debate continued in negotiations. Developing nations favored extending the Kyoto Protocol for developed countries while devising a new, separate plan for poor developing countries. Developed nations preferred to merge the Kyoto Protocol into a single new accord that obliged all nations to reduce greenhouse gas emissions. As reported in the *Earth Negotiations Bulletin* (International Institute for Sustainable Development 2010), many developed nations favored a single track because they feared signing a binding agreement while the United States, not a signatory, slipped by with a less strict regime.

The United States, Canada, Japan, Australia, New Zealand, and the Russian Federation consistently opposed a legally binding agreement, while the European Union favored one. The U.S. position was to reject a binding commitment without the inclusion of developing economies such as China. But developing countries refused to reduce their carbon emissions unless developed countries financed their emissions technologies, provided compensation for reduced deforestation, and implemented adaptation measures against rising sea levels and extreme weather events.

COP-15 failed to resolve the conflicts between developed and developing nations and to produce a new, legally binding agreement to replace the Kyoto Protocol. A last-minute closed-door session was led by the U.S. delegation and President Barack Obama; the only developing nations represented were China, India, and Saudi Arabia. This small group devised the Copenhagen Accord, a minimalist framework agreement that advocated a deadline at the end of 2010 for transforming the text of the accord into a legally binding text; set a target to limit global warming to 2 degrees Celsius over pre-industrial times; promised $100 billion in annual aid to developing nations without identifying the source of the aid; and set a deadline of January 31, 2011, for submitting national emissions reduction plans to the United Nations. This relatively weak plan also failed to win consensus support. Instead, the records simply "noted" the Copenhagen Accord.

Many were discouraged by COP-15's failure. Christopher Flavin of the WorldWatch Institute concluded that the failure signaled a limited role for future international negotiations on climate. Progress on climate change, he argued, "will be driven more by domestic economics and politics . . . than [by] the international negotiating process" (Flavin 2009). Alden Meyer of the Union of Concerned Scientists observed that the way the accord was negotiated created considerable uncertainty about where future negotiations would occur: "It remains to be seen whether elaboration of the Accord takes place under the auspices of the UN process, through other multilateral processes such as the Major Economies Forum (MEF) launched by President Obama or the G-20 Economic Summit meetings, or most likely, through some combination of the two" (Meyer 2009).

In January 2010, fifty-five developed and developing countries, accounting for 78 percent of global greenhouse gas emissions, acceded to the Copenhagen Accord by submitting emissions reduction plans to the United Nations (Broder 2010b). But many remained skeptical. Meyer wrote, "The pledges put on the table to date do not put us on track to meet that goal and will make it very difficult for us politically and technically beyond 2020 to meet that target" (Meyer 2009).

The meeting of the UN Ad Hoc Working Group–Long-term Cooperative Action (AWG-LCA) and UN Ad Hoc Working Group–Kyoto Protocol (AWG-KP) held in March 2010 was less well attended than previous meetings (International Institute for Sustainable Development 2010). The participants' main task was to establish the textual basis for further negotiations in 2010 to ensure that COP-16 delivered a meaningful global response to climate change. The meeting was plagued by controversy over two issues: the relevance of the Copenhagen Accord and whether to increase cooperation between the two negotiating tracks (International Institute for Sustainable Development 2010).

Debate over the accord's relevance was manifested in deciding two issues: (1) whether to give the chairperson of the AWG-LCA a mandate to prepare a new draft negotiating text prior to meetings in June; and (2) whether to use the Copenhagen Accord in that text. Many developed countries favored the accord, while many developing countries opposed it, citing their exclusion from the process that produced it (International Institute for Sustainable Development 2010). The decisions were to allow the chairperson to prepare a draft negotiating text and use the accord in its preparation.

The second controversy centered on whether to increase cooperation between the two negotiating tracks: one for countries that were not committed to mandatory limits and a second building on the Kyoto Protocol. A proposed text said that the chairperson of the AWG-LCA would meet with the chairperson of the AWG-KP to identify common concerns about developed nations' commitments. Developed countries favored the text, but the larger developing countries opposed it. The compromise replaced "to identify issues of common concerns" with "to identify information on developed countries['] commitments" (International Institute for Sustainable Development 2010).

COP-16, held in Cancun, Mexico, in 2010 produced the Cancun Agreements, which give the more than 190 participating countries another year to decide whether to extend the Kyoto Protocol. The agreement established a new fund to help developing countries adapt to climate changes, created new mechanisms for transferring clean energy technology, provided compensation for the preservation of tropical forests, and strengthened pledges to reduce emissions made at the previous climate change meeting. But the agreement left unresolved the source of the $100 billion in annual climate-related aid that the wealthy nations promised to provide. As John Broder (2010a) writes, "The United Nations climate change conference began with modest aims and ended . . . with modest achievements. The agreement fell well short of the broad changes scientists say are needed to avoid dangerous climate change in coming decades."

Climate Change Deniers

At a U.S. Senate committee hearing in June 1988, James Hansen, a climatologist with NASA, testified that he was 99 percent sure that the greenhouse effect was changing the planet's climate (Begley 2007). Corporations and industry associations representing petroleum, coal, steel, auto, and utilities immediately pushed back by forming lobbying groups aimed at recruiting doubters to cast global warming as theory rather than fact (Begley 2007). With the first Earth Summit in 1992, the burgeoning movement to deny climate change went international. The Global Climate Coalition, Information Council on the Environment, and conservative George C. Marshall Institute lobbied against a global treaty to reduce greenhouse gas emissions and claimed success in the treaty's stipulation of voluntary reductions.

The scientific evidence has been challenged especially since the IPCC issued its report in 1995 affirming anthropogenic global warming. The IPCC itself has been criticized, and climate scientists have been threatened (Gelbspan 1995; Girling 2010; Ravilious 2009). The phenomenon referred to as "climate change denial" is generally understood as attempts to minimize the extent and significance of global warming or its anthropogenic source to protect financial interests. Using advertisements, op-ed articles, lobbying, and publicity, deniers typically use one or more of the following arguments (Revkin 2009b):

- No conclusive evidence proves that climate change is occurring.
- Measured temperature changes are part of nature's cycle.
- Even if the changes are anthropogenic, the danger is not sufficient to make changes that are not cost-effective.
- The economic impact of cuts in greenhouse gas emissions on the scale suggested by the IPCC is too large.
- The dire predictions of global warming are based on computer models, but those models do not include correlated data such as the effects of sun spots and natural temperature changes.

Denial of climate change is associated with the energy lobby, other corporate advocates, conservative think tanks, and some elected officials, often in the United States (Adams 2005, 2006; Greenpeace 2003; Hoggan and Littlemore 2009). The campaign is frequently compared to earlier efforts by the tobacco industry to undermine scientific evidence of the dangers of second-hand smoke (Oreskes and Conway 2010).

In a meeting hosted by the American Petroleum Institute in 1998, called to ensure that President Clinton did not sign the Kyoto Protocol, a small group of climate change deniers, including the Marshall Institute and representatives of Exxon Mobil Corporation, discussed strategies to influence public opinion. A public relations specialist for the American Petroleum Institute summarized the discussion in an eight-page memo sent to industry and conservative political groups that opposed the treaty (Hoggan and Littlemore 2009). The memo was leaked to the *New York Times,* which published it. It revealed deniers' plan to spend $5 million to recruit scientists who share the oil industry's view of climate change and train them in public relations so they could convince journalists, politicians, and the public that the risk of global warming was too uncertain to justify mandatory controls on greenhouse gas emissions (Begley 2007).

Much of the documented evidence on climate change deniers' funding sources emphasizes the role of Exxon Mobil (Oreskes and Conway 2010; Greenpeace 2003). An inquiry conducted by the United Kingdom's Royal Society in 2006 found that Exxon Mobil gave $2.9 million to U.S. groups that misinformed the public about climate change and that thirty-nine of the groups misrepresented the science of climate change by outright denial (Adams 2006). The Royal Society demanded in a private letter that Exxon Mobil withdraw funding for climate change denial. When the letter was leaked to the media, critics chastised the society, arguing that the letter demonstrated the society's attempt to politicize private funding of science and to censor scientific debate (Adams 2006).

Exxon Mobil's efforts to influence opinion on climate change were revealed again in 2007. The American Enterprise Institute offered British, U.S., and other nations' scientists $10,000 plus travel expenses to publish articles critical of the IPCC's assessment in 2006 (Hoggan and Littlemore 2009). Letters were sent that criticized the IPCC as resistant to reasonable dissent and as promoting conclusions that were poorly supported by analytical work (Hoggan and Littlemore 2009). The American Enterprise Institute not only had received more than $1.6 million from Exxon Mobil; it also had a vice-chairman of trustees who was the former head of that corporation.

Exxon Mobil denied the accusations. A spokesman stated that Exxon Mobil supports research but does not act to influence outcomes. Yet Jonathan Owen and Paul Bignell (2010) reported that Exxon Mobil granted hundreds of thousands of dollars to think tanks such as the Atlas Economic Research Foundation in the United States and the International Policy Network in the United Kingdom to host conferences on climate change denial. The Heartland Institute, funded by Exxon Mobil, hosted climate change deniers at a meeting in March 2009 titled "Global Warming: Was It Ever Really a Crisis?" The Atlas Economic Research Foundation used funds from Exxon Mobil to support more than thirty other think tanks that deny climate change.

In November 2009, an unauthorized person gained access to thousands of e-mails and other documents from the Climatic Research Unit (CRU) at the University of East Anglia (Hickman 2009). Shortly afterward, the materials were widely publicized on climate change deniers' blogs and subsequently in the media (Pearce 2010). The deniers alleged that the hacked e-mails proved manipulation of data by climate scientists (Hickman 2009) and that dissenting scientific papers were being suppressed (Moore 2009). Their allegations were quickly publicized by the media, provoking the controversy dubbed "Climategate" (Hickman 2009; Revkin 2009a).

The university and the CRU issued rebuttals. Academics and climate change researchers dismissed the allegations (Moore 2009). An independent review by the Associated Press concluded that the e-mails did not affect evidence that human-made global warming is truly a threat and said that the e-mails were misrepresented to support unfounded claims of scientific misconduct (Satter 2010). An independent report by the Science and Technology Select Committee of the

British House of Commons concluded that no evidence proved malpractice by researchers at the CRU (Satter 2010).

Climategate revivified climate change denial and attacks on climate scientists. In a letter published in the journal *Science* in May 2010, more than 250 members of the U.S. National Academy of Sciences, including eleven Nobel Prize laureates, condemned the increased political assaults on scientists who argue that greenhouse gas emissions are warming the planet. They likened the situation to the McCarthy era and wrote, "Many recent assaults on climate science and, more disturbingly, on climate scientists by climate change deniers are typically driven by special interests or dogma, not by an honest effort to provide an alternative theory that credibly satisfies the evidence" (Gray 2010).

Transnational corporations have succeeded in persuading many people who do not have vested interests that climate change science is methodologically unsound by simultaneously highlighting the uncertainty of that science and playing into popular conceptions of science as truth and certainty to manipulate fears. The implications of climate science are scary. Change—such as changing to renewable energy—is also scary. Climate change deniers tell us what we all secretly want to hear.

The Transnational Corporate State and Democracy

In reference to the challenges of global economic integration, Robert Paehlke (2004: 2) writes, "Democracy's dilemma is this: global economic integration virtually requires some form of corresponding political integration, but the very notion of global government in any form is worrisome, especially perhaps to those with strong liberal democratic instincts."

The political system's purpose is social control: to protect and advance the economic system by legitimating it, spreading the supportive ideology of corporate rationalization, and abusing its authority to withhold and release information strategically. Authoritarian governments may spread their hegemonic ideology, and they certainly abuse their authority. But their corruption is frequently flagrant and conspicuous, endangering governments' legitimacy. Such was the case in Egypt, Libya, and Syria.

Apparent democracies fare better than authoritarian regimes at social control of the public. The rhetoric of democratic freedom and family values, plus some opportunities for electoral participation, persuade us that the government is looking out for us. Few states have the power to temper corporate interests with beefed-up democratic procedures and concerns for the collective well-being. Developed nations are disingenuous in pressing democratic reform abroad while whittling away at their own democratic processes.

Globalization is the only game in town, and it's play or pay. Citizens' calls for greater participatory political processes will not be answered in the petro-dependent world because increased democratic participation would inevitably reveal the man behind the curtain once and for all. Democracy—*true* democracy—is antithetical to petro-dependency.

Petro-dependency and democracy are incompatible. The inequities are too great; the resources are too limited; and the world's diverse voices are too muted by the consistent pounding drumbeat of corporate environmentalism. Petro-dependency and sustainability are irreconcilable, and democracy and sustainability are inseparable.

And so?

And so, in the final chapter, I take up analytical hammer and tongs to fashion a response to myself. How bad could it get? What needs to be done differently? Will we do what needs to be done?

IV

And So . . .

12

Once There Was a Planet in the Milky Way Galaxy . . .

... a beautiful blue and white orb, spinning gracefully through space. All life lived in harmony with the surroundings. Then a strange blight crept over the planet, leaving in its wake illness, conflict, and barrenness. No witchcraft, no enemy action had deadened this stricken planet. The people had done it themselves. (With apologies to Rachel Carson and *Silent Spring* [1962])

National and international environmental policies fail because our mode of subsistence does not work. Land and food are not commodities; they are basic necessities of life that should be accessible to all. Cost-benefit analyses that hang price tags on human life and the biospheric life support system are ludicrous and insulting. "Sustainable growth" is nonsensical: growth is not sustainable because resources are not infinite. Petro-dependency is intrinsically unsustainable—no changes in policymaking can rectify it. We must change our mode of subsistence, if we are to survive.

We have no silver bullet, no magic spell. We have only our individual and collective will to survive. Is that enough?

An ancient Chinese proverb says, "If we do not change the direction we are going, we will surely end up where we are headed." In this chapter, I examine the direction we are going and where we might end up, and I offer some suggestions for changing our direction.

The Direction We Are Going: Moving Away from Sustainability

Hunters and gatherers flourished for 2 million years, seasonally migrating to collect food from natural habitats. Their environmental impacts were negligible and localized. No policies were needed. Humans broke from the boundaries of ecological principles, first with the transformation to agriculturalism and then with the shift to petro-dependency. Environmental degradation steadily increased. We developed environmental policies and created coordinated bureaucratic infrastructures for policy formulation and implementation. We have attempted to erect international policies as environmental impacts have escalated in scale, magnitude, and toxicity. But the gap between policies and impacts is now a chasm, and widening.

The Use of Surplus in Altering the Biosphere

Agriculturalism's fundamental alteration of the biosphere was our first significant lurch away from sustainability. Replacing natural selection processes with human selection processes, we designed production systems specifically to continue expanding surpluses. Both ecosystems and economic systems experience production surplus. But utilization of surplus in the two systems differs in ways that carry significant implications for environmental degradation (Schnaiberg 1980).

The surplus produced in ecosystems derives from favorable living conditions and is manifested in increased availability of the fundamental resource of every organism in the ecological hierarchy: energy in the form of food, beginning with plants' use of solar energy for photosynthetic processes that produce the stored chemical energy that organisms require. Ecosystem surpluses are entirely absorbed in the production of new biomass through the natural processes of birth, growth, and decay. Population growth is greatest in species that are lower in the food chain. Populations continue to increase until the surplus is fully absorbed and population size stabilizes again. In this way, ecosystems maintain a steady-state equilibrium, operating within ecological limits, because surpluses are used as quickly as they appear in the production of biomass.

One species in that biospheric hierarchy attempted to break away from ecological limits. We humans deliberately designed agricultural systems to enlarge the supply of foods we desired. A portion of the surplus was inevitably expended in increased biomass—population growth. But the rest of the surplus was purposely diverted to ends that ensured the accumulation of ever larger future surpluses.

A second portion of the surplus was exploited to generate wealth and create institutionalized stratification systems. With more food produced than needed to sustain the population, some individuals managed to obtain more than others. The sociocultural invention of a monetary system allowed us to deal concretely with future surpluses. As a symbol of resource ownership, money was the medium used to develop techniques and tools for more efficient extraction and use of natural resources. Status systems transformed from tribal hierarchies based on non-transferable individual traits such as hunting prowess to institutionalized stratification systems based on the unequal distribution of surplus in the form of money.

A third portion of the surplus generated a treadmill of consumption. Agriculturalism allowed permanent settlements to be formed and freed some of the population from the task of securing food. In the complex division of labor that resulted, some surplus was devoted to the production and trading of a variety of objects that were *not* required for survival: luxury foods such as spices and fruit, luxury clothing such as cotton coats and silk dresses, and luxury shelters such as pyramids and palaces. The unequal distribution of consumables marked and reinforced social strata.

In this way, agricultural and manufacturing production continually expanded in pursuit of ever larger future surpluses. Agricultural systems *accumulated* surplus rather than absorbed it, as ecosystems do.

The Creation of the Risk Society: Poisoning the Biosphere

Our second lurch away from sustainability is petro-dependency's creation of the risk society. Petro-dependent technology exacerbated the impact of agricultural-ism and upped the ecological ante by substantially increasing the use of petro-leum, relying more heavily on the use of noxious substances such as radioactive materials and heavy metals, and introducing toxic substances to production processes. John McNeill (2000: 3) refers to these production changes as a gigantic uncontrolled experiment with unique consequences: "This is the first time in human history that we have altered ecosystems with such intensity, on such scale and with such speed."

Petro-dependency's unique ecological hazards are the basis for many analysts' references to contemporary societies as "risk societies" (Beck 1992, 1995, 1996; Douglas and Wildavsky 1982; Eder 1996; Gare 1995; Giddens 1990; Habermas 1984; Jameson 1991; Offe 1984; Perrow 1984). Petro-technologies are consciously developed to replace human labor with greater energy inputs to increase surplus and profits. Hazardous production substances and the complexity and tight coupling of technical systems combine to pose threats of potentially catastrophic accidents, such as the partial reactor meltdown at the Three Mile Island nuclear power plant; the release of lethal gas from the pesticide plant in Bhopal, India; the fire and explosion at the Chernobyl nuclear power plant; and the Deepwater Horizon oil spill in the Gulf of Mexico. The prevalence of risky technical systems makes accidents so inevitable that Charles Perrow (1984) refers to them as "nor-mal" accidents.

The development of hazardous and complex technical systems and the incor-poration of adequate safety measures demand that scientists play substantial roles in economic development, elevating them to prominence in policy debates. The resultant highly politicized policy context is characterized by symbiotic relation-ships among scientific experts seeking research funds, corporate actors seeking ever higher profits, and state actors seeking economic growth to protect the nation's wealth and fund social programs to maintain the state's legitimacy.

Such symbiosis makes risk societies' members doubly vulnerable. We are vul-nerable because the ubiquity of hazardous substances ensures high rates of risky exposure. And we are vulnerable because knowledge of hazardous risks is rou-tinely kept from the public (Cable, Shriver, and Mix 2008). Technical knowledge is considered a proprietary commodity by corporations and a national security issue by the state. Scientists serve as the hired interpreters of knowledge. The use of institutional power to withhold critical information from the public denies citi-zens the opportunity to influence policies that adversely affect them, stifling the democratic process.

The ubiquity of hazardous substances and the institutionally imposed igno-rance of exposure is a prescription for widespread illnesses. Since the early 1980s, citizens' complaints have increased about illnesses attributable to hazardous exposure. Symptoms such as chronic fatigue, memory loss, immune system defi-ciencies, previously rare tumors, and chronic headaches are now so common that analysts refer to them as "environmental illnesses." But those who become ill frequently go undiagnosed and untreated. The link between exposure and illness is difficult to establish because of the long latency period of the risks and the vagueness of symptoms. Such illnesses could eventually become a defining characteristic of risk societies.

The petro-dependent mode of production carries several critical implications for human sustainability:

- In the same way that land was the basis for wealth in the agricultural mode of subsistence, oil is the basis for wealth in the petro-dependent mode. As a strategic productive resource that is nonrenewable and nearing peak production, oil will remain the center of growing conflict and warfare.
- Representatives of TNCs, nations, and international banks cooperate in international groups such as the World Trade Organization deliberately to steer global economic integration according to neoliberal principles that benefit wealthy petro-dependent societies. The result is a global treadmill of production and a global stratification system in which elites in rich countries direct development in poor countries, pressuring them onto the petro-intensive path. But the world is different today from when developed nations began to accumulate wealth: neither imperial expansion to secure cheap natural resources nor enslavement to ensure cheap labor is a possible tactic for developing nations. Poor nations are forced to import oil, paying for it with the agricultural exports that rich nations will buy and distorting their production decisions to suit the demands of the global market. The consequence is greater discrepancies between rich and poor.
- The petro-dependent mode of subsistence substantially reinforces and fuels our biological hubris. The ability to manipulate nature to produce unnatural chemicals, organisms, and elements feeds the belief that our cleverness can overcome any problem. Biological hubris tells us that we are exempt from the biospheric laws that govern all other life forms and blinds us to the fate awaiting us if we do not turn away from petro-dependency.

Where We Might End Up

The entire biosphere is treated as a commodity to be seized, controlled, extracted, manipulated, contorted, drained, and discarded—for a price. Transnational corporations concentrate global power, assisted by political systems that have been downgraded to instruments of the TNCs that function to ensure favorable conditions in which to accumulate surpluses. Surplus begets ever larger surplus, and wealth multiplies at the expense of our biospheric life support system. The starkly uneven distribution of wealth emphasizes our differences instead of our similarities, playing to our dark side and precipitating prejudice, conflict, and genocide. Discrepancies between rich and poor produce the contradiction of disease and food insecurity in the midst of fantastic wealth.

Under such conditions, a truly noble idea such as democracy is reduced to a tool for the political system to distort in servicing the economy. We have democratic veneer rather than democracy. It is not ugly for a species with a high level of self-awareness to try to sustain itself—what is ugly is being unfair about it.

Economy and ecology are not just connected—"economy" is merely an abstract term for the material environment. The economy *is* the environment. Economists' routine use of growth in the gross domestic product as an indicator of national health and progress is an absurd contradiction. Such growth actually indicates increased consumption per person of finite resources and the destruction of the biospheric life support system.

We began as a species by obtaining food, clothing, and shelter for a day or so at a time. Now, we in developed nations produce and consume more food than we should, more clothes than needed to keep us clean for a day or so, more shelters in greater variety and larger than we can possibly inhabit, plus multiple luxuries that further differentiate people. Human survival is doomed if we continue this path. How bad could it get?

Human civilization could collapse. Jared Diamond (2005: 6) analyzes the conditions associated with "unintended ecological suicide," identifying eight categories of problems that doomed some ancient societies: deforestation and habitat destruction; soil erosion, salinization of soil, and fertility losses; water management problems; overhunting; overfishing; introduced species; human population growth; and increased environmental impact per capita. These problems are identical to contemporary ones. Petro-dependency adds three more categories of problems that could collapse societies: anthropogenic climate change, bioaccumulation of petrochemicals and other hazardous substances, and energy shortages.

Citing claims that most of these threats will become globally critical within a few decades, Diamond believes that civilization is at risk of collapse. Doomed ancient societies collapsed in isolation, but globalization will prevent such segregation. According to Diamond (2005: 23), "Any society in turmoil today can cause trouble for prosperous societies on other continents. For the first time in history, we face the risk of a global decline." It won't be societies that collapse but human civilization.

Or our actions may even kill off the human species. Approximately 99 percent of all species that ever evolved on the planet are now extinct—extinction is part of a natural process of population growth, stability, and decline. Human actions have already hastened the extinction of numerous species and are increasing the pressure on many others. Our alteration and poisoning of the biosphere in a headlong pursuit of wealth could change the biospheric life support system so substantially that we will be unable to adapt in time to survive, because biological adaptation takes far more time than does cultural adaptation. Thus our sojourn on the planet could prove embarrassingly short, as I demonstrate with a planetary timeline.

> *Fifteen to eighteen billion years ago*, physical and chemical processes involving energy and matter created the universe. The Milky Way Galaxy formed approximately 12 billion years ago. The Earth formed 4.6 billion years ago from a cloud of interstellar gas and dust that created an atmosphere of hydrogen and hydrogen-based gases.

Four billion years ago, Earth's gases and water vapor were exposed to an energy source (such as sunlight or lightning), initiating chemical reactions that produced amino acid molecules. Complex molecules developed that constantly formed, broke down, and re-formed. Eventually, instead of breaking down, a complex molecule reproduced itself and passed on its structural organization. Life began. Approximately 3.5 billion years ago, increasingly complex molecules assembled to form cells that used genes to store and pass along information about cell function and production. Life prospered as single-celled microbes expanded into the new environment. The evolutionary processes—reproduction, random mutation, and natural selection—began to increase the diversity of the new life. Random mutation (errors in the reproduction process) introduced genetic variations, some of which were favored in natural selection processes because the changes enhanced the organism's ability to survive and produce offspring that carried the mutation. Multicellular plants and animals appeared .5 billion years ago.

Once established, all species undergo stages of population growth, stability, decline, and extinction. Populations grow exponentially as long as resources are available to support them. Stability occurs as habitat changes or restrictions limit the species' reproduction and survival rates. Some organisms adapt to the changes. With sufficient time and genetic variation in the species, mutations appear that favor survival in the changed environment, and evolution continues. Stability is inevitably followed by decline and extinction because, eventually, environmental changes or limitations are too rapid or too great to permit continued adaptation.

Two and a half million years ago, an evolutionary product arose that possessed enhanced self-awareness and learning abilities: humans. These new creatures made their living as hunters and gatherers and evolved rapidly.

Self-awareness and learning abilities foster the development of culture through symbolic systems of meaning (such as language) shared by a group or society. Learned information that facilitates adaptation to the biophysical environment is passed to the next generation through these communication systems. This *cultural* evolution occurs on the scale of the human lifetime, markedly faster than biological evolution.

Ten thousand years ago, human culture had developed sufficiently that the population began to increase rapidly. In more than 2 million years of hunting and gathering by small populations of humans, the impact on the planet had been relatively minor. But all of that began to change. Hunting and gathering gave way to ever-expanding agriculture, and mere subsistence gave way to abundance and even surplus. These dramatic new pressures on the environment began to radically alter the biosphere.

Within the last century, cultural evolution has brought the human species to activities that extend beyond mere radical alteration of the biosphere: humans have begun to poison the biosphere to a significant degree. For the whole of human evolution, we have pushed the limits of our one and only biosphere.

Now our poisoned biosphere is beginning to push back, as humans are being increasingly harmed through environmental illness and scarcity of resources.

Such harm could eventually extend to the premature extinction of the human species. Humans can cause environmental changes rapidly through cultural evolution. But humans can adapt to those changes only slowly, through biological evolution. Unless humans are truly the only species ever to be exempted from the laws of population dynamics, we may find that our economic activities have changed the Earth so much that we will be unable to survive in our altered and damaged environment.

Figure 12.1 illustrates the downward spiral of the human species from our appearance as hunters and gatherers, through our continual intensification of agriculture, to our suicidal path of petro-dependency.

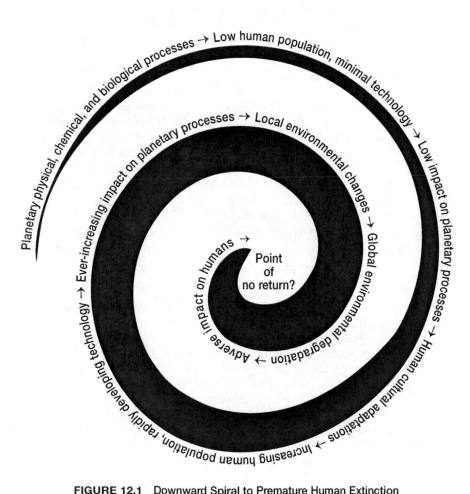

FIGURE 12.1   Downward Spiral to Premature Human Extinction

Some analysts believe that we may extinguish our own species in the process of eroding biological diversity to the point of a sixth mass extinction. "Unrestrained, *Homo sapiens* might not only be the agent of the sixth extinction but also risks being one of its victims" (Leakey and Lewin 1995: 249). If we reduce our capacity for destruction and avoid hastening our end, we are likely to persist for another million years or so. We must change our direction.

Changing Our Direction

Albert Einstein has been quoted as saying, "You cannot solve a problem from the same consciousness that created it. You must learn to see the world anew." This advice is crucial for changing our direction to a sustainable path. We can avoid the collapse of human civilization and the premature extinction of the human species by tailoring a sustainable mode of subsistence to secure food, clothing, and shelter. We can re-create our economic institution with technologies and energy sources that comply with ecological principles. We can apply our species' unique gift of consciousness to infuse social institutions with democratic principles, ensuring that neither the costs nor the benefits of our sustenance are unequally borne. The United States, as the world's first petro-dependent society, is obligated to lead the way to sustainability and survival.

Imagine a sustainable mode of subsistence—not hunting and gathering, but draw clues from that mode. Imagine a perpetual energy source, food grown and consumed locally, more human and less energy-intensive labor, reduced use of noxious substances, and elimination or prudent selection of toxic substances. I contend that a sustainable society acknowledges ecological principles, recognizes the link between economic activities and ecological stability, and enacts democratic principles of fairness and justice. I use these guidelines to identify some critical characteristics of a sustainable society. None represents a truly new idea. Instead, I place the characteristics in a context that suggests a social structure for sustainability. Piecemeal efforts will not save us. Using petro-dependent consciousness will not save us.

A sustainable society acknowledges four ecological principles.
Ecological principle 1 is that the biosphere is an elaborate network in which all component parts are intrinsically linked to others. We cannot intervene without ecological consequences. Characteristics related to this principle are sustainable agriculture, protection of biodiversity, and local power generation. Sustainable agriculture features organic farming, considerable reduction of the surplus, and the domestication of more indigenous plants and fewer animals. Food is produced and consumed locally. Biodiversity is prized and protected to maintain ecological stability and complexity. Electrical power is provided by small, decentralized power-generating stations using solar, wind, and hydro power and biofuels.

Agriculture is the foundation of an economy. Since sustainable agriculture is local, economic systems are local. Such systems have been referred to as bioregionalism, a political, cultural, and environmental system based on areas defined by physical and environmental features, usually watershed boundaries plus soil and terrain characteristics (Berg and Dasmann 1977). All human activities are organized according to bioregional characteristics, including political systems. Bioregions are largely self-sufficient in the production and distribution of food, other consumables, and services.

Ecological principle 2 is that ecosystems are perfect recycling systems, recycling the same atoms over and over. We never "create" matter; we only transform and manipulate nature's materials. The characteristics of a sustainable society pertaining to this principle are resource conservation and renewable energy sources.

Resource conservation includes the management of natural resources such as forests, soil, and grasslands and of waste. The waste stream is substantially diminished through source reduction (such as packaging on consumer products), the absence of toxins, and the recycling and re-use of materials. Remaining wastes are safely landfilled.

The hallmarks of the sustainable society are the use of renewable solar, wind, geothermal, and hydro forms of energy for power generation and the use of human muscle power instead of machines, which leads to fuller employment. Fossil fuels are not burned. Dwindling oil supplies are reserved for the manufacture of critical pharmaceuticals and plastics for vital applications such as surgical instruments. Transportation systems are public and plentiful, powered by the sun or alternative fuels.

Ecological principle 3 states that nature provides a limited array of substances essential to life that have been tested through Earth time by natural selection processes. When we transform and manipulate nature's provisions to produce something novel, we poison life. Production in the sustainable society relies almost entirely on natural substances. Unnatural substances are used only after substantial research proves them safe.

Many have described this approach to regulation as the precautionary principle. Joel Tickner (2003) describes it as driving policies that protect human health and the environment in the face of uncertain risks, even if cause–effect relationships are not fully established scientifically. Romeo Quijano (2003) identifies the elements of the precautionary principle: the focus of decision making is preventing exposure rather than mitigating exposure, producers rather than potential victims are responsible for safety, and the basic human right to health and a safe environment takes precedence over economic and proprietary rights. The precautionary principle requires public access to information.

Ecological principle 4 states that disrupted ecological systems sooner or later severely threaten human fertility, morbidity, and mortality. We can neither run nor hide from the effects of our unsustainable lifestyles. A sustainable society lives within its means and pays its debts on time. The environmental costs of production are internalized, reflected in prices.

A sustainable society recognizes the link between economic activities and environmental stability.

Involved parties in the sustainable society are the state, corporations, labor, and the polity. The sustainable society separates the corporate state into its constituent parts. The state emphasizes its legitimation function over capital accumulation, since sustainability requires a reduced surplus. Legitimation derives from the state's provisions for and regulation of the production and distribution of food, clothing, and shelter to citizens.

Corporations no longer have the legal rights of citizens; corporate members are legally accountable as individuals for their actions. The relevant political institution grants charters for corporations to contribute to the public good. Economic development is planned at the bioregional level. Charters charge corporations with social responsibility, emphasizing safe working conditions and fair wages for labor. The polity is provided with information by the state and corporations to generate public discourse on issues that affect it.

A sustainable society enacts democratic principles of fairness and justice.

Environmental justice is impossible without social justice. Translating John Rawls's (1999) model into structural terms, a sustainable and just society has a social structure that guarantees individual rights, including political participation in decisions that affect individuals; seeks an equal distribution of occupational opportunity; and seeks fairness in the distribution of wealth.

The social institutions of a sustainable, democratic, and just society feature the following attributes:

- The political institution supersedes the economic institution. Its representatives construct and enforce rules that guarantee civil liberties and democratic processes, maintain equal occupational opportunities, and ensure that discrepancies in wealth are just. The physically and mentally impaired are protected from poverty with an adequate social safety net and universal health care. The political institution uses science to maintain sustainability.
- The economic institution is based on bioregionalism: local production of food, clothing, and shelter. Corporations are chartered by the local political authority. Social mobility permits movement up and down the economic ladder.
- The educational institution provides equal education for all to ensure equality of occupational opportunity. Education aims at removing our cultural blinders to recognize that humans are not exempt from biospheric laws. A hands-on education reinvigorates humans' recognition of our dependence on the biospheric life support system as part of the web of life. Student involvement in farming projects begins in nursery school with school farms and community farms. National service in agriculture and natural resource management after high school provides college scholarships similar to the GI Bill.
- The institution of the family is stabilized and bolstered by a fairer distribution of wealth and access to education. Family problems do not become social problems.

Last Word

A political-economic system firmly founded on individual greed can only make us behave badly. Why do we so often make decisions that bring out the worst in us instead of the best?

Because nobody eats us.

This has to do with the predator's intention and the prey's place in the food chain. Humans are *not* the usual prey of the organisms that occasionally—almost accidentally—eat us, such as polar and grizzly bears, mountain lions, and bacteria. Humans are not the usual prey of *any* critter. If we were, we would be more sensitive to ecological limits.

Because nobody eats us, we are out of touch with the environment that supports us. Human reality is unique in that it is not a direct response to our immediate physical environment. Instead, we respond directly to our cultural *interpretations* of that environment. The farther we have moved from the material base of life, the more lost we have become in our constructed realities. A peculiarly human dilemma is that we are interpretive creatures designing and living in a symbolic world while we are wholly dependent on the material world.

That 1945 threshold at which humankind briefly was poised revealed an alluring promise of vastly increased wealth and higher standards of living for more people. But the promise of the petro-dependent mode of subsistence is actually a deal with the Devil. We stepped through the threshold; we struck the deal; and although we can ignore the costs momentarily, we will eventually have the Devil to pay.

Is it too late to pay down the hellish debt? The sixty-five years of our deal with oil is far less than the tick of a clock when compared with our 10,000 years in the agricultural mode of subsistence, and it is nothing at all compared with our nearly 2 million years as hunters and gatherers.

Lester Milbrath (1989) has devised a cleverly effective way to examine human activities in Earth time rather than in human time. He asks us to imagine a movie, representing all time since the Earth's origin. The movie starts on January 1 and runs for a year. Each frame of the movie is one year; each minute is 8,752 years; each hour is 525,740 years; and each day is 12,602,240 years. In this year-long movie of the Earth's history, no life appears until March, when microbial life develops. More complex forms of life do not evolve until August and September. Multicellular organisms appear only in November. Dinosaurs finally show up on December 13 but are extinct by December 26. Mammals appear on December 15. December 31 is a momentous day in this year-long movie—for humans, at least. The genus *Homo* develops on December 31, at approximately 7 P.M. Modern humans develop at about 11:49 P.M. Human civilization appears at 11:59. Industrialized agriculture begins in the last two seconds of the movie. And petro-dependency? December 31, at 11:59:58.5 P.M.—less than the blink of an eye.

We can we do it if we choose to do it. I envision an Environmental Revolution: not an overnight phenomenon deliberately guided by human hands but a gradual process of transformative change. I imagine the Environmental Revolution as similar to the Neolithic Revolution—so slow that you cannot see much progress in one lifetime, but it is inexorable.

We are obligated to do it: we owe the rest of the world's creatures and future generations. Human consciousness is a joy and a curse. It is also a responsibility.

Websites and Mission Statements

NGO Partners for the Global Plan of Action
for the Protection of the Marine Environment
from Land-Based Activities

Advisory Committee on Protection of the Sea (ACOPS)
http://www.acops.org.uk

Primary Objective: Environmental protection

ACOPS seeks cost-effective, long-term global development strategies for coastal and marine environments. Organizational efforts include policy research and public outreach.

American Crop Protection Association (ACPA)
http://www.croplifeamerica.org

Primary Objective: Industry promotion

ACPA is a trade organization established in 1933. From its headquarters in Washington, D.C., ACPA supports agriculture and pest management. Claiming to be "the voice of the industry," ACPA encourages the safe and responsible use of pesticides. The staff consists of thirty lobbyists, lawyers, and science, regulatory, and communications experts.

Center for International Environmental Law (CIEL)
http://www.ciel.org

Primary Objective: Environmental protection

CIEL is a nonprofit organization applying international law in pursuit of environmental protection, human health, and a sustainable society. The website offers services such as legal counsel, policy research, advocacy, and education.

Chlorine Chemistry Division of the American Chemistry Council
http://chlorine.americanchemistry.com

Primary Objective: Industry promotion

The Chlorine Chemistry Division of the American Chemistry Council represents major producers and users of chlorine in the United States. Claiming that chlorine chemistry contributes more than $46 billion to the U.S. economy each year, the organization advocates application of this technology to enhance safety, reduce energy consumption, and facilitate expansion of renewable energy.

Chlorine Institute

http://www.chlorineinstitute.org

Primary Objective: Industry promotion

The Chlorine Institute supports the chlor-alkali industry, advocating voluntary industry regulation over command-and-control government regulation. The institute works with government agencies and other stakeholders to encourage the use of science and technology in policymaking decisions.

Cousteau Society

http://www.cousteau.org

Primary Objective: Environmental protection

According to its website, the Cousteau Society is supported by more than 50,000 members worldwide. Since 1973, this nonprofit organization has sponsored unique explorations and ecosystem observations that have helped people understand and appreciate the fragility of life in the oceans.

Earth Action

http://www.earthaction.org

Primary Objective: Environmental protection

Earth Action's mission statement identifies organizational aims to "inform and inspire people to turn their concern, passion, and outrage into meaningful action for a more just, peaceful, and sustainable world." Earth Action claims to be the world's largest action network, with more than 2,600 organizations in 165 countries.

Environmental and Energy Study Institute (EESI)

http://www.eesi.org

Primary Objective: Industry promotion

The EESI is a nonprofit organization established in 1984 by bipartisan, bicameral members of the U.S. Congress to provide information for developing environmental policy. The EESI accomplishes these objectives by educating policymakers, networking and building coalitions, and recommending policies.

Environmental Defense Fund (EDF)

http://www.edf.org

Primary Objective: Environmental protection

The EDF is a national nonprofit organization formed in 1967 that claims to represent more than 700,000 members. The EDF states its mission as protecting the environmental rights of all people, including future generations.

European Chemical Industry Council (Cefic)

http://www.cefic.org

Primary Objective: Industry promotion

Cefic represents the European chemical industry and claims to be one of the "largest and most efficient advocacy networks" among European and global industry trade organizations.

European Crop Protection Association (ECPA)

http://www.ecpa.eu

Primary Objective: Industry promotion

The ECPA represents the crop protection industry in Europe, promoting competitive agriculture through the use of chemical pesticides. The ECPA advocates European Union policies grounded in science-based risk assessments and rewards for new technology and practices.

Foundation for International Environmental Law and Development (FIELD)

http://www.field.org.uk

Primary Objective: Environmental protection

FIELD is a group of international public lawyers committed to "helping vulnerable countries, communities, and campaigners negotiate for fairer international environmental laws." Members work with local partners, national and international NGOs, and institutions, providing pro bono services when possible.

Friends of the Earth

http://www.foe.org

Primary Objective: Environmental protection

Friends of the Earth is a network of grassroots groups in seventy-seven countries. The organization describes its members as "progressive environmental advocates who pull no punches and speak sometimes uncomfortable truths to power." Campaigns focus on clean energy and solutions to global warming; protecting people from toxic technology; and promoting smarter, low-pollution transportation alternatives.

Greenpeace International

http://www.greenpeace.org/international/en/

Primary Objective: Environmental protection

Greenpeace is a global organization aimed at protecting the environment by changing attitudes and behavior. Greenpeace relies on individual donations and foundation grants rather than soliciting or accepting funding from governments, corporations, or political parties.

International Association of Ports and Harbors (IAPH)

http://www.iaphworldports.org

Primary Objective: Industry promotion

The IAPH advocates cooperation among all global ports and harbors, emphasizing the significance of ports in global trade. The organization's motto is "World Peace Through World Trade—World Trade Through World Ports."

International Council of Chemical Associations (ICCA)

http://www.icca-chem.org

Primary Objective: Industry promotion

The ICCA seeks to strengthen cooperation on chemicals management among global organizations such as the United Nations Environmental Programme, the United Nations Institute for Training and Research, the Organisation for Economic Co-operation and Development, and NGOs. The association's vision is that "the global chemical industry will be widely valued and supported for its economic, social, and environmental contributions to society."

International Council of Environmental Law (ICEL)

http://www.i-c-e-l.org/indexen.html

Primary Objective: Industry promotion

The ICEL is a public interest organization that aims to promote and support exchange of information on legal, administrative, and policy aspects of environmental conservation and development. The ICEL is supported by the Karl-Schmitz-Scholl Foundation and the Elizabeth Haub Foundations for Environmental Law and Policy.

International Fertilizer Industry Association (IFA)

http://www.fertilizer.org

Primary Objective: Industry promotion

The IFA is a nonprofit organization that represents the global fertilizer industry. About half of its 525 member companies are in developing countries.

International Union for Conservation of Nature (IUCN; formerly World Conservation Union)

http://www.iucn.org

Primary Objective: Environmental protection

The IUCN manages global projects to resolve issues between developers and environmentalists. The organization aims to bring together governments, NGOs, United Nations agencies, corporations, and local communities to develop policy and best practices. It is funded by governments, bilateral and multilateral agencies, foundations, member organizations, and corporations.

National Academy of Sciences (NAS)

http://www.nasonline.org

Primary Objective: Environmental protection

The NAS is an honorific society established in 1863 that consists of scientific and engineering scholars who use their skills for the general welfare. The NAS has served to "investigate, examine, experiment, and report upon any subject of science or art" when requested by the federal government.

Society of Chemical Manufacturers and Affiliates (SOCMA)

http://www.socma.com

Primary Objective: Industry promotion

SOCMA is an international trade association for chemical manufacturers. It advocates enactment of flexible regulatory policies rather than command-and-control government regulation.

Woods Hole Oceanographic Institution (WHOI)

http://www.whoi.edu

Primary Objective: Environmental protection

WHOI is a nonprofit oceanographic institution dedicated to research and higher education to advance and promote understanding of the seas.

World Resources Institute (WRI)

http://www.wri.org

Primary Objective: Environmental protection

The WRI is an environmental think tank. Its mission is to "move human society to live in ways that protect the Earth's environment and its capacity to provide for the needs and aspirations of current and future generations."

World Wide Fund for Nature/World Wildlife Fund (WWF)

http://www.worldwildlife.org

Primary Objective: Environmental protection

The WWF is an international nature conservation organization. Members advance scientific knowledge to preserve the diversity and abundance of life and the health of ecological systems.

The World Wildlife Fund Network was established in 1961 as an international organization. In 1986, the organization changed its name to World Wide Fund for Nature, retaining the WWF acronym. Chapters in the United States and Canada continue to operate under the original name, the World Wildlife Fund.

References

Adams, David. 2005. Oil firms fund climate change "denial." *The Guardian,* January 27.

———. 2006. Royal Society tells Exxon: Stop funding climate change denial. *The Guardian,* September 20.

Allen, David S. 2005. *Democracy Inc.: The press and law in the corporate rationalization of the public sphere.* Urbana: University of Illinois Press.

American Institute of Physics. 2001. New research shows mountain glaciers shrinking world wide. *Science Daily,* May 30.

Andrews, Richard N. L. 1999. *Managing the environment, managing ourselves: A history of American environmental policy.* New Haven, Conn.: Yale University Press.

———. 2006. Risk-based decision making: Policy, science, and politics. In *Environmental policy: New directions for the twenty-first century,* 6th ed., ed. Norman J. Vig and Michael E. Kraft, 215–238. Washington, D.C.: Congressional Quarterly Press.

Archibold, Randal C. 2007. A century later, Los Angeles atones for water sins. *New York Times,* January 1. Available online at http://www.nytimes.com/2007/01/01/us/01water.html?_4=1&pagewanted=print&oref=slogin (accessed August 5, 2008).

Associated Press. 2008a. Controlled drugs dumped uncontrolled into water. September 16. Available online at http://www.comcast.net/articles/news-health/20080916/PharmaWater.Narcotics (accessed September 17, 2008).

———. 2008b. Court says no deadline for EPA on global warming. June 26. Available online at http://www.comcast.net/articles/news-science/20080626/EPA.Global.Warming (accessed June 27, 2008).

———. 2008c. Food crunch opens doors to bioengineered crops. November 30. Available online at http://www.comcast.net/articles/news-science/20081130/Food_s.Future.GM.Crops (accessed December 1, 2008).

———. 2008d. G-8 climate scorecard shows U.S. last. Available online at http://www.comcast.net/articles/news-science/20080703/Germany.Climate.Scorecards (accessed July 5, 2008).

———. 2008e. Global warming pollution increases 3 percent. Available online at http://www.comcast.net/articles/news-science/20080925/Warming.Emissions (accessed September 26, 2008).

———. 2008f. Group sues over crop subsidies on US forest land. July 1. Available online at http://www.comcast.net/articles/news-finance/20080701/Farm.Scene.Forest.Farming (accessed July 1, 2008).

———. 2008g. NOAA report: U.S. coral reefs in severe decline. Available online at http://www.comcast.net/articles/news-national/20080707/Coral.Reef.Threats (accessed July 18, 2008).

———. 2008h. Pollution curbs turn Beijing into urban laboratory. August 3. Available online at http://www.comcast.net/articles/news-science/20080803/OLY.Olympics.Laboratory (accessed August 4, 2008).

———. 2008i. R[hode] I[sland] high court overturns lead paint verdict. July 1. Available online at http://www.comcast.net/articles/news-finance/20080701/Lead.Paint.Lawsuit (accessed July 1, 2008).

———. 2008j. Rocky Mountain conservation deal tops $500 million. June 30. Available online at http://www.comcast.net/articles/news-science/20080701/Conservation.Land.Deal (accessed July 1, 2008).

———. 2008k. Scientists: One in four mammals faces extinction. October 6. Available online at http://www.comcast.net/articles/news-science/20081006/SCI.Endangered.Mammals (accessed October 7, 2008).

———. 2008l. White House rejects regulating greenhouse gases. Available online at http://www.comcast.net/articles/news-science/20080713/Bush.Global.Warming (accessed July 16, 2008).

Athanasiou, Tom. 1996. The age of greenwashing. *Capitalism, Nature, Socialism* 7:1–36.

Austin, Andrew. 2002. Advancing accumulation and managing its discontents: The U.S. anti-environmental countermovement. *Sociological Spectrum* 22 (1): 71–105.

Barlett, Donald L., and James B. Steele. 1998 Corporate welfare. *Time,* November 9, 36–39.

Beck, Eckardt C. 1979. The Love Canal tragedy. EPA website. January. Available online at http://www.epa.gov/history/topics/lovecanal/01.htm (accessed August 7, 2008).

Beck, Ulrich. 1992. *Risk Society: Towards a New Modernity.* London: Sage.

———. 1995. *Ecological Enlightenment: Essays on the Politics of the Risk Society.* Atlantic Highlands, N.J.: Humanities Press.

———. 1996. "Risk Society and the Provident State." In *Risk, Environment and Modernity: Towards a New Ecology,* ed. S. Lash, B. Szerszynski, and B. Wynne, 27–43. London: Sage.

Begley, Sharon. 2007. The truth about denial. *Newsweek,* August 13. Available online at http://www.newsweek.com/id/32482 (accessed May 20, 2010).

Bennis, Phyllis. 2000. *Calling the shots: How Washington dominates today's UN.* New York: Olive Branch.

Berg, Peter, and Raymond Dasmann. 1977. Reinhabiting California. *The Ecologist* 7 (10): 399–401.

Betsill, Michele M., and Elisabeth Corell. 2008. *NGO diplomacy: The influence of nongovernmental organizations in international environmental negotiations.* Cambridge, Mass.: MIT Press.

Block, Ben. 2008. Report calls for better animal waste treatment. Worldwatch Institute. Available online at http://www.enn.com/agriculture/article/35646 (accessed July 4, 2008).

Block, Fred. 1977. The ruling class does not rule: Notes on the Marxist theory of the state. *Socialist Review* 7 (May–June): 6–28.

Bonfatti, John F., and Brian Hayden. 2008. Thirty years later, Love Canal legacy lingers: Transformation hasn't allayed fears many have on safety. *Buffalo News,* August 4. Available online at http://www.buffalonews.com/cityregion/niagaracounty/story/405306.html (accessed August 8, 2008).

Brannon, Nancy. 2007. Ground water: A community's management of the invaluable resource beneath its feet. Ph.D. diss., University of Tennessee, Knoxville.

Braverman, Harry. 1998. *Labor and monopoly capital: The degradation of work in the twentieth century.* New York: Monthly Review Press.

Broder, John M. 2010a. Climate talks end with modest deal on emissions. *New York Times,* December 11. Available online at http://www.nytimes.com/2010/12/12/science/earth/12climate.html (accessed September 27, 2011).

———. 2010b. Countries submit emission goals. *New York Times,* February 2. Available online at http://www.nytimes.com/2010/02/02/science/earth/02copenhagen.html (accessed May 14, 2010).

Brown, Lester R. 2006. *Plan B 2.0.* New York: W. W. Norton.

Brown, Phil. 1991. The popular epidemiology approach to toxic waste contamination. In *Communities at risk: Collective responses to technological hazards,* ed. Stephen Robert Couch and J. Stephen Kroll-Smith, 133–155. New York: Peter Lang.

———. 2000. Popular epidemiology and toxic waste contamination: Lay and professional ways of knowing. In *Illness and the environment: A reader in contested medicine,* ed. Steve Kroll-Smith, Phil Brown, and Valerie J. Gunter, 364–383. New York: New York University Press.

Bruno, Kenny, and Joshua Karliner. 2002. *Earthsummit.biz: The corporate takeover of sustainable development.* Oakland, Calif.: Food First Books.

Bryce, Robert. 2009. If Reid, Obama kill Yucca Mountain, where will nuclear waste go? Think fusion. *U.S. News and World Report,* June 24. Available online at http://www.usnews.com/articles/opinion/2009/06/24/if-reid-obama-kill-yucca-mountain-where-will-nuclear-waste-go-think-fusion.html (accessed July 26, 2009).

Buck, Susan. 1996. *Understanding environmental administration and law.* Washington, D.C.: Island Press.

Burdeau, Cain, and Harry R. Weber. 2011. Vigils, claims mark spill. *Knoxville News Sentinel,* April 21, A1.

Burke, William K. 1994. The wise use movement: Right-wing anti-environmentalism. *Propaganda Review* 11 (Spring): 4–10.

Burris, Val. 2005. Interlocking directorates and political cohesion among corporate elites. *American Sociological Review* 45:821–841.

Cable, Sherry, and Michael Benson. 1993. Acting locally: Environmental injustice and the emergence of grassroots environmental organizations. *Social Problems* 40 (4): 464–477.

Cable, Sherry, and Charles Cable. 1995. *Environmental problems, grassroots solutions: The politics of grassroots environmental conflict.* New York: St. Martin's Press.

Cable, Sherry, Donald W. Hastings, and Tamara L. Mix. 2002. Different voices, different venues: Environmental racism claims by activists, researchers, and lawyers. *Human Ecology Review* 9 (1): 26–42.

Cable, Sherry, and Thomas Shriver. 1995. The production and extrapolation of meaning in the Environmental Justice Movement. *Sociological Spectrum* 15:419–442.

Cable, Sherry, Thomas E. Shriver, and Donald W. Hastings. 1999. The silenced majority: Quiescence and social control on the Oak Ridge Nuclear Reservation. *Research in Social Problems and Public Policy* 6:59–81.

Cable, Sherry, Thomas E. Shriver, and Tamara L. Mix. 2008. Risk society and contested illness: The case of nuclear weapons workers. *American Sociological Review* 73 (3): 380–401.

Carey, Alex. 1997. *Taking the risk out of democracy: Corporate propaganda versus freedom and liberty.* Urbana: University of Illinois Press.

Carson, Rachel. 1962. *Silent spring.* Boston: Houghton Mifflin.

Catton, William R. 1982. *Overshoot: The ecological basis of revolutionary change.* Urbana: University of Illinois Press.

Chatterjee, Rhitu. 2007. Are you ready for the scary, largely unregulated brave new world of nanotechnology? Organic Consumers Association. Available online at http://www.organicconsumer.org/articles/article_8414.cfm (accessed August 12, 2009).

CNN (Cable News Network). 2002. India heat wave toll tops 1,000. May 22.

Coglianese, Cary. 2007. Business interests and information in environmental rulemaking. In *Business and environmental policy: Corporate interests in the American political system,* ed. Michael E. Kraft and Sheldon Kamieniecki, 185–210. Cambridge, Mass.: MIT Press.

Cohen, Aaron J., H. Ross Anderson, Bart Ostro, Kiran Dev Pandey, Michal Krzyzanowski, Nino Künzli, Kersten Gutschmidt, C. Arden Pope III, Isabelle Romieu, Jonathan M. Samet, and Kirk R. Smith. 1996. Urban air pollution. *The World Health Report 1996.* World Health Organization.

Commoner, Barry. 1992. *Making peace with the planet.* New York: New Press.

Connor, Steve. 2009. Warning: Oil supplies are running out fast. *The Independent,* August 3. Available online at http://license.icopyright.net/user/viewFreeUse.act?fuid=NDM2Nz AzOQ%3D%3D (accessed August 4, 2009).

Cornell University Program on Breast Cancer and Environmental Risk Factors in New York State, Institute for Comparative and Environmental Toxicology. 2000. Cornell Center for the Environment fact sheet 37, June.

Cruger, Roberta. 2010. "Nicotine bees" population restored with neonicotinoid bans. May 15. Available online at http://www.treehugger.com/files/2010/05/nicotine-bees-population -restored-with-neonicotinoids-ban.php (accessed June 26, 2010).

Dahl-Jensen, Dorthe. 2000. The Greenland ice sheet reacts. *Science* 289 (July 21): 404–405.

Davis, Mike. 2007. *Planet of slums.* New York: Verso.

Denoeux, G. 2007. Corruption in Morocco: Old forces, new dynamics, and a say forward. *Middle East Policy* 14 (4): 134–151.

Department of Public Health, Commonwealth of Massachusetts. 2006. Ashland Nyanza Health Study final report. April. Available online at http://archives.lib.state.ma.us:8080/dspace/ html/2452/35441/ocm70287798-1.pdf (accessed August 11, 2008).

Derber, Charles. 1998. *Corporation nation: How corporations are taking over our lives and what we can do about it.* New York: St. Martin's Press.

Diamond, Jared. 1999. *Guns, germs, and steel: The fates of human societies.* New York: W. W. Norton.

———. 2005. *Collapse: How societies choose to fail or succeed.* New York: Viking.

Dickson, David. 1988. *The new politics of science.* Chicago: University of Chicago Press.

Dietz, Thomas M., and Robert W. Rycroft. 1987. *The risk professionals.* New York: Russell Sage Foundation.

Dolbeare, Kenneth. 1974. *Political change in the United States.* New York: McGraw-Hill.

Domhoff, G. William. 2002. *Who rules America? Power and politics.* Boston: McGraw-Hill.

Donn, Jeff. 2011. AP investigation: At aging U.S. nuke plants Feds are repeatedly weakening safety standards or simply failing to enforce them. EneNews, June 20. Available online at http://enenews.com/ap-investigation-aging-nuke-plants-feds-repeatedly-weakening -safety-standards-simply-failing-enforce (accessed April 5, 2012).

Douglas, Mary, and Aaron Wildavsky. 1982. *Risk and culture.* Berkeley: University of California Press.

Down, Jeff, Martha Mendoza, and Justin Pritchard. 2008. AP probe finds drugs in drinking water. Associated Press. Available online at http://www6.comcast.net/news/articles/ health/2008/03/09/PharmaWater.I (accessed July 5, 2008).

Duffy, Robert J. 2007. Business, elections, and the environment. In *Business and environmental policy: Corporate interests in the American political system,* ed. Michael E. Kraft and Sheldon Kamieniecki, 61–90. Cambridge, Mass.: MIT Press.

Dunham, Will. 2008. Fivefold dust increase chokes the West. Environmental News Network. Available online at http://www.enn.com/top_stories/article/31688 (accessed July 4, 2008).

Dye, Thomas R. 1995. *Who's running America? The Clinton years,* 6th ed. Upper Saddle River, N.J.: Prentice Hall.

The Economist. 2007. The risk in nanotechnology: A little risky business. November 22. Available online at http://www.economist.com/node/10171212 (accessed March 23, 2012).

Eder, Klaus. 1996. *The social construction of nature: A sociology of ecological enlightenment.* London: Sage.

Energy Watch Group. 2007. *Crude oil: The supply outlook,* October 11. Available online at http://www.energywatchgroup.org/fileadmin/global/pdf/EWG_Oilreport_10-2007.pdf (accessed August 4, 2009).

Environmental News Service. 2004. U.S. gives public lands away for pennies. Available online at http://www.ens-newswire.com/ens/2004/2004-05-11-02.asp (accessed July 4, 2008).

Erikson, Erik. 1991. In *Communities at risk: Collective responses to technological hazards*. New York: Peter Lang.

Evans, David. 1997. *A history of nature conservation in Britain*, 2d ed. New York: Routledge.

Flavin, Christopher. 2009. Escape from Copenhagen. Worldwatch Institute, December 23. Available online at http://www.worldwatch.org/node/6354 (accessed January 19, 2010).

Flessner, Dave. 2009. TVA forging ahead on new nuclear reactor. *Knoxville News-Sentinel*, July 21, B1.

Foster, John Bellamy. 1996. Wise use and workers. *Dollars and Sense* 204 (March–April): 7.

———. 2005. The vulnerable planet. In *Environmental sociology: From analysis to action*, ed. Leslie King and Deborah McCarthy, 3–15. New York: Rowman and Littlefield.

———. 2008. Peak oil and energy imperialism. *Monthly Review* (July–August). Available online at http://www.monthlyreview.org/080707foster.php (accessed September 27, 2008).

French, Hilary F. 2002. Reshaping global governance. *State of the world, 2002*. New York: W. W. Norton.

Freudenburg, William, Robert Gramling, and Debra J. Davidson. 2008. Scientific Certainty Argumentation Methods (SCAMs): Science and the politics of doubt. *Sociological Inquiry* 78 (1): 2–38.

Furlong, Scott R. 2007. Businesses and the environment: Influencing agency policymaking. In *Business and environmental policy: Corporate interests in the American political system*, ed. Michael E. Kraft and Sheldon Kamieniecki, 155–184. Cambridge, Mass.: MIT Press.

Gaffin, Stuart R. 1997. *High water blues: Impacts of sea level rise on selected coasts and islands*. Washington, D.C.: Environmental Defense Fund.

Gare, Arran E. 1995. *Postmodernism and the environmental crisis*. London: Routledge.

Gelbspan, Ross. 1995. The heat is on: The warming of the world's climate sparks a blaze of denial. *Harper's Magazine*, December, 31–37.

Giddens, Anthony. 1990. *The consequences of modernity*. Stanford, Calif.: Stanford University Press.

Gimpel, Jean. 1976. *The medieval machine*. New York: Penguin Books.

Girling, Richard. 2009. The leak was bad: Then came the death threats. *Sunday Times*, February 7.

Goodstein, David. 2004. *Out of gas: The end of the age of Oil*. New York: W. W. Norton.

Gottlieb, Robert. 1995. *Reducing toxics: A new approach to policy and industrial decision-making*. Washington, D.C.: Island Press.

Goudsblom, Johan. 1994. *Fire and civilization*. New York: Penguin.

Governor's Independent Investigation Panel. 2011. *Upper Big Branch—the April 5, 2010 explosion: A failure of basic coal mine safety practices*. Charleston, W.V., May. Available online at http://www.nttc.edu/ubb (accessed September 6, 2011).

Graham, Otis L., Jr. 1976. *Toward a planned society: From Roosevelt to Nixon*. New York: Oxford University Press.

Gray, Louise. 2010. Scientists speak out against climate change deniers' McCarthy-like threats. *The Telegraph*, May 6.

Greenpeace. 2002. Denial and deception: A chronicle of Exxon Mobil's efforts to corrupt the debate on global warming. August 14. Available online at http://www.stopesso.com/pdf/exxon_denial.pdf (accessed June 27, 2008).

Greider, William. 1992. *Who will tell the people?* New York: Simon and Schuster.

Guber, Deborah Lynn, and Christopher J. Bosso. 2007. Framing ANWR: Citizens, consumers, and the privileged position of business. In *Business and environmental policy: Corporate interests in the American political system*, ed. Michael E. Kraft and Sheldon Kamieniecki, 35–59. Cambridge, Mass.: MIT Press.

Gulf dead zone likely to set record. 2008. *U.S. News and World Report*, June 12. Available online at http://www.usnews.com/articles/news/2008/06/12/gulf-dead-zone-likely-to-set-record (accessed July 5, 2008).

Habermas, Jürgen. 1970. *Toward a rational society: Student protest, science, and politics.* Boston: Beacon Press.

———. 2001. *The postnational constellation: Political essays.* Cambridge, Mass.: MIT Press.

Hansen, Eric. 2002. Hot peaks. *OnEarth* (Fall). Available online at http://www.nrdc.org/onearth/02fal/briefings.asp (accessed July 27, 2008).

Hardin, Garrett. 1993. *Living within limits: Ecology, economics, and population taboos.* New York: Oxford University Press.

Harding, Thomas, Danny Kennedy, and Pratap Chatterjee. 1992. *Whose summit is it anyway? An investigative report on the corporate sponsorship of the Earth Summit.* Rio de Janeiro: Asian Society for Entrepreneurship Education and Development–International Youth Network.

Harper, Charles L. 2004. *Environment and society: Human perspectives on environmental issues,* 3d ed. Upper Saddle River, N.J.: Prentice Hall.

———. 2008. *Environment and society: Human perspectives on environmental issues.* 4th ed. Upper Saddle River, N.J.: Prentice Hall.

Harper, Charles L., and Bryan F. LeBeau. 2003. *Food, society, and environment.* Upper Saddle River, N.J.: Prentice Hall.

Harris, Jonathan M., and Neva R. Goodwin. 2003. Reconciling growth and the environment. Global Development and Environment Institute working paper no. 03-03. Tufts University, Medford, Mass.

Hawken, Paul. 1993. *The ecology of commerce: A declaration of sustainability.* New York: HarperCollins.

Hays, Samuel P. 2000. *A history of environmental politics since 1945.* Pittsburgh: University of Pittsburgh Press.

Hebert, Josef. 2009. Nuclear energy becomes pivotal in climate debate. Associated Press, October 25. Available online at http://www.comcast.net/articles/news-science/20091028/US.Nuclear.Climate/print (accessed October 30, 2009).

Heinberg, Richard. 2004. *Power down: Options and actions for a post-carbon world.* Gabriola Island, Canada: New Society.

Helvarg, David. 1997. *The war against the greens: The "wise-use" movement, the New Right, and anti-environmental violence.* San Francisco: Sierra Club Books.

Hertz, Noreena. 2001. *The silent takeover: Global capitalism and the death of democracy.* New York: Free Press.

Heywood, P. 1997. Political corruption: Problems and perspectives. *Political Studies* 45:417–435.

Hickman, Leo. 2009. Climate sceptics claim leaked emails are evidence of collusion among scientists. *The Guardian,* November 20. Available online at http://www.guardian.co.uk/environment/2009/nov/20/climate-sceptics-hackers-leaked-emails (accessed June 26, 2010).

Hoggan, James, and Richard Littlemore. 2009. *Climate cover-up: The crusade to deny global warming.* Vancouver: Greystone Books.

Huber, Tim, and Vicki Smith. 2011. Feds: Mine owner kept fake safety records. *Knoxville News Sentinel,* June 30, B1.

Hughes, J. Donald. 1994. *Pan's travail: Environmental problems of the ancient Greeks and Romans.* Baltimore: Johns Hopkins University Press.

Humphreys, David. 2008. NGO influence on international policy on forest conservation. In *NGO diplomacy: The influence of nongovernmental organizations in international environmental negotiations,* ed. Michele M. Betsill and Elisabeth Corell, 149–176. Cambridge, Mass.: MIT Press.

Hytrek, Gary, and Kristine M. Zentgraf. 2008. *America transformed: Globalization, inequality, and power.* New York: Oxford University Press.

Intergovernmental Panel on Climate Change (IPCC). 2007a. Climate change 2007: Fourth assessment report of the International Governmental Panel on Climate Change. Geneva: United Nations.

———. 2007b. Climate change 2007: Synthesis report—Summary for policymakers. November. Available online at http://www.ipcc.ch/pdf/assessment-report/ar4/syr/ar4_syr_spm .pdf (accessed October 30, 2009).

International Court of Justice. 1974. Fisheries jurisdiction case: Judgment of 25 July 1974. Available online at http://www.icj-cij.org/docket/files/55/5979.pdf (accessed July 17, 2010).

———. 2001. Maritime delimitation and territorial questions between Qatar and Bahrain (*Qatar v. Bahrain*): Judgment of 16 March 2001. Available online at http://www.icj-cij .org/docket/index.php?p1=3&p2=3&k=61&case=87&code=qb&p3=5 (accessed July 17, 2010).

International Institute for Sustainable Development. 2010. A brief analysis of AWG-LCA 9 and AWG-KP 11. *Earth Negotiations Bulletin* 12, no. 460 (April 14): 10–12.

Isaacs, Tony. 2008. Our disappearing minerals and their vital health role. NaturalNews.com. Available online at http://www.naturalnews.com/023237_minerals_health_soil.html (accessed July 4, 2008).

Jacobsen, Rowan. 2008. *Fruitless fall: The collapse of the honey bee and the coming agricultural crisis.* New York: Bloomsbury.

Jain, Arvind K. 2001. Power, politics, and corruption. In *The political economy of corruption,* ed. Arvind K. Jain, 3–10. New York: Routledge.

Kaufmann, D. 1998. Research on corruption: Critical empirical issues. In *Economics of corruption,* ed. Arvind K. Jain, 129–176. Boston: Kluwer Academic.

Kerbo, Harold R. 2009. *Social stratification and inequality: Class conflict in historical, comparative, and global perspective.* New York: McGraw-Hill.

Klapp, Merrie. 1992. *Bargaining with uncertainty: Decisionmaking in public health, technological safety, and environmental quality.* New York: Auburn House.

Klare, Michael T. 2004. *Blood and oil.* New York: Henry Holt.

Klinenberg, Eric. 2003. *Heat wave: A social autopsy of disaster in Chicago.* Chicago: University of Chicago Press.

Korten, David C. 2001. *When corporations rule the world,* 2d ed. Bloomfield, Conn.: Kumarian Press.

Kraft, Michael E., and Sheldon Kamieniecki. 2007. Analyzing the role of business in environmental policy. In *Business and environmental policy: Corporate interests in the American political system,* ed. Michael E. Kraft and Sheldon Kamieniecki, 3–31. Cambridge, Mass.: MIT Press.

Kubasek, Nancy K., and Gary S. Silverman. 2008. *Environmental law,* 6th ed. Upper Saddle River, N.J.: Prentice Hall.

Kunstler, James Howard. 2005. *The long emergency: Surviving the end of oil, climate change, and other converging catastrophes of the twenty-first century.* New York: Grove Press.

Lang, Susan S. 2006. "Slow, insidious" soil erosion threatens human health and welfare as well as the environment, Cornell study asserts. Chronicle Online. Available online at http:// www.news.cornell.edu/stories/March06/soil.erosion.threat.ssl.html (accessed July 4, 2008).

Lapp, Ralph E. 1965. *The new priesthood: The scientific elite and the uses of power.* New York: Harper and Row.

Larsen, Janet. 2003. Record heat wave in Europe takes 35,000 lives. *Eco-economy Update,* October 9. Washington, D.C.: Earth Policy Institute.

Lavelle, M., and M. Coyle. 1993. Unequal protection: The racial divide in environmental law. *National Law Journal* 21 (September): S1–S12.

Layzer, Judith A. 2007. Deep freeze: How business has shaped the global warming debate in Congress. In *Business and environmental policy: Corporate interests in the American political system*, ed. Michael E. Kraft and Sheldon Kamieniecki, 93–151. Cambridge, Mass.: MIT Press.

Leakey, Richard, and Roger Lewin. 1995. *The sixth extinction: Patterns of life and the future of humankind.* New York: Anchor Books.

Leistner, Marilyn. 1985. The Times Beach story. *Proceedings of the Third Annual Hazardous Materials Management Conference*, Philadelphia, June 4–6. Available online at http://www.greens.org/s-r/078/07-09.html (accessed August 12, 2008).

Levine, Adeline. 1982. *Love Canal: Science, politics, and people.* Lexington, Mass.: Lexington Books.

Lewis, C. S. 1947. *The abolition of man or reflections on education with special reference to the teaching of English in the upper forms of schools.* New York: HarperOne.

Logan, John, and Harvey Molotch. 1987. *Urban fortunes: The political economy of place.* Berkeley: University of California Press.

Los Angeles Department of Water and Power. 2008. A hundred or a thousand fold more important. Available online at http://wsoweb.ladwp.com/Aqueduct/historyoflaa/hundred.htm (accessed August 5, 2008).

Lustgarten, Abrahim, and Ryan Knutson. 2010. Documents show history of BP problems. *Knoxville News Sentinel,* June 13, A14.

Lynn, Frances M. 1986. The interplay of science and values in assessing and regulating environmental risks. *Science, Technology, and Human Values* 11 (2): 40–50.

Macalister, Terry. 2009. Oil: Future world shortages are being drastically underplayed, say experts. *The Guardian,* November 12. Available online at http://www.guardian.co.uk/business/2009/nov/12/oil.shortage.uppsala-aleklett (accessed December 21, 2009.).

Manning, Richard. 2004. *Against the grain: How agriculture has hijacked civilization.* New York: North Point Press.

Marcum, Ed. 2012. NRC sets hearing on Watts Bar. *Knoxville News Sentinel,* April 7, B1.

Marger, Martin N. 1987. *Elites and masses: An introduction to political sociology,* 2d ed. Belmont, Calif.: Wadsworth.

Martin, Brian. 1999. Suppression of dissent in science. *Research in Social Problems and Public Policy* 7:105–135.

McAdam, Doug. 1982. Political process and the development of black insurgency, 1930–1970. Chicago: University of Chicago Press.

McKinney, Michael L., and Robert M. Schoch. 1996. *Environmental science: Systems and solutions.* New York: West Publishing.

McNeill, John R. 2000. *Something new under the sun: An environmental history of the twentieth-century world.* New York. W. W. Norton.

Menon, Ajay, and Anil Menon. 1997. Enviropreneurial marketing strategy: The emergence of corporate environmentalism as market strategy. *Journal of Marketing* 61:51–68.

The Merriam-Webster Dictionary. 1995. Springfield, Mass.: Merriam-Webster.

Meyer, Alden. 2009. The Copenhagen Accord: Not everything we wanted, but something to build on. Union of Concerned Scientists, December 23. Available online at http://www.ucsusa.org/global_warming/solutions/big_picture_solutions/the-copenhagen-accord.html (accessed January 10, 2009).

Milbrath, Lester W. 1989. Envisioning a sustainable society: Learning our way out. Albany: State University of New York Press.

Miller, G. Tyler, Jr. 1991. *Environmental science: Sustaining the earth,* 3d ed. Belmont, Calif.: Wadsworth Publishing.

———. 2008. *Living in the environment: Principles, connections, and solutions.* Pacific Grove, Calif.: Brooks Cole.

Minerals Management Service (MMS). 2010. Press release, June 21. Available online at http://www.mms.gov/ooc/press/2010/press0621.html (accessed July 15, 2010).

Mitchell, Lawrence. 2007. *The speculation economy: How finance triumphed over industry.* San Francisco: Berrett-Koehler Publisher.

Molotch, Harvey. 1976. The city as a growth machine: Toward a political economy of place. *American Journal of Sociology* 82 (2): 309–332.

Montague, Peter. 2006. Some chemicals are more harmful than anyone ever suspected. *Rachel's Democracy and Health News,* no. 876 (October 12).

Montinola, G., and R. Jackman. 2002. Sources of corruption: A cross-country study. *British Journal of Political Science* 32:147–170.

Moore, Matthew. 2009. Climate change scientists face calls for public inquiry over data manipulation claims. *Daily Telegraph,* November 24. Available online at http://www.webcitation.org/5mdXqWeCz (accessed January 10, 2010).

Morris, Stephen D. 1991. *Corruption and politics in contemporary Mexico.* Tuscaloosa: University of Alabama Press.

Murphy, Brian. 2009. UN: Growth of slums boosting natural disaster risk. Associated Press, May 17. Available online at http://www.comcast.net/articles/news-science/20090517/ML.UN.Disaster.Risks (accessed May 18, 2009).

NanoXchange. 2004. Lux Research releases 'The Nanotech Report 2004' key findings. Available online at http://www.nanoxchange.com/NewsFinancial.asp?ID=264) (accessed March 23, 2012).

National Academy of Sciences. 2005. *Joint science academies' statement: Global response to climate change.* Available online at http://nationalacademies.org/onpi/06072005.pdf (accessed February 19, 2010).

———. 2007. *Evaluating progress of the U.S. climate change science program: Methods and preliminary results.* Available online at http://dels.nas.edu/Report/Evaluating-Progress/11934 (accessed February 18, 2010).

———. 2008. *Understanding and responding to climate change* Available online at http://dels.nas.edu/resources/static-assets/materials-based-on-reports/booklets/climate_change_2008_final.pdf (accessed February 19, 2010).

———. 2009. *Ecological impacts of climate change.* Available online at http://dels-old.nas.edu/dels/rpt_briefs/ecological_impacts.pdf (accessed February 19, 2010).

National Center for Atmospheric Research (NCAR). 2005. Drought's growing reach: NCAR study points to global warming as key factor. January 10. Available online at http://www.ucar.edu/news/releases/2005/drought_research.shtml (accessed August 4, 2009).

National Oceanic and Atmospheric Administration (NOAA). 2008a. International scientists find "acidified" water on the continental shelf from Canada to Mexico. May 22. Available online at http://www.noaanews.noaa.gov/stories2008/20080522_oceanacid.html (accessed July 18, 2008).

———. 2008b. Nutrient pollution of coastal waters: Too much of a good thing. Available online at http://coastalscience.noaa.gov/news/feature/01112008.html (accessed July 18, 2008).

Natural Resources Defense Council. 2001. Hostile environment: How activist judges threaten our air, water and soil. Available online at http://www.nrdc.org/legislation/hostile/hostinx.asp (accessed October 2, 2001).

Netherlands Environmental Assessment Agency. 2006. Global greenhouse gas emissions increased 75 percent since 1970. Available online at http://www.pbl.nl/en/dossiers/Climatechange/TrendGHGemissions1990-2004.html (accessed January 11, 2010).

Offe, Claus. 1984. *Contradictions of the welfare state.* Cambridge, Mass.: MIT Press.

O'Leary, Rosemary. 1993. *Environmental change: Federal courts and the EPA.* Philadelphia: Temple University Press.

————. 2006. Environmental policy in the courts. In *Environmental policy,* 6th ed., ed. Norman J. Vig and Michael E. Kraft, 148–168. Washington, D.C.: Congressional Quarterly Press.

Olson, Kevin. 2006. *Reflexive democracy: Political equality and the welfare state.* Cambridge, Mass.: MIT Press.

Oreskes, Naomi, and Erik M. Conway. 2010. *Merchants of doubt: How a handful of scientists obscured the truth on issues from tobacco smoke to global warming.* New York: Bloomsbury Press.

O'Sullivan, Mary A. 2000. *Contests for corporate control: Corporate governance and economic performance in the United States and Germany.* New York: Oxford University Press.

Owen, Jonathan, and Paul Bignell. 2010. Think-tanks take oil money and use it to fund climate deniers. *The Independent,* February 7. Available online at http://license.icopyright.net/user/viewFreeUse.act?fuid=NzAwMDQ0OQ%3D%3D (accessed February 8, 2010).

Ozawa, Connie. 2005. Science in environmental conflicts. In *Environmental sociology: From analysis to action,* ed. Leslie King and Deborah McCarthy, 326–338. New York: Rowman and Littlefield.

Paehlke, Robert C. 2004. *Democracy's dilemma: Environment, social equity, and the global economy.* Cambridge, Mass.: MIT Press.

Parmesan, Camille, and Hector Galbraith. 2004. *Observed impacts of global climate change in the U.S.* Arlington, Va.: Pew Center on Global Climate Change.

The peak of Mt. Kilimanjaro as it has not been seen for 11,000 years. 2005. *The Guardian,* March 14.

Pearce, Evans. 2010. Climate emails: Were they really hacked or just sitting in cyberspace? *The Guardian,* February 4. Available online at http://www.guardian.co.uk/environment/2010/feb/04/climate-change-email-hacker-police-investigation (accessed August 8, 2010).

Pena, Devon G. 1997. *The terror of the machine: Technology, work, gender, and ecology on the U.S.–Mexico border.* Austin: Center for Mexican American Studies, University of Texas.

Perrow, Charles. 1984. *Normal accidents: Living with high risk technologies.* New York: Basic.

Phillips, Kevin. 2008. *Bad money: Reckless finance, failed politics, and the global crisis of American capitalism.* New York: Viking.

Pirages, Dennis, and Paul R. Ehrlich. 1974. *ARK II.* New York: W. H. Freeman.

Polanyi, Michael. 1972. The republic of science: Its political and economic theory. *Minerva* 1:54–73.

Ponting, Clive. 1991. *A green history of the world: The environment and the collapse of great civilizations.* New York: Penguin.

Popper, Karl R. 1959. *The logic of scientific discovery.* New York: Basic Books.

Porter, David, and Chester L. Mirsky. 2002. *Megamall on the Hudson: Planning, Wal-Mart, and grassroots resistance.* Victoria, Canada: Trafford.

Price, Don K. 1965. *The scientific estate.* Cambridge, Mass.: Harvard University Press.

Pring, George W., and Penelope Canan. 1993. SLAPPs: "Strategic lawsuits against public participation" in government—diagnosis and treatment of the newest civil rights abuse. In *Civil rights litigation and attorney fees annual handbook,* vol. 9, ed. Barbara Wolvovitz, 378–386. New York: Clark Boardman.

Prüss-Üstün, Annette, and Carlos Corvalán. 2006. Preventing disease through healthy environments: Towards an estimate of the environmental burden of disease. Geneva: World Health Organization Press. Available online at http://www.quapawtribe.com (accessed November 22, 2008).

Quijano, Romeo F. 2003. Elements of the precautionary principle. In *Environmental science and preventive public policy,* ed. Joel A. Tickner, 21–27. Washington, D.C.: Island Press.

Ravilious, Kate. 2009. Hacked email climate scientists receive death threats. *The Guardian,* December 12. Available online at http://www.guardian.co.uk/environment/2009/dec/08/hacked-climate-emails-death-threats (accessed January 15, 2010).

Rawls, John. 1999. *A theory of justice.* Cambridge, Mass.: Harvard University Press.

Redman, Charles L. 1999. *Human impact on ancient environments.* Tucson: University of Arizona Press.

Reisner, Marc. 1993. *Cadillac desert: The American West and its disappearing water.* New York: Penguin.

Revkin, Andrew C. 2009a. Hacked email is new fodder for climate dispute. *New York Times,* November 20. Available online at http://www.nytimes.com/2009/11/21/science/earth/21climate.html?_r=3 (accessed January 15, 2010).

———. 2009b. Industry ignored its scientists on climate. *New York Times,* April 23. Available online at http://www.nytimes.com/2009/04/24/science/earth/24deny.html?ref=andrewc revkin (accessed January 15, 2010).

Roach, Brian. 2007. *Corporate power in a global economy.* Medford, Mass.: Global Development and Environment Institute, Tufts University. Available online at http://www.e3net work.org/teaching/Roach_Corporate_Power_in_a_Global_Economy.pdf (accessed January 28, 2010).

Roberts, J. Timmons, and Bradley C. Parks. 2007. *A climate of injustice: Global inequality, North-South politics, and climate policy.* Cambridge, Mass.: MIT Press.

Roberts, Paul. 2004. *The end of oil: On the edge of a perilous New World.* New York: Houghton Mifflin.

Rose-Ackerman, Susan. 1998. In *Economics of corruption,* ed. Arvind K. Jain, 35–62. Boston: Kluwer Academic.

Rosenbaum, Walter A. 2002. *Environmental politics and policy,* 5th ed. Washington, D.C.: Congressional Quarterly Press.

Rosner, David, and Gerald Markowitz. 1991. *Deadly dust: Silicosis and the politics of occupational disease in twentieth-century America.* Princeton, N.J.: Princeton University Press.

Rowell, Andrew. 1996. *Green backlash: Global subversion of the environmental movement.* New York: Routledge.

Satter, Raphael G. 2010. U.K. "Climategate" inquiry largely clears scientists. Associated Press, March 30. Available online at http://news.yahoo.com/s/ap/20100330/ap_on_re_us/climate _hacked_e_mails (accessed August 4, 2010).

Schlozman, Kay Lehman, and John T. Tierney. 1986. *Organized interests and American democracy.* New York: Harper and Row.

Schmid, Randolph E. 2009. Study: Arctic sea ice melting faster than expected. Associated Press, April 3. Available online at http://www.comcast.net/articles/news-science/2009 0402/SCI.Sea.Ice (accessed April 3, 2009).

Schmidheiny, Stephan, and World Business Council for Sustainable Development. 1992. *Changing course: A global business perspective on development and the environment.* Boston: MIT Press.

Schnaiberg, Allan. 1980. *The environment: From surplus to scarcity.* New York: Oxford.

Schulte, Constanze. 2004. *Compliance with decisions of the International Court of Justice.* New York: Oxford University Press.

Scorecard. 2008a. Hazardous air pollutants. Available online at http://www.scorecard.com (accessed June 29, 2008).

———. 2008b. Pollution releases ranked by ozone depleting potential. Available online at http://www.scorecard.org/env-releases/us-ozone-detail.tcl (accessed July 7, 2008).

Shah, Sonia. 2004. *Crude: The story of oil.* New York: Seven Stories.

Shand, Hope, and Kathy Jo Wetter. 2006. Shrinking science: An introduction to nanotechnology. In *State of the world: 2006,* ed. Lind Starke, 78–95. New York: W. W. Norton.

Shefner, Jon. 2004. Global economic change, protest, and its implications for U.S. policymakers. In *Agenda for social justice,* ed. Kathleen Ferraro, JoAnn Miller, Robert Perrucci, and Paula Rodriguez Rust, 31–42. Knoxville, Tenn.: Society for the Study of Social Problems.

Shepherd, Andrew. 2003. Larsen ice sheet has progressively thinned. *Science* 302 (October 31): 856–859.

Shleifer, Andrei, and Robert W. Vishny. 1993. Corruption. *Quarterly Journal of Economics* 108 (3): 599–617.

Shriver, Thomas E., Sherry Cable, and Dennis Kennedy. 2008. Mining for conflict and staking claims: Contested illness at the Tar Creek Superfund site. *Sociological Inquiry* 78 (4): 558–579.

Sjoberg, Gideon. 1960. *The preindustrial city: Past and present.* New York: Free Press.

Smith, James. 1991. *The idea brokers: Think tanks and the rise of the new policy elite.* New York: Free Press.

Soliman, Hussein, and Sherry Cable. 2011. Sinking under the weight of corruption: Neoliberal reform, political accountability, and justice. *Current Sociology* 59 (6): 735–753

Solomon, Susan, Gian-Kasper Plattner, Reto Knutti, and Pierre Friedlingstein. 2009. Irreversible climate change due to carbon dioxide emissions. *Proceedings of the National Academy of Sciences* 106 (6): 1704–1709.

Starkey, B., M. A. Boyer, and J. Wilkenfeld. 2005. *Negotiating in a complex world: An introduction to international negotiation,* 2d ed. Lanham, Md.: Rowman and Littlefield.

Stausberg, Matthias. 2009. Business leaders are key to solving the climate crisis. Available online at http://unglobalcompact.org/NewsAndEvents/news_archives/2009_12_12.html (accessed February 16, 2010).

Stefancic, Jean, and Richard Delgado. 1996. *No mercy: How conservative think tanks and foundations changed America's social agenda.* Philadelphia: Temple University Press.

Stokstad, Erik. 2004. Defrosting the carbon freezer of the North. *Science* 304 (June 11): 1618–1620.

Tavernise, Sabrina. 2011. Report faults mine owner for explosion that killed 29. *New York Times,* May 18. Available online at http://www.nytimes.com/2011/05/20/us/20mine.html?pagewanted=all (accessed September 6, 2011).

Tickner, Joel A., ed. 2003. *Environmental science and preventive public policy.* Washington, D.C.: Island Press.

Tokar, Brian. 1997. *Earth for sale: Reclaiming ecology in the age of corporate greenwash.* Boston: South End.

United Nations. 2003. Convention against corruption. Available at http://www.unodc.org/documents/treaties/UNCAC/Publications/Convention/08-50026_E.pdf (accessed June 8, 2010).

———. 2005a. Millennium Ecosystem Assessment—Ecosystems and human well-being: Synthesis. Washington, D.C.: Island Press.

———. 2005b. Millennium Ecosystem Assessment—Overview of the Millennium Ecosystem Assessment. Available online at http://www.millenniumassessment.org/cn/About.aspx (accessed August 5, 2009).

———. 2010. Secretary-general warns corruption "threat to development, democracy, and stability." Available online at http://www.un.org/News/Press/docs/2010/sgsm13292.doc.htm (accessed April 27, 2012).

United Nations Convention against Corruption. 2009. Available online at www.unodc.org/yournocounts/en/about-the-campaign/sgs-message-on-anti-corruption (accessed June 8, 2010).

United Nations Environmental Programme (UNEP). 2005. *Register of international treaties and other agreements in the field of the environment.* Geneva: United Nations. Available online at http://www.unep.org/law/PDF/register_Int_treaties_contents.pdf (accessed October 10, 2009).

United Nations Framework Convention on Climate Change. 2001. Bonn climate talks make progress on fleshing out specifics of global climate change regime. Press release, June 11.

Available online at http://unfccc.int/files/press/news_room/press_releases_and_advisories/application/pdf/20101106_pr_closing_june.pdf (accessed August 2, 2010).

United Nations World Commission on Environment and Development. 1987. *Our common future: From one Earth to one world.* Geneva: United Nations. Available online at http://www.un-documents.net/ocf-ov.htm (accessed September 19, 2009).

Urbina, Ian. 2011. Regulation lax as gas wells' tainted water hits rivers. *New York Times,* February 26. Available online at http://www.nytimes.com/2011/02/27/us/27gas.html?ref=ianurbina (accessed September 6, 2011).

U.S. Department of Agriculture. 2005. Crop production. Washington, D.C.: National Agricultural Statistics Service.

——. 2010. Questions and answers: Colony collapse disorder. Washington, D.C.: U.S. Department of Agriculture. Available online at http://www.ars.usda.gov/News/docs.htm?docid=15572 (accessed June 26, 2010).

U.S. Environmental Protection Agency (EPA). 1989. Occidental Chemical signs consent order for storage and destruction of Love Canal wastes. Press release, June 1. Available online at http://www.epa.gov/history/topics/lovecanal/05.htm (accessed August 7, 2008).

——. 2002. *EPA Office of Compliance Sector Notebook Project: Profile of the Organic Chemical Industry,* 2d ed. Report no. EPA/310-R02-001. Washington, D.C.: U.S. Environmental Protection Agency.

——. 2007. Air Quality Index Report. Available online at http://iaspub.epa.gov/airsdata/adaqs.aqi?geotype=us&geocode=usa&geoinfo=us%7Eusa%7EUnited+States&year=2007&sumtype=ms&fld=gname&fld=gcode&fld=stabbr&fld=regn&rpp=25 (accessed July 19, 2008).

——. 2008a. National Priorities List (NPL). Available online at http://www.epa.gov/superfund (accessed August 11, 2008).

——. 2008b. Superfund Information Systems. Available online at http://www.epa.gov/superfund/sites/query (accessed August 11, 2008).

——. 2008c. 2006 Toxic Release Inventory (TRI) Public Data Release Report. Available online at http://www.epa.gov/tri (accessed July 23, 2008).

——. 2010. Radiation protection: Health effects. Available online at http://www.epa.gov/rpdweb00/understand/health_effects.html (accessed June 25, 2010).

U.S. Office of the General Counsel for the Commission on Civil Rights. 1994. Not in my backyard: Executive Order 12,898 and Title VI as tools for achieving environmental justice. *Federal Register* 59, no. 32, available online at http://www.archives.gov/federal-register/executive-orders/pdf/12898.pdf (accessed June 15, 2008).

Vanden Heuvel, Katrina. 2011. Twenty-nine miners and Massey's coal crimes. *The Nation,* June 26. Available online at http://www.thenation.com/blog/161658/29-miners-and-masseys-coal-crimes (accessed September 6, 2011).

Vicini, James. 2008. *Exxon Valdez* oil spill ruling overturned. Reuters, June 25. Available online at http://up.nytimes.com?d=3&h=&g=news&u=%2Fbin%2Fprintfriendly.php&hs=&t=&r=http%3A%2F%2Fwww.iht.com%2Farticles%2Freuters%2F2008%2F06%2F25%2Fnews%2FOUKWD-UK-EXXON-VALDEZ-COURT.php (accessed June 25, 2008).

——. 2010. Landmark U.S. ruling allows corporate political cash. Reuters, January 21. Available online at http://www.reuters.com/assets/print?aid=USN2123222420100121 (accessed January 28, 2010).

Wade, R. 1985. The market for public office: Why the Indian state is not better at development. *World Development* 13 (4): 467–497.

Wallach, Lori, and Michelle Sforza. 1999. *Whose trade organization?* Washington, D.C.: Public Citizen.

Weidenbaum, Murray. 2004. Surveying the global marketplace. *USA Today Magazine,* January, 26–27.

Weiss, Rick. 2007. Synthetic DNA on the brink of yielding new life forms. *Washington Post,* December 17, A01.

Weissman, Evan. 2005. Food Security in the 21st Century: Lessons from Cuban agriculture for materializing realities. Master's thesis, University of Tennessee, Knoxville.

Whitney, M. T. 2007a. Global warming will directly impact children's health with increase in fevers, emergency visits. NaturalNews.com. Available online at http://www.naturalnews .com/z021712.html (accessed July 5, 2008).

———. 2007b. When old electronics meet their end, much ends up becoming toxic waste in China. NaturalNews.com. Available online at http://www.naturalnews.com/z021578.html (accessed July 2, 2008).

Williams, Gwyndaf. 1996. Manchester. *Cities* 13 (3): 203–212.

Wolf, Eric. 1966. *Peasants.* Englewood Cliffs, N.J.: Prentice Hall.

World oil pollution: Causes, prevention and clean-up. N.d. Available online at http://www .oceanlink.info/ocean_matters/oil.html (accessed August 12, 2009).

World's frog species face extinction due to pollution and climate change, scientists warn. 2006. NaturalNews.com, July 7. Available online at http://www.naturalnews.com/z019586 .html (accessed July 23, 2008).

World Trade Organization. 2012. About the organization. Available online at http://www .wto.org/english/thewto_e/thewto_e.htm (accessed April 12, 2012).

World Wildlife Fund. 2006. *Living planet report 2006.* Gland, Switzerland: Ropress.

Wright, Will. 2007. The worst major oil spills in history. Available online at http://www .associatedcontent.com/article/454782/the_worst_major_oil_spills_in_history.html ?cat=37 (accessed June 30, 2010).

Wynne, Brian. 1992. Uncertainty and environmental learning: Reconceiving science and policy in the preventive paradigm. *Global Environmental Change* 2:111–127.

Yeomans, Matthew. 2004. *Oil: A concise guide to the most important product on earth.* New York: New Press.

Yohe, Evelyne. 2004. Sizing up the earth's glaciers. NASA Earth Observatory. June 22. Available online at http://earthobservatory.nasa.gov/Features/GLIMS (accessed August 2, 2010).

Zeller, Tom, Jr. 2011. Gas drilling technique is labeled violation. *New York Times,* January 31. Available online at http://www.nytimes.com/2011/02/01/business/energy-environment/ 01gas.html (accessed September 6, 2011).

Zimmerman, R. 1993. Social equity and environmental risk. *Risk Analysis* 13:649–666.

Zupko, Ronald E., and Robert A. Laures. 1996. *Straws in the wind: Medieval urban environmental law—The case of northern Italy.* Boulder, Colo.: Westview Press.

Zwerdling, Daniel. 2009. India's farming "revolution" heading for collapse. National Public Radio, April 14. Available online at http://www.npr.org/templates/story/story.php?story Id=102893816 (accessed April 14, 2009).

Index